# JOHN ECHOLS

DISCOVER THE SECRETS OF "MIND CONTROL"
AND TRANSFORM YOUR DREAMS INTO *REALITY!*

# Praise for...
# MIND CONTROLOGY®
*And John Echols*

***"John Echols writes about the amazing human spirit that inspires passion and desire to go after what you want. Fun, interesting and creative... an optimistic read about possibility within."***

-Dr. Karyl McBride, PhD, LMFT
Renowned Behavioral Psychologist
Author, *"Will I Ever Be Good Enough?"*

***"Invigorating, motivational and inspirational... A book the likes of Covey, Carnegie, Robbins and Tice. This book will fire up the soul of those who desire change."***

-Michael Grover
President, *G-6 Turnaround Consulting*
*DuPont,* Six Sigma Operations Expert

***"Insightful, interesting, and accurate."***

-Dr. Fred R. David
Francis Marion University School of Business
Professor of Strategic Management
Author, *"Strategic Management"*

***"'Mind Contrology®,' by John Echols, is really something special in the world of personal and business success development...I look forward to sharing this book with clients worldwide."***

-Danny Creed
Best-selling Author, *"A Life Best Lived"*
CEO, *FocalPoint Business Coaching of Arizona*

***"Interesting!"***

-Dr. Katherine Sherif, MD
Vice Chair and Professor, Department of Medicine
Thomas Jefferson University

***"This book offers an opportunity to tap into positive energy and move toward self-actualization...and offers examples of how to apply this positive energy to almost every discipline."***

-Jack F. Downs
Inspector General of Pennsylvania, PSD

***"Highly recommended reading for all who have brains and wish to use them more productively to achieve spectacular things in their lives and careers."***

-Victoria Ipri
Nationally Recognized Social Media Expert
Author, *"LinkedIn for the Clueless"*

***"MIND BLOWING! An inspirational piece of literary genius... Now those that are 'ordinary' have the chance to be extraordinary. John, in my opinion, has given everyone the tools to become their best possible self. This book is a success!"***

-Pamela Denise Brown
President & Publisher, *Books Speak for You*
Author of More than 120 Children's Books

***"This book serves as an operating manual for your brain, enabling you to...harness the power of your mind to evolve into the highest version of yourself."***

-Kristin Swarcheck, M.Ed., CPC, ELI-MP

***"The kind of guy I want on my team."***

-Andy Hildalgo
CEO, Telecom Giant, *WPCS*

***"John Echols is an extraordinary human being. This book not only reflects his higher wisdom and how to apply sage advice to modern human endeavors but also his extraordinary moral compass and profound ethos for humanity."***

-Dr. Rachel Wellner, MD, MPH, FACS
Fox News, ABC, MBC-TV, Featured Medical Expert

***"Powerful, riveting, and thought-provoking. This book opens the door to endless possibilities...for people who want to make a positive change in their lives and careers. The ultimate guide to mastering the mind."***

-Scott W. Clarke
CEO/Executive Chef
*Blue Monkey Catering*

***"Intriguing and informative from the start... Author John Echols has tapped into something great, and well worth the read."***

-Julie Downs
DeSales University, Marketing Communications

***"This stuff is like Sun Tzu 'Art of War' tactics!"***

-Dan York
President, *Stellar Marketing Group*

***"Perhaps the most remarkable thing about John is this: His experience and insightfulness are built almost entirely upon a foundation of self-education. And since we know that the leader who never stops learning never stops growing, it's safe to say that John will always be found among that elite group of leaders."***

-Howard Bernstein
President, *Nuts to You, Inc.*

***Mind...Business...and Beyond!***

**Mindbiz Coaching & Consulting, Inc.**
**2001 Market Street, Suite 2500**
**Philadelphia, PA 19103**
**mindbizinc.com**

For special discounts regarding bulk purchasing, contact Mindbiz Coaching & Consulting, Inc.

(267) 628-6242

Visit us on the web at *mindbizinc.com*



Mindbiz, Inc.

ISBN-13: 978-0692810156
ISBN-10: 0692810153



*Mind Contrology*® printed and assembled in the United States by Mindbiz Coaching & Consulting, Inc.

*Dedicated to my wife Denise;*
*our children "Smidgeon" and Tyler;*
*and our Rottweiler, Odie…*
*You are what make life worth living for me*
*This book is for you*

# Contents

The 4th Element of the DAF: Harness the Force of Belief



The 5th Element of the DAF: Become a Goal Scientist



The 6th Element of the DAF: Master the Art of Strategic Living



The Final Element: Take Action unto Excellence!



## Epilogue

# A Day at the Office

It was a typical day at the office—except, I was soaring across the country at 400 mph in a corporate jet and babysitting an aging, Hollywood celebrity…

He was a friend of Jamie's, the CEO of the company I was working for. He was also interested in making a rather large investment in the company and wanted a private tour of corporate headquarters. Guess who got the assignment?

"So, what qualifies *you* to be my handler today, kid?" asked the star. Glass and ice clinked as he used his finger to stir his third drink since take-off—just 50 minutes ago.

I closed my laptop, sat up straight, and loosened my tie. "For starters, I'm president of the management consultancy that Jamie uses. My firm's client list includes Fortune-level CEOs and nationally recognized surgeons, as well as numerous regional brands and small businesses. I'm also the only coach who our mutual friend, Jamie, trusts on matters of performance psychology. So, whadaya think, am I qualified?"

"Ah, yes, the *Mind Guru,"* my guest slurred then swigged. "Jamie says you're a true authority on the human mind. Says you're a regular celebrity around the firm. Hey, is it true that you can…"

"Read people's minds?" I blurted out. "Once you unlock the hidden powers of your mind, outpacing other folks' thoughts will be the least of what you can do. Take me, for instance, I never received an Ivy League MBA. In fact, the only degree I possess is from the University of Hard Knocks. Yet, for the past several years, I've been teaching executives who are twice my age and who possess university MBAs how to achieve peak performance."

My guest's brow crinkled curiously. "And just how do you manage *that?*"

As if conducting a TV interview, I returned. "I help my clients use their mind to master their lives, careers, relationships, and finances."

"So, you're a...*mind control* expert? Kid, your life sounds like a movie script my agent once had me read. It's all very intriguing." The star glanced into the passing clouds and released a pitiful sigh. "Unfortunately for me, my life has begun to resemble the plot to some B-rated horror flick. And it keeps getting *scarier* by the day."

"What's seems to be the problem?" I ventured.

"Everything." The actor went on to unleash a laundry list of career troubles, relationship problems, and, strangely enough, financial woes. "That's why I'm making this investment. I'm hoping it pulls my life out of the crapper, because, most days, I don't even feel like getting out of bed in the morning."

This guy was a nervous wreck. I have to say, it was troubling to see this actor whose on-screen heroics had brought me so much inspiration over the years acting so utterly helpless. It was time to make some magic happen...

"Let's try an exercise, shall we?" I offered. By employing some cognitive priming techniques designed to accelerate rapport-building, I was able to convince the actor that I could help him regain control of his life. Next, I directed him to, "Relax. Close your eyes and breathe rhythmically. Now, go to your Mental Theater—that place in your mind in which you *see* images, *hear* messages, and generate the associated *feelings* that affect your physiology. Next, draw upon the memory of waking up in bed this morning, long before we met. Tell me when you've got it."

Jet engines backgrounded a lengthy pause. Then, "Okay, I *see* it!"

"Excellent. Your alarm clock rings. You're opening your eyes for the first time this morning. Now, tell me what you see and hear."

"That's easy. I see my wife and hear my dogs bark..."

"No, no. I'm not interested in what you see with your eyes and hear with your ears. Tell me what you see and hear...in your mind.

What images and messages are playing inside your Mental Theater which make you *feel* like not getting out of bed? Take your time. Pinpoint that internal audio-animated activity."

The actor squinted tightly. His eyes darted beneath his lids, automatic responses of his attempt to gain mental clarity. "Okay, kid. I'm dialed in now."

"What do you see and hear?"

"I'm picturing myself calling my agent after my trip. He's giving me the same old story. There are zero projects that fit my profile."

"What else is going on in your head?" I coached.

"*Debt*. Lots and lots of debt. The actor's fingers clutched the arms of his seat. His forehead beaded with sweat and his chest pounded under his fashionable outfit. "I imagine my place in Greece going into foreclosure. Then my home in L.A. I can see my wife crying. I can hear her calling me…a failure. I keep thinking, 'I've got to make this investment work, because if it fails, I'm doomed'!"

"Consumed from the moment you awake by notions of joblessness, debt, foreclosures, failure, and impending doom, is it any wonder why you *feel* your life is spinning hopelessly out of control?" I asked.

He peeked at me with one eye, and then quickly shut it back as if embarrassed.

"You've just learned that your own thoughts are fueling your anxiety and exaggerating your loss of control. You're not only starring in that horror show you say your life has become; my friend, you're the one *directing* it."

"Geez, kid," the actor drew a sobering breath, "I've become my own worst enemy. How could I have been so stupid?'

"It's not a question of IQ," I explained. "It's a matter of understanding your mind and how it works. Unfortunately, the human mind doesn't come with an owner's manual. So, like 99% of the population, you lacked the basic know-how to master your thinking. As a result, your mind began running the show. Congratulations, you're now among the 1% of the population that understands the fundamental principle of mind control—mental focus reigns supreme. Later, I'll teach you how to reprogram your inner-voice and reconstruct your belief system to your advantage. But, right now, let's redirect your mental focus and get you back on the road to success. Ready to take back control of your life?"

"Kid," my guest confidently returned, "I was born ready."

The purr of jet engines provided a soothing musical backdrop as I introduced the star to just a few of the revolutionary principles and strategies I have developed through a decade of studies in the fields of mind science and peak performance. When all was said and done, the actor had a profound, new outlook on life and was in a better position than ever before to take charge of his mind, his life, and his future.

"Wow, kid! I feel…reborn. I never realized that I could control what goes on inside my head. This stuff you taught me is amazing. No, it's…"

"Miraculous?" I ventured. "I've got news for you. We've only scratched the surface of what the mind can do. What if I told you that you not only have the ability to alter your emotional and physiological states but possess irrevocable power to manipulate circumstances to your benefit, to design a new-and-improved identity, and to transform your wildest dreams into your waking reality?

"I'd say, sign me up for Mind School. But first, kid, I gotta' say. You make the Beverly Hills shrinks I've been to look like first-year psychology students. Where on Earth did you learn all this stuff?"

"That's an interesting story," I offered. At the risk of stirring up old ghosts, I admitted, "Long before I became a CEO, business consultant, and mind expert, and kept the company of elite professionals, I struggled long and hard with substance abuse issues—a consuming problem which left me homeless, penniless, and at the brink of insanity. Worst of all, I had no idea *why* I was destroying myself or how to make the madness stop."

The actor sneered at his glass. "Yeah, I know what you mean."

"Anyway, nearing the end of my downward spiral, a friend of mine—a wealthy friend who never allowed his success to tarnish his heart of gold—asked me to meet with him to discuss my dilemma. During our meeting, Mike said, 'Johnny, I know what your problem is. You forgot who you are.' I thought long and hard about Mike's words before I realized he was wrong. I hadn't forgotten who I was. Actually, I'd placed too much emphasis on my current, *limited* self and too little emphasis on who I wanted to *become* in life. I'd left my destiny to chance and it nearly cost me my life."

"This is good stuff, kid," said the actor. He walked to the snack cabinet, grabbed a bag of popcorn, and then sat back down and started munching. "I'm all ears. Please continue."

"It was perhaps by an act of Providence that I became fascinated with the human mind and how it works. So, on a quest to decode the mysteries of mentality and peak performance, I began studying the human mind and researching the lives of nearly 500 of the world's most fascinating figures. And as I did, a *science* began to emerge—a science hidden behind the scenes of every great life ever lived and every dream ever fulfilled."

The star chewed, gawked.

"Eager to put this science to work, I constructed bold dreams for my life, career, relationships, and finances, and then used what I learned to trade my old, chemical dependent identity for that of the successful businessman, husband, and father you see today."

The star nodded. "That's what I call getting into character."

"That's just the beginning. After constructing a vision for my future, powers I never knew I possessed were suddenly awakened within me and my life took on bold, new meaning. Virtually overnight, amazing and seeming unexplainable things began to happen. Lucrative ideas flooded into my brain and helpful people began crossing my path at every turn. Opportunities were presented to me at just the right time and events began to unfold in my favor. It seemed as if the entire Universe was operating on the axis of my recalibrated mentality, and all of the resources I needed to fulfill my dreams became increasingly available to me, as if being provided by the Heavens above."

"S-t-r-a-n-g-e," whispered the actor with narrowing eyes.

"I'll say. It was as if, from the moment I had taken control of my mind, the world and everything in it began to *cooperate* with the plan that I had for my future."

The actor stopped chewing. "You telling me your mind was *influencing*...reality?"

"That's exactly what I'm saying."

"So, our mind and world are connected?" ventured the actor.

"Inextricably linked. Furthermore, my extensive research in the fields of mind science and peak performance, and my personal experiences with this 'Mind/Reality Relationship,' have taught me that one's ability to alter one's reality is exponentially increased when one takes a *systematic* approach to success in life and business. In fact, I've spent 10 years and 10,000 hours fashioning everything that I've learned about mind control and peak performance into a system which anyone can use to transform dreams into reality…with scientific precision. I call it the '*Dream Acquisition Formula*'."

Popcorn crumbs fell from the actor's lap as he moved to the edge of his seat. "This *formula?* It really works?"

"Anyone who's ever fulfilled an 'impossible dream' or achieved some great feat has used it. It is more often used by accident than by design, but *always* with destiny-defining ramifications. Take me, for instance. An application of this Dream Acquisition Formula is my secret for rising from the gutter to 30,000 feet above sea-level. What's more, I did it in a fraction of the time it takes most people just to reach the second floor. And I'm just getting started. Does the formula work? It works with the unfailing precision of the interplanetary rotation of our solar system. And the activating ingredient is mind control."

Just then, the pilot came over the intercom. Clear skies welcomed our 3-hour ETA for Philadelphia.

The actor and I spent the rest of the flight discussing the secrets of mind control, the mysteries of the Mind/Reality Relationship, and the seven elements of my revolutionary formula for transforming dreams into reality.

"Kid, your star is on the rise," wooed the actor as he reached into his sport coat and produced a pair of cigars. "Cohiba?"

I grasped one in appreciation. "You really *are* my hero."

"I'll never forget what you did for me today," vowed my newest fan. He reached over to light my cigar, smirked, and admitted, "You know, I would have paid $100 grand for the feeling I have right now."

“What a coincidence,” I replied, puffing my stogie and opening my laptop. “That happens to be my fee.”

The actor roared. “You know, kid, there are millions of folks out there who could use an hour on your couch—people who could really benefit from your expertise in mind science and peak performance. Ever think about writing a book?”

“Actually…” I produced a grin while twisting my laptop toward the star. “My book is called, *‘Mind Contrology.’* It’s due to begin hitting shelves later this year.”

“Mind Guru, that book of yours is going to empower the masses.”

Cigar clenched between my teeth, I closed my eyes and imagined my readers flipping to the first chapter…mastering their minds…revolutionizing their lives…fulfilling their dreams.

Yeah,” I whispered, breathing rhythmically, “That’s exactly how I imagine it.”

# MASTER YOUR MIND

*The "Precursor" to the Dream Acquisition Formula (DAF)*

# 1

# The Amazing Brain

*Workshop of Legendary Genius*

*"The potential powers of your mind are beyond comprehension."*
-Dr. Napoleon Hill

Think you're making the best possible use of your brain? Chances are, you're not even *close* to maximum cognitive performance.

Harvard psychologist William James observed that, "Most people live, whether physically, intellectually or morally, in a very restricted circle of their potential being. They make use of a very small portion of their available consciousness." A landmark Stanford University study similarly revealed that most people employ as little as 5% of their total brain capacity. Furthermore, *Mind Contrology's* decade-long research of a large cross-section of America's 320 million citizens has shown that less than 5% of the population understands the 1st Rule of Mentality: *The mind rises to the challenges placed before it.*

Well, what if I told you that you could *learn* to operate at 50%, 75%, or a full 100% of the intellectual, imaginative, and other mental resources that represent your total cognitive output?

Before you write this feat off as impossible, consider this…

Legendary genius Thomas Edison was one of the greatest *Mind Contrologists* of the 20th century. Edison routinely spent 100 hours per week managing his Jersey-based lab; building Edison, Inc. into a global energy empire; and amassing a fortune worth billions by today's standards. What's more, he managed to maintain this level of mental and physical productivity into his 70's.

In 1912, while working through the night on a quest to produce a starter motor for the Ford Model-T, Edison, 65, barged into his R&D department where a young engineer was laboring at a workstation strewn with tools, charts, and experimental motors.

"What say you and I put our heads together and conquer this project tonight?" hollered a nearly deaf Edison through a cheek full of tobacco.

Already well into the evening, the engineer, perhaps indulging his pocket watch for effect, protested, "Mr. Edison, I've been at this puzzle for weeks and have pursued every reasonable solution I could conjure, to no avail. The hour is late. Perhaps a night's rest will bring progress."

The Master Inventor produced a knowing smile. "Dear boy, a life's worth of experience has taught me this—reasonable approaches never work. Thank God you are out of sensible approaches. Now we can think-up the *unreasonable solution* this project requires!"

The question is: How did Thomas Edison—a self-educated, hearing impaired paperboy from Ohio—manage to summon forth the mental, physical, and spiritual energies by which to overcome his "limitations" and accomplish more throughout his lifetime than 1,000 other men combined…without skipping a beat…well into his golden years?

Think Edison was born with superior intelligence or some super-gene which predisposed him to the grand scale success that elevated him from the shadows of obscurity to the pages of history? "That's not true," Edison once responded to that very line of questioning. "Any other bright-minded fellow can accomplish just as much if he will stick like hell and remember that nothing works by itself, just to please you. You've got to make the damn thing work!"

Simply put, Edison regularly operated according to the 1st Rule of Mentality*: The mind rises to the challenges placed before it.*

By applying this simple rule to your own life, career, relationships, and finances, you, too, can…

1. Tap into reservoirs of mentality you never knew existed
2. Increase your authority over your life and world to an astonishing degree

Once you've begun to master the operations of your amazing brain, you'll open the door to powers and potentialities you've never dreamed of possessing, and there'll be no limit to what you can do.

## Your Amazing Brain

*Fascinating Facts about the "Physical Mind"*

*"At the top of your spinal cord...sits the most complex and amazing object on Earth—the human brain."*
-Dr. Maggie Greenwood-Robinson

The entire Universe is made up of only two elements: energy and matter. Step in front of a mirror and you will discover the most powerful marriage of these two elements known to man—your *amazing brain.*

Following are some stimulating facts about your brain.

• Your amazing brain is a 3-pound, self-governing superstructure made up of about 100 billion neurons (or brain cells,) each equipped with its *own* miniature brain.

• Your brain and body love to communicate. Your central nervous system (consisting of your brain and spinal cord) exchanges near-instantaneous electrochemical messages with your body's more than 600 muscles over a vast and intricate fiber-optic, neural network. If stretched lengthwise, this network would span from New York to Paris, and *back again.* Messages travel this network at speeds of 5.8 miles per second!

• Cooperation between your cerebral cortex and brain stem allow you to process a staggering 25 million bits of stored information and environmental data in little more time than it takes to blink an eye.

And that's only the beginning...

*"Your brain weighs only three pounds, yet it is the most complex object in the solar system."*
-Michio Kaku, PhD

• Your neurological power plant contains electrochemical ionic transfers capable of energizing a 25-watt light bulb. If converted into pure energy, however, your amazing brain could supply the energy demands of a small country for about four years.

• Haven't been taking care of your brain? Don't panic. It's entirely possible to reverse *years' worth* of cognitive atrophy caused by cerebral inactivity. Forging new habits of mental and physical exercise forces your brain to build new synapses (neural bridges) and dendrites (receptor stations) through a process called "neural connectivity." Healthy lifestyle choices (including smart eating and sleeping habits) have also been shown to prevent mental aging, increase brain mass, and even *regenerate* brain cells.

• A full 25% of your daily caloric and oxygen intake is used by your brain as it regulates more than 6,000 physiological processes and generates your mind's precious energy—your *thoughts.*

• *Your brain gives a whole new meaning to the term* "team player." If one region becomes damaged, healthy regions have been known to compensate by taking over the functions assigned to the impaired regions! Science refers to this miracle as "neural plasticity."

Your amazing brain is the supreme power-source behind all that you think, say, and do. Whether you're drawing the morning's first breath or brushing your teeth, accessing your favorite memory or visualizing your future, feeling down in the dumps or motivated to excel, your *brain* is in charge. And your brain's critical role as life-systems overlord never ends. Regulating your respiratory and circulatory systems 24/7, your brain is responsible for keeping you alive, even as you sleep.

Separated from your brain, your heart would stop beating and life as you know it would cease to exist. Of course, if you take charge of this vital resource—and award it the reverence and attention it deserves—peak performance will become the norm for you, and the possibilities will multiply by the second.

*"The mind is the great lever of all things; human thought is the process by which all human ends are ultimately answered."*
-Daniel Webster

## The Only "Average Brain" is an *Unchallenged* Brain

The human brain is a vast storehouse of unlimited potential waiting to be unleashed.

Super-CEO Jack Welch stumbled upon this fact during the 1980s and 1990s while managing General Electric through one of the most impressive growth spurts in the history of business. Dr. Welch had many brilliant ideas during his legendary tenure at the helm of America's largest manufacturer, including the orchestration of a series of profitable acquisitions and the introduction of Six Sigma. Jack's most revolutionary idea, however, was that of tapping the collective "brain-power" of his *entire* organization.

Sensing that buried within GE's ranks existed a deep pool of human intellect waiting to be discovered, Welch directed his senior managers to begin cultivating the ideas and suggestions of every GE employee, regardless of title, rank or pay-rate.

The results were nothing less than astonishing.

During a seminar designed to invite new ideas from among the ranks, a production worker normally assigned to mundane tasks was encouraged to help brainstorm a solution to a complex operational dilemma. Instructors assured the worker that his ideas would be taken seriously, and implemented if feasible. Confident that his opinion mattered, the worker performed a small miracle.

In a display that typifies the power of the unobstructed mind, the emboldened worker leapt to the front of the classroom and scribbled onto the blackboard the solution to a manufacturing riddle which had been plaguing GE executives for months!

**POINT TO PONDER:** The solution to General Electric's problem had been lying dormant inside the amazing brain of an "average worker" who, until that day, had never been asked to use his brain instead of his brawn.

This was not an isolated incident. Similar results were replicated throughout the company, enabling Dr. Welch to transform General Electric from a bureaucratic $30 billion conglomerate into a high-performance "learning organization" once valued at over $500 billion!

*"Thoughts rule the world.*
*Beware when the Great God lets loose*
*a thinker on the planet."*
-Ralph Waldo Emerson

**GURU'S TIP**: The 1st Rule of Mentality states: *The mind rises to the challenges placed before it.*

When you aim high and challenge yourself by directing your thoughts toward challenging goals, you stimulate "neural connectivity," you open the door to lucrative ideas and unstoppable inner-resources, and you set the stage for personal and professional milestones you never dreamed possible.

*"As intricate a mass as your brain is, you are still only using a fraction of its available power."*
-Marilyn vos Savant
World's Smartest Person

So, if the average brain houses such extraordinary resources, why don't more people harness these powers and use them to revolutionize their *lives* the way Jack Welch revolutionized GE?

Quite simply, as much as 99.9% of the population is in the dark about the life-altering forces which are available to them within their mind. After all, no one was ever given an "operating manual" by which to understand the brain and unleash the mind's limitless powers.

That is, until now...

# 2

# Discovering Your Mental Theater

*Neural Universe of Magic and Wonder*

*"The mind is a dangerous weapon, even to the possessor, if he knows not how to use it."*
-Miquel de Montaigne

Close your eyes and you will discover—your "Mental Theater."

Housed inside your skull but in no way limited to flesh, fluid, and neurons, your *Mental Theater* can best be described as a living machine of fascinating neurological features and powerful mental processes. By placing these features and processes under your control, you will discover an extraordinary capacity for managing your life, career, relationships, and finances.

The primary components of your Mental Theater include:

- **Cerebrum:** The facilitator of learning and intelligence

- **"Mental Language" Center**: The epicenter of all the communication that takes place between you, your mind, and your world

- **Memory**: The part of your brain that enables you to draw upon the inspiration of your greatest experiences in the blink of an eye

- **Internal Messaging System (IMS)**: Through your IMS, you may *record* and *replay* the audible messages of your choosing

• **Limbic System**: The feature of your Mental Theater that enables you to generate *passion* to fuel your dreams

By bringing your Mental Theater under your command, you bring within your grasp everything else under the sun. You may begin this process now by gaining an intimate knowledge of the fascinating features that represent your neural universe of magic and wonder.

Consider this chapter an "operating manual" for your amazing brain…

## The Cerebrum

*Taking Charge of Your Rational Mind*

*"Every man's reason is every man's oracle."*
-Henry St. John

Your cerebrum, working as a team with your cerebral cortex, plays the role of your "rational mind." Assisted by its cortex, your cerebrum—the birthplace of logic and reason—governs a host of *left-brain* activities ranging from speech, reading, and decision-making, to creating, learning, and foresight.

Together, your cerebrum and cerebral cortex enable you to perform everyday tasks such as: reading your watch (transforming numbers and dials into the concept of *time,)* transforming thoughts into dialogue, processing mathematical equations like 2+2=4, and managing your money. Your cerebral hemispheres also house the intellectual capacity by which you may skillfully manage the complex affairs of your personal and professional agendas.

Without your cerebrum, your existence would be little more than a blank stare from a motionless body. Applied to a quest for embetterment, however, your rational mind can elevate you to the highest plateaus of peak performance.

## Leonardo da Vinci's Secret to *Mind Control* and *Peak Performance*:

*Cerebral Stimulation through Self-education*

The habit of self-education isn't only a wonderful way to stimulate your cerebrum; it's the key to personal advancement regardless of circumstances.

Consider Leonardo da Vinci...

Born in 1452, Leonardo da Vinci was the illegitimate son of an attorney and his peasant lover. Raised in the village of Vinci in Tuscany, Italy, Leonardo wasn't born into money. He never attended college. And his IQ, most experts agree, was about average. Nevertheless, Leonardo managed to excel in more than a dozen different fields.

At age 15, da Vinci began an apprenticeship with a local sculptor. After earning his Master's Certification in art by age 24, Leonardo began his first commissioned sculpture in 1482 at the age of 30. The 20' statue earned the sculptor instant celebrity across Italy and France. That same year, da Vinci—possessing no prior experience related to his desired positions—convinced Duke Sforza of Milan to bring him on as a structural engineering consultant and, oddly, a self-taught military strategist.

It was while working as an engineer and military strategist that Leonardo adopted the habit of studying the methods of current experts in the fields in which he wished to excel. And da Vinci used this strategy often. When he wasn't working for Duke Sforza or creating artistic masterpieces, da Vinci took on roles including: inventor, craftsman, writer, mathematician, and businessman.

Throughout his legendary life, Leonardo invented the catapult, drew up plans for a primitive helicopter, engineered an armored vehicle, devised brilliant war strategies, wrote about "solar power," and built the first calculator. Leonardo also contributed to the world of medicine (da Vinci is credited with performing one of the first known autopsies.)

Of course, da Vinci also created the "Mona Lisa." Although Leonardo would later in life conclude that "I have not labored at my art as I should have," da Vinci's Mona Lisa now reigns amongst the world's most valuable artistic treasures.

*"The rational mind is a faithful servant."*
-Albert Einstein

So, how did Leonardo da Vinci—an illegitimate child who possessed no formal schooling—manage to master the dozen-plus professions that delivered him wealth, fame, and a legacy which has survived the ages? Quite simply, da Vinci dreamed big, and consistently *stimulated his cerebrum* through the habit of self-education. And his brain faithfully rose to each progressive challenge. Like da Vinci, your ability to learn, do, and conquer is not dependent on who your parents are, where you grew up, how far you went in school, or how much money you have in the bank. All that matters is what you want to accomplish and when you want to get started.

Is there some great feat you wish to accomplish? Educate yourself according to your goal, take action—and make it happen.

## "Mental Language" Center

*How to Master the Mental Language Barrier*

*"We are to employ the mind to rule,*
*the body rather to serve."*
-Sallust

Albert Einstein asserted that one's mind should act as one's obedient servant. Fortunately, it doesn't take an IQ of Einsteinian proportions to assume the role of *master* in the relationship between yourself and your mind. In fact, getting your brain to obey your wishes is a relatively straightforward task once you learn to speak the "language" by which your mind *communicates.*

To illustrate the importance of speaking in your mind's native tongue, consider the following.

Let's say you're a busy restaurant owner who's trying to train a new chef who speaks a foreign language. Through much frustrated effort, you get your employee to follow a *few* of your instructions, but most of your important wants and needs continue to get lost in translation. The "language barrier" is preventing you from realizing the benefits of your servant's vast abilities, and, as a result, progress has come to a standstill.

Because you believe that your chef possesses enormous potential, you want the relationship to work. Outsmarting the situation, you take a course in your employee's native tongue and, with a little effort, you not only begin to understand everything your servant has been trying to tell you, but your every command is soon being carried out with explicit attention to detail.

Mastering the mind works this way.

By learning to *speak* the mind's *language,* you are enabled to (1) interpret with ease the information your brain is attempting to send you, and (2) feed your brain the specific instructions you wish it to carry out. When you speak "mind," your every wish is your brain's command.

So, just what is the mind's special language?

## The Mind's Language

*External Sensory Perception and Internal Audio-animation*

Around the clock, you are in constant communication with both the external world and your innermost self. This unceasing interplay of communication represents a neuro-language, which, when understood, provides the basis for your ability to navigate effectively through life.

The language of the mind may be broken into two major dialects:

1) **External Sensory Perception**: What you see, smell, touch, taste, and hear as you move through your environment.

2) **Internal Audio-animation:** The *images* (accessed memories or future projections) you "see," and the *messages* you "hear" within your Mental Theater. Audio-animation also includes the *bodily sensations* you experience as a result of these images and messages.

*"The strong man is the one who is able to interpret at will the communication between the mind and the senses."*
-Napoleon Bonaparte

### The Subliminal Influence of Internal Audio-animation

The constant stream of images, messages, and feelings which we generate inside of our Mental Theater (and experience in our body) is an unrivaled director of human behavior. Just how much influence does this unceasing stream of internal communication exert over the quality of our lives? Consider this…

In 1974, American companies were banned by the federal government from advertising by way of flashing brief images of their products on movie and television screens. The reason? The practice of broadcasting lively images of products (such as a close-up of a fizzling, ice-cold soda) was found to have rendered an "unethical level" of influence over the behavior of those being shown the images.

Simply put, flash-image advertising was corralling unsuspecting moviegoers to concession stands like herds of mindless cattle.

Now just imagine the influence your *own* Mental Theater—which flashes anywhere from 60,000 to 100,000 discernable thoughts across the "viewing screen" inside your mind during any given 24-hour period—has over what you think, say, and do.

This is why it is so important that you move from a position of *responding* to the activity taking place inside your Mental Theater, to one of *directing* it.

Speaking mind is largely a matter of forging the habits of taking control of your thoughts, self-talk, and feelings; and of proactively managing the communication that takes place between your mind and your world. In doing so, the mental "language barrier" will become a thing of the past, and you will be well on your way not only to managing your mind, but to mastering it.

### You Will Learn to Speak "Mind"… and Much More

Before you finish this book, you will gain unprecedented control over your mind by learning to communicate fluently in the least understood, yet most important, dialect of mental language—*internal audio-animation.* Along your journey to becoming a 21st century *Mind Contrologist…*

- You'll learn to manage your *Mental Theater*, deciding for yourself what images, messages, and feelings drive your days.
- You'll discover the *"7 Pillars of "Mind Control!"*—a set of mind control principles you can use to begin taking immediate control of your life, career, relationships, and finances.
- You'll find out how to produce and direct your own *"Mental Movies,"* an advanced mental mastery technique which will enable you to script your own destiny and maximize your God-given potential.
- You'll also discover the *"Mind/Reality Relationship,"* and learn how to use this thought-activated relationship between your mind and your world to the benefit of you, your family, and your fellows.

Right now, let's delve deeper into the functions of your Mental Theater…

## The Human Memory

*Leveraging Your Interactive Library of Life Experiences*

*"The power of memory is great, very great, my God. It is a vast and infinite profundity."*
-Saint Augustine

Located within your hippocampus is an expansive "interactive library" of still-framed images and streaming motion pictures.

Exhibiting an audio-visual reference capacity of 2.8x10$_{2}$ (the equivalent of about 10 million 1000-page books,) your brain is a vast archive of past experiences stored primarily in the contexts of sight and sound. Through the miracle of command-of-thought, you're able to access decades-old memories, with lightning speed and pinpoint accuracy, as if these experiences had taken place just *moments* ago. Your most dominating memories (whether painful or pleasant) can retain potency, affecting you for worse or for better, for as long as you live.

## How Memories Influence Mood and Behavior

Research has shown that the mind has a hard time distinguishing between real and imagined events. For some people, this presents a real problem.

For instance, drivers often develop a paralyzing fear of the road following a major car wreck. Why? Distraught drivers "show themselves" detailed images of their recent accident. Memory drives this fear despite statistics that prove chances of a second wreck drop off markedly after a major accident.

Fortunately, there's a flipside. Your *favorite* memories are just as effective at enhancing your mood and physiology as your worst memories are at destroying them. Accessing your most cherished memories puts a smile on your face and pep in your step, and also "tricks" your brain into releasing endorphins—your brain's *feel-good* neurotransmitter. By proactively accessing your fondest memories, you get to relive your greatest moments, and improve your overall well-being in the process, at any time you wish.

## 3 Empowering Purposes of Memory

*(1) Past experiences* teach you what works and what doesn't, providing the basis for sound decision-making.

(2) Your *semantic memory* enables you to retain the facts, concepts, information, and experiences that represent your body of knowledge.

(3) *Pleasant* memories elevate your mood and enrich your life.

**GURU'S TIP**: Memory is a standard neurological feature which holds enormous power to either ruin or enrich your days, depending upon which memories you habitually access. Exploit your memory to your advantage by calling upon only the happiest, most motivating memories in your interactive library.

## Your "Internal Messaging System" (IMS):

*Decoding the Mystery of Your Inner-voice*

*"None of us will ever accomplish anything excellent or commanding, except when he listens to the voice that is heard by him alone."*

-Ralph Waldo Emerson

One of the most baffling mysteries of the human mind can be found in your ability to "hear" audible messages through the "audio system" (or left inferior frontal gyrus) within your Mental Theater. While these messages are initially interpreted through your physical ears, they are "recorded" and "played back" through your mental audio system in much the same way that you may download and listen to songs on your iPod.

Sources of these messages can include: parents and friends, teachers and classmates, bosses and coworkers, media and entertainment, religious sermons, marketing and advertising, as well as the audible translations of your *own* deepest thoughts.

The neurological audio system which enables you to experience all of this dialogue may be referred to as your "Internal Messaging System"—or IMS.

## Worst Enemy IMS vs. Wise, Old Mentor IMS

The quality of the messages we choose to download, replay, and *internalize* directly contributes to the quality of our mental and emotional states, our physiology (or body language,) and our overall quality of life.

For instance, imagine yourself strolling along a tranquil path at your favorite park. You're enjoying Nature's bounty and contemplating your goals for the future when suddenly a filthy vagrant springs from the bushes, berating you with a barrage of degrading comments like, "You're stupid, ugly, weak, out of shape, and you'll never amount to anything!"

You feel cornered, violated, and angry. So, what do you do? Chances are you'll either pick up the pace and ditch this loser or give your verbal assailant a stiff dose of his own medicine. Surely no one in their right mind would endure this kind of abuse without taking bold, decisive action.

Of course, many folks *do* put up with this kind of abuse—inside their own heads—not just for minutes, hours or days, but for *years* and *decades!*

*"If you hear a voice in your head say,*
*'you cannot paint,' then by all means paint,*
*and that voice will be silenced."*
-Vincent van Gogh

Now consider another scenario. While walking along your chosen path in life, you're accompanied by a wise, old mentor. Wanting only the best for you, your mentor reminds you of your best attributes and focuses you on your goals. Supporting you in your bold plans for the future, this person reminds you of truths like; "You can achieve anything you set your mind to," and, "You're capable of far more than you realize." As you continue along your journey, increasingly motivated and empowered, your wise, old mentor guides you along beautiful paths you never knew existed, paths which provide short-cuts to all the places in life you've always wanted to go.

We all talk to ourselves. We've all got an *inner-voice.* For some of us, the Internal Messaging System (IMS) is an enemy which keeps its "hostage" locked in a prison of criticism, defeatism, and seemingly unexplainable failures. For others, the inner-messenger is a wise, old mentor who guides its "beloved apprentice" along an enchanted path of sound advice, priceless encouragement, and unceasing progress.

The question is: How does the person who suffers from any number of self-defeating prerecorded messages move from the role of a self-ascribed hostage to that of one's own best friend and trusted advisor?

## Mastering Your Internal Messaging System

*How to Transform Your Inner-voice into that of a Wise, Old Mentor*

(1) **Guard the gate:** Never accept a defeating message from your own inner-voice (or from anyone else.)

(2) **"Delete" unwelcome messages:** The instant an undesirable message surfaces, break the cycle by verbalizing an overriding command like, *"Stop," "Wrong," "Correction,"* etc.

(3) **"Record" superior messages**: Immediately declare a new, empowering message which *directly counters* any unwanted message. Is that little voice of doubt whispering, "No, you can't?" Boldly silence that voice by shouting aloud, "Yes…I *can!*"

(4) **"Implant" chosen messages daily**: Start each day (and end each night) by proactively *implanting* an optimistic message of encouragement into your Internal Messaging System.

Say it out loud and with conviction.

**GURU'S TIP:** Remember, you retain unquestionable authority over what goes on inside your head. Program your IMS with empowering messages on a daily basis until your inner-voice has taken on a life of its own—that of a wise, old mentor!

# The Limbic System

*Deciphering the Secrets of Your "Emotional" Brain*

*"Anyone who is capable of stimulating his or her mind to produce intense desire is capable also of the achievement of that desire."*
-Dr. Dennis Kimbro

Located in the mid-brain, your *limbic system* produces the bodily sensations you associate with "emotion." Your limbic system fires electrochemical messages (traveling at more than 300 mph) to create the natural, physical sensations you know as joy and pain, fear and intrigue, sexual excitement, and even...*love*.

Your limbic system, working in concert with external sensory perception and internal audio-animation, also triggers your Internal Motivation Mechanism (IMM,) which generates the motivating force we refer to as "passion."

## How "Passion" Works

To understand how *passion* works, let's turn to Michelangelo. What was the "magic recipe" that fueled Michelangelo's passion for painting and enabled him to create such legendary masterpieces as the Sistine Chapel?

It was a combination of the following:

(1) **External Sensory Perception**: Michelangelo enjoyed the sight of the chapel's enormous, vaulted ceiling—his *canvas.* He craved the compliments of clients and admirers, and loved to be referred to as the "Pride of Italy." The scent and colors of the paint and the feel of the brush in his hand also stimulated the artist's senses. And Michelangelo thrived on the company of his assistants.

(2) **Internal Audio-animation**: What motivated Michelangelo internally? Visualizing the finished product—the biblical mural—certainly excited the artist. The Italian sought prosperity, and surely

imagined what he'd buy with the 500 ducats (5 times the average artist's *annual* salary) he received just for *beginning* the project. Michelangelo also fanned the flames of his passion by way of empowering beliefs and self-labeling. The Italian insisted that a "fortunate alignment of the stars" predestined him to mastery of the arts, and often referred to himself as the "world's greatest artist."

**GURU'S TIP:** For Michelangelo, the above combination of external sensory data and internal audio-animation was the "magic recipe" that triggered his limbic system into generating the neurophysiological drive (or passion) which enabled him to create a lifelong series of legendary masterpieces.

To discover your own "magic recipe" for passion, simply determine what combination of external sensory data and internal audio-animation triggers your unique limbic system into action. In later chapters, you'll discover the "magic recipe" for passion by which you may get motivated—and sustain momentum—24/7.

In the meantime, remember this about your limbic system: The bodily sensations we associate with *emotion,* and the neurophysiological drive we refer to as *passion,* are both entirely manufactured in the brain.

*"Unlock your mind,*
*you have the magic power."*
-Pat Croche

## The "Physical Mind"

*in a Nutshell*

Over the last two chapters you've learned quite a bit about your *amazing brain.*

You know that you've been operating on only a small portion of your total neurological capabilities, and that your brain will rise to the challenges and expectations you place upon yourself.

You've discovered your Mental Theater—the epicenter of your past, present, and future. Within your Mental Theater exists the uncultivated seed of all that you will experience, acquire, and become. Your Mental Theater is the place where all of your limitations end, and your dreams begin.

You've already learned more about your mind than perhaps 1,000 average individuals combined. However, we've only scratched the surface of what your mind can do.

What if I told you that deep within your mind you possess the power to overcome horrific circumstances, to forge the superior "reality" of your choosing, and to perform certifiable miracles of progress in your life, career, relationships, and finances?

Interested? Then turn the page, and let's explore the world of *mental miracles...*

# 3

# Mental Miracles

*The Limitless Power of the Human Mind*

*"We have found that by reaching for what appears to be impossible, we actually do the impossible."*
-Dr. Jack Welch
CEO, GE

Go beyond the physical brain and you will discover the miraculous resources of the *human mind.* Your mind is a limitless storehouse of intellect, energy, creativity, willpower, possibility, and strength which must be summoned forth and experienced to be fully appreciated. Great personal breakthroughs and "unexplainable" feats of superhuman ability become suddenly possible for those who—by accident or design—awaken the hidden forces of the mind and set them in motion.

For instance, Laura Schultz (a 62 year-old grandmother) lifted a car from her injured grandson in Tallassee, Florida in 1977. Indiana's Ralph Braun (confined to a wheelchair at age 14) overcame muscular dystrophy by going on to build a $200 million company. And in 2016, Patrick Downs completed the Boston Marathon in 5 hours and 56 minutes, in spite of his so-called "limitation" of having only one leg.

These are the stories that raise the bar on hope, redefine what the world considers possible, and incite a level of awe which takes one's breath away. And underlying each of these stories are the miraculous forces of the *human mind.*

A conscious awakening of the mind's powers enables one to take charge of one's life, to alter one's immediate and future circumstances, and to improve one's world in ways that only a true *Mind Contrologist* can. Genesis 1:27-28 tells us that we are created in the likeness of God and admonishes us to "bring the Earth under your control." In no other fashion is man's divinity more clearly demonstrated than in our inborn ability to perform our very own miracles of triumph over circumstance.

## Performance Miracles

*The "Unexplainable Phenomenon" of Superhuman Feats*

*"We are really just beginning to understand the tremendous powers of the mind and how it works."*
-Michael LeBoeuf, PhD

It was during WWII in 1943 that the 26 year-old captain of gunboat PT-109 accidentally awakened the unlimited powers within him, forces that would mean the difference between life and death for him and his men.

Somewhere in the South Pacific, among a cluster of untraveled islands, the gunboat full of American seamen was afloat under the cover of pitch-black nightfall. Suddenly…tragedy struck. The crew of PT-109 never saw the 2,000-ton Japanese naval destroyer which rammed their gunboat broadside, ripping the smaller vessel in two. As the destroyer sailed off into the night, the crew of U.S. seamen struggled to keep from drowning in the cold, black waters. Watching the first of his men perish, the young captain engaged his mighty mind, summoning deep, dormant powers which recognize no limits, create their own rules, and transcend even the most dire of circumstances. Fighting to get his bearings, the skinny captain searched the endless waters, spotted what looked like land upon the horizon, and then dragged his remaining crew members to a nearby, deserted island.

Later, trapped on a sliver of land in the middle of nowhere, with no food, water or operable radio equipment, the captain's crew surrendered their destinies into the hands of fate. The captain, however, focused on a way out…and prepared to *master* fate.

It was miles, estimated the hero, to the nearest island where he could locate help for his ailing men. So, driven by a mind alive with visions of saving his crew, the captain summoned forth the energy he would need to reach his impossible destination, and then took to the shark-infested water in the dead of night.

One can only imagine the shock of the deserted crew members when the captain returned with the rescuers who would deliver them to safety!

That naval hero later turned his focus to politics, launched his first congressional campaign at age 29, and then took the White House by storm at age 44—becoming one of the most beloved American presidents in recent history. Who was the captain of PT-109? John F. Kennedy. Once asked what triggered the unstoppable drive that had fueled his wartime heroics, Kennedy modestly replied, "It was involuntary. They sunk my ship."

*"Whenever you hear about someone performing unbelievable feats...it is because of the power of their mind."*
-Arnold Schwarzenegger

**POINT TO PONDER:** The mind's hidden powers are often discovered accidentally in the course of some unexpected emergency. So, imagine the vast scope of superior performance capabilities that become available to the person who learns to access the mind's reservoirs of energy and might on *purpose*.

## Miracles of Personal Achievement

*The Infinite Possibilities of the Human Mind*

*"Slumbering in every human being lies an infinity of possibilities, which one should not arouse in vain."*
-Elias Canetti

Magnificent success stories are rarely created by folks who enjoy the advantages of exceptional brains, unlimited finances, and perfect circumstances. To the contrary, the most inspiring accounts of human triumph this world has ever known have been engineered by ordinary—and often highly *disadvantaged*—men, women, and children who have awakened the dormant resources of the human mind while in pursuit of some "impossible" dream or goal.

Take Napoleon Bonaparte, for instance.

Born in 1769 on the Italian island of Corsica, Napoleon Bonaparte was short, sickly, and strange-looking. He also disliked school. On a school exam that typified Napoleon's academic hardships, the youngster placed 15th out of the 16 students in his class. However, what the boy lacked in height, looks, and academics, he made up for in bold aspirations of greatness.

In 1780, Bonaparte entered military school at age 11. There, he grew in confidence and began to excel. By the time he graduated some five years later, Napoleon had adopted the personal mantra, "With audacity, one can undertake anything." Operating according to this newfound philosophy, Napoleon developed a dream of becoming a prestigious military officer.

Suddenly compelled to abandon his homeland of Corsica, Bonaparte, 16, pledged allegiance to France and joined the French army as a second lieutenant in an artillery regiment. While struggling merely to speak and write French, Napoleon skillfully ascended the ranks of the military by befriending superiors, favoring peers who treated him kindly, scolding anyone who dared challenge him, and bewildering the brass with his broad, self-taught knowledge of military strategy.

By 1794, less than a decade after infiltrating the French military, Napoleon Bonaparte finagled himself a promotion to general. He was just 25 years old.

In 1795, after having become one of the youngest generals in the history of the French military, Bonaparte recalibrated his mental horizons. This time, Napoleon's vision included the *throne* of France.

Bonaparte's loftier mental focus brought about an equally heightened degree of strategic brilliance. Carefully setting the stage for his role as emperor, Napoleon spent the next several years helping the French government conquer its neighboring towns. Through his victories as a "loyal general," Bonaparte's scope of command increased, his alliances multiplied, and his public popularity grew.

At last, it was time to carry out his plan.

Confident that the people of France were on his side, Bonaparte began recruiting members of his own family into key military positions. Then, after quietly and brilliantly assembling across France a loyal, personal army of relatives who refused to betray him and lackeys who were too afraid to dissent, Napoleon used his private army to overthrow France's government and place himself into power.

In 1804, at the age of 35, Napoleon Bonaparte, a short, weak, unattractive slacker from the slums of Corsica became a living testament to his personal philosophies "I create circumstances" and "Impossible is the adjective of fools" by achieving the unthinkable—crowning *himself* emperor of France!

Want to achieve a miracle of peak performance? Engage your mind by developing a dream for your life, career, relationships, and finances. As Napoleon Bonaparte has shown, the *hidden forces* of your mentality will stop at nothing on your behalf once you have awakened these functions and placed them under your control by focusing your thoughts on some specific, energizing purpose of good.

*"What pulls the strings is*
*the Force hidden within."*
-Marcus Aurelius

Still not convinced that you can do anything you set your mind to? You'll find all the proof you need in the following story about Helen Keller's astonishing triumph over the most horrific set of circumstances...

Born in 1880 in Tuscumbia, Alabama, Helen Keller was just 19 months old when a mysterious illness stole away her sight and hearing. Helen's parents were devastated, and after consulting with a series of doctors who labeled their daughter's condition as "hopeless," the Kellers found themselves running out of places to turn for help. Helen was seven when Alexander Graham Bell, a Keller family friend and educator of the deaf, referred the child to a legally blind teacher named Anne Sullivan.

Sullivan became Helen's guardian angel. Daily, the teacher supplied her student with clever methods for *focusing her mind's-eye away from what she couldn't do, and toward what she could do*. Sullivan taught Helen to "hear" by touching the throats of others, and how to "speak" by spelling out her desires through a method that resembled Morse code. Keller was soon reading both Braille and lips. Suddenly rescued from her dark and lonely pit of despair and exposed to a world of language and learning, something magical happened—Helen experienced an awakening of her dormant personal powers.

Setting her sights on a whole new realm of possibilities, Helen began attending lectures with Sullivan by her side translating the lectures into her hands. It was while attending a conference with Sullivan that Helen began to *visualize* what she wanted to do with her future, boldly declaring, "I long to achieve a great and noble task." Keller's task? To earn a college degree and become a success.

In 1900, Helen, 20 years old and newly empowered by her can-do attitude, enrolled at Ratcliffe College where she mastered English, French, Latin, and Greek; penned her autobiography "The Story of My Life" in 1903; and then graduated with honors in 1904. Once labeled "hopelessly catatonic" by a local doctor, Helen went on to perform her own miracle of personal achievement by becoming an educated scholar, famous author, captivating orator, and brave crusader for the rights of the sensory impaired.

*"Conscious power exists in the mind of everyone...*
*to develop it is to individualize all that is best within you,*
*and offer it to the world."*
-James Russell Lowell

So, how does Helen Keller describe the moment at which she discovered her internal eyesight, awakened her inner-potential, and seized control of her life? Keller says, "A *potent force* within me impelled me…to try my strength against the standards of those who see and hear." Keller insists, "One must never consent to creep when one feels the impulse to soar!"

**GURU'S TIP**: The Forces of Fate eagerly align on the side of the person whose mind becomes focused on *possibilities* instead of limitations.

## Professional Miracles

*Willpower: Source of Business Genius and Vast Wealth*

The human will is nothing short of miraculous. By simply determining what you want and channeling the combined forces of your thoughts and actions in that direction, you can take control of your life and begin transforming your wildest fantasies into your waking reality.

*"Great things do not come by accident;*
*they are manufactured by the human will."*
-Vincent van Gogh

Ross Perot was born in 1930 in Texarkana, Texas. Young Ross's compact stature kept him from dominating the football field and his large ears (exaggerated by his skinny frame) and battered nose (the result of a costly misstep while breaking his father's horse) made him shy around girls. However, what Ross lacked in size and looks he made up for in smarts, guts, and an appetite for progress.

While still in grade school, Perot's cleverness and ability to master circumstances could already be seen operating in plain sight. For instance, at age 13, Ross began searching for a way to earn a *bigger* paycheck. Perot quickly increased his income to twice the going rate by negotiating from his boss a raise for delivering newspapers on horseback to the Texas slums which other delivery boys were too afraid to enter.

It was shortly after his salary renegotiation victory that Ross found the courage to make a prediction which would come to prove legendary. With his mind focused on future success, young Perot began proclaiming to his friends his destiny of one day becoming an executive on the board of directors at General Motors.

After graduating high school in 1947, Perot attended Texarkana Junior College until 1949, joined the Naval Academy in Annapolis that same year, and then spent eight years ascending the ranks in the Navy. And all the while, Ross's subconscious mind was patiently planning a way to bring his childhood dream to fruition.

In 1957, Ross, 27, was fresh out of the Navy and searching for a career in the civilian world. Driven by his penchant for progress, Ross landed a job in sales at IBM. After proving himself a master salesman, Perot asked to be placed on the company's toughest accounts. Within 12 months, Perot was making good money doing what he enjoyed. In spite of his success, however, Ross wasn't content. Something inside of the salesman assured him that there was greater satisfaction to be gained beyond IBM. Perot's discontentedness bubbled to the surface while casually flipping through the pages of a *"Reader's Digest"* magazine. It was as his eyes stumbled upon Henry David Thoreau's famous quote, "The masses of men lead lives of quiet desperation," that Ross's *executive dreams* came back into focus.

With the magazine still in his hands, Ross made the decision to begin taking charge of his professional and financial destinies.

Determined not to be counted among the "desperate masses," Perot quit his job at IBM, and then used a mere $1,000 to launch his own data processing firm, EDS. Perot built EDS around providing data services to the banking and insurance industries; as well as to the federal government, a pioneering business strategy which increased EDS's gross revenues from $400,000 in 1964 to a market value of $230 million following EDS's initial public offering in 1968. Then, just 18 months later, EDS's soaring shares multiplied Ross's net worth to a staggering $1.5 billion.

At last, Perot's subconscious mind figured out a way to make Ross's boyhood dreams real. In 1984, Ross Perot sold EDS to General Motors at a personal gain of $930 million. Later that year, Ross fulfilled is youthful prophesy by attending his first meeting among the board of directors at General Motors!

*"Nothing can resist the human will."*
-Benjamin Disraeli

**GURU'S TIP:** Maybe you, like Napoleon Bonaparte, have dreams of achieving some spectacular feat in spite of one or more "limitations" which have long held you back. Perhaps you imagine overcoming some grave mental or physical barrier as the legendary Helen Keller has shown us to be entirely possible. Or maybe you, like Ross Perot, foresee yourself starting a business and transforming $1000 into a billion dollar empire in just a few, short years.

Whatever *your* dream may be, making your desired reality the object of your daily mental focus is the first step to making it real. By doing so, you will recruit the hidden forces of your mind to the task. And before long, you will come to understand this universal truth: The only thing stopping you from achieving all that you've ever dreamed of and more, is *you*…

# 4

# Medical Miracles

*Evidence of the Mind's Authority over the Physical Being*

*"The human consciousness is capable of manifesting powers which contradict psychological knowledge, just as the human body is capable of manifesting powers which contradict medical knowledge. Both powers and phenomenon may seem miraculous, but they issue forth from the Hidden Laws of man's own being."*
-Paul Brunton

The world of medicine is chockfull of examples of the mind's leading role in matters such as health and wellness, accelerated recovery from injury, longevity, and more. French mathematician Blaise Pascal once wrote, "It is impossible on reasonable grounds to disbelieve in miracles." After ingesting the following stories about the mind's ability to influence—and even *direct*—external circumstances of every kind, you're likely to share Pascal's sentiments...

## Mind Over Matter

Dr. Milton Erickson was born in 1902 in Germany.

In 1919, at the age of 17, Milton contracted polio. Like so many unwitting victims of inaccurate medical prognoses, Erickson was informed by his doctors that he likely would not survive. Milton, fortunately, had other plans.

Virtually paralyzed from the disease which was ravishing his body, Erickson spent his time in the hospital thinking about how to recover. While lying in bed under the spell of polio, Erickson recalled something which would change his life. Milton remembered that, as a child just learning the alphabet, the task seemed at the time to be an undertaking of impossible proportions. Yet, over time, reading and writing the alphabet had become to him as natural as breathing. It was this realization that inspired Erickson to begin the massive undertaking of bringing his body back under the control of his mind.

Through much concentrated effort, Milton managed to regain total control of his motor functions. And it was through this victory over illness that Erickson discovered, and became fascinated with, the phenomenon of *mind over matter.*

After earning his diploma in psycho-analytics in Vienna at age 31, Dr. Milton Erickson would devote his career to the advancement of the field of hypnosis. Over the course of his legendary career, Erickson assisted countless patients in overcoming lifelong barriers such as OCD, mental illnesses, and phobias by helping them use their *own* mind's power to produce cures, as he had done as a teenager.

Erickson's techniques continue to be employed by trained clinical hypnotists around the world.

Acclaimed hypnotherapist Roberta Temes, PhD has witnessed the power of mind over matter taking place on multiple occasions during her hypnosis sessions. While employing the techniques of Ericksonian hypnosis, Temes has reported witnessing her clients producing "red spots" and even *blisters* by accessing memories or visualizing scenarios in which hot objects were being placed on the patient's skin.

Clinical hypnotists often coach their patients into using their mind's power to accentuate the benefits of the mind-body relationship. For instance, hypnotic suggestion has been used to accelerate the healing of broken bones, to remove warts, to speed recovery from horrible burns, and to overcome phobias related to everything from snakes to flying, virtually overnight.

## Mind Over Injury

Evidence of the human mind's authority over the physical being go on and on…

In 1994, Dr. Bruce Moseley was studying the effects of knee surgery on arthritic patients when the hidden powers of his patients' mind took center stage.

Moseley's 165-patient study focused on two groups: Group #1 included patients who received *actual* arthroscopic surgery. Group #2 was comprised of patients who received *mock* surgery. (For this group, Moseley staged elaborate, phony procedures to convince his patients that they were actually undergoing the knife.)

Over the next 24-months, both groups were monitored to assess overall improvement as measured by increased mobility and strength, and absence of pain. The shocking results? The group that *thought* they'd received surgery exhibited recovery characteristics identical to those of the group that underwent actual surgery.

To Dr. Moseley's surprise, his patients' minds proved just as effective at healing knee injuries as the advanced surgical procedures he'd trained for years to perform, and which cost thousands of dollars!

After studying the influence of the human mind over matters of health and wellness on some 2,000 patients, Dr. Norman Cousins, a pioneer in the field of psychoneuroimmunology (or the science of mind over being) recognized, "The body tends to move in the direction of one's expectations, plus or minus."

In Cousins' ground-breaking book *Anatomy of an Illness*, Cousins journals the story of Pablo Casals, an elderly conductor and cellist who fell victim to a crippling form of arthritis. At his weakest point, Casals became bedridden with limbs so stiffened that he could barely go about his daily routine. But when Casals' disease threatened to come between him and his instrument, the musician *reversed* the crippling spell of arthritis using nothing more than a mind focused on his desire to play music. Even until age 95, Casals could be found playing his cello with the effortless passion of a man half his age.

After witnessing Casals' self-willed triumph, Cousins reported, "No one need fear death. We need only fear that we may die without ever having known our greatest power."

*"Look deep into your mind,*
*amazing wonders are there."*
-Norman Vincent Peale

I, too, have had many experiences with the *great power* of mind over matter. During the winter of 2011, for instance, I had the opportunity to put the power of my mind to the task of accelerated healing…

It was just before Christmas and I was carrying a heavy bag on my shoulder when I slipped on a patch of black ice and landed directly on my shoulder. More embarrassed than hurt, I picked myself up and thought little of the fall—until I went home, took off my shirt, and saw the severe bruising which covered my entire shoulder.

An MRI would later show that I'd torn ligaments and muscles in my shoulder. As a result, I was recommended for surgery. Adamantly against going under the knife, and certain that my injury didn't necessitate it, I told my doctor that physical therapy would do just fine and underwent PT as directed. It was during my first session with a therapist named Lydia that I received the shocking news I could hardly stomach.

"No overhead exercises for the next three months," said Lydia.

"WHAT! Three months?" As a lifelong fitness buff, I had not gone three weeks without military presses since the age of 15. This was a devastating blow.

Over the next three months, I attended therapy once per week and followed Lydia's instructions to the letter. And while my shoulder certainly healed, I'd also lost massive amounts of hard-earned muscle and strength. I realized that I had serious work ahead of me if I wanted to return to my pre-injury levels of fitness. But fortunately, I understood the power of the mind/body relationship.

After finally returning to the gym, I went to great lengths to "get in the zone" prior to each routine. Understanding the advantage of a focused mind, I took supplements proven to help improve concentration and build muscle, loaded my iPod with my favorite music, and visualized a speedy recovery. Committed to returning to 100% within 90 days, I started each routine by "grounding" myself mentally and physically (a focusing technique pioneered by Arnold Schwarzenegger,) and cut myself off from distractions such as my cell phone. On shoulder day, I particularly zeroed in on rebuilding in the shortest timeframe the deltoids that had atrophied during my hiatus.

The results of these efforts were astounding.

Over a period of just 45 days (working shoulders once per week to allow for maximum recovery) my military press shot up from 95 pounds for 8 reps to 225 pounds for 6 reps. Ordinarily, an increase of just 5 pounds per week on this exercise would be fabulous. So, this average increase of 21 pounds every week for 6 weeks straight exceeded even my own expectations of what was possible.

Moreover, my top overhead press of 225 pounds for 6 reps outshined even my pre-injury levels of shoulder strength!

How could I accomplish this without the surgery for which I was originally recommended? I attribute my full recovery to visualizing and expecting a full, speedy recovery *on my own terms*, not the doctor's.

*"We carry within us the wonders we seek without."*
-Sir Thomas Browne

## Mind Over Health, Wellness—and More

Apparently, the mind also has dominion over the quality of your health and wellness. Keeping your thoughts trained on health and happiness has been linked to such benefits as decreased blood pressure, improved energy levels, reduced aches and pains, relief from headaches, mitigated stress, less frequency of injury, elevated mood, and a supercharged immune system.

Now may be a good time to ask yourself two questions: *How long do I expect to live?* And, *does my thinking support this expectation?* Science suggests it better…

In her brilliant book, "20/20 Thinking," Dr. Maggie Greenwood-Robinson reveals the details of a compelling study conducted by psychologists at the Mayo Clinic in Rochester, Minnesota. Over a 30-year period, patients were studied to gauge the effects of optimistic mindsets versus pessimistic mindsets on longevity.

The eye-opening results? In the final analysis, pessimists fell 19% short of the average lifespan, while optimists *far outlived* average life expectancy rates.

As it turns out, a positive mindset not only helps you live *longer,* but can vastly improve the *quality* of the years you get to enjoy. According to Greenwood-Robinson, pessimists are more prone to experience anxiety, depression, high blood pressure, and disease; while optimists enjoy about twice the immunity to infectious disease as scrooges. Optimists generally feel better, and enjoy superior health and happiness over the long-term.

"Clearly," says Greenwood-Robinson, "If you have a positive outlook, you'll enjoy better health, greater happiness, and live longer."

Dr. George Vailliant came to a similar conclusion through his own, lengthy study.

Dr. Vaillant was a Harvard psychiatrist and professor who, in 1942, began to suspect that the human mind was the epicenter of one's *physiological* wellbeing. On a quest for answers, Vaillant launched an unprecedented long-term study. Vaillant's study targeted 185 of his own medical students and followed the students' lives over a period of 40 years.

The amazing findings? Dr. Vaillant discovered that of the 59 men with the *best mental outlook,* only two suffered chronic or fatal illnesses before age 53. Of an opposing group of men who possessed the *worst mental outlook*, 18 suffered chronic illness or premature death.

In other words, those who possessed a superior mental disposition lived longer and enjoyed better health, by a margin of nearly 10-to-1!

*"Man is more powerful than matter."*
-Benjamin Disraeli

Perhaps your mind's most amazing power is its ability to extend its energy—your *thoughts*—beyond the limits of your physical being. Just how far-reaching *is* the power of positive thinking? One study suggests *at least* 15 miles.

Dr. Larry Dossey, author of "Healing Words," conducted a 5-year study of 130 experiments related to the power of prayer. Dossey's studies included a fascinating experiment in which a prayer group focused their prayers on retarding the growth of a fungus housed in a laboratory some 15 miles away. The stunning outcome? While non-prayed-for cultures continued to breed as expected, the fungus targeted by prayer exhibited retarded growth in 100% of the trials conducted!

## Creating Your *Own* Medical Miracles

In this chapter, you learned that a conscious focus on health and wellness, instead of on disease and ailments, is a reliable facilitator of the kind of *medical miracles* that confound practitioners of modern medical science on a daily basis. You also discovered that positive thinking is *not* just "in your head." Much like sound waves, gravity, and ultraviolet rays, the thoughts you produce represent an invisible force which exerts visible, measurable effects on the world around you.

Is there some medical miracle you'd like to make happen in *your* life? Always begin by consulting with your doctor. If you don't agree with your doctor's diagnosis, by all means, get a second opinion. Then, awaken your mind to your cause by making this desired medical miracle the object of your daily, mental focus. A specific, energizing purpose acts as a direct mental command that tells your mind, "This is what I want—find a way to make it happen!" Finally, add faith and prayer to the equation.

As a result of your superior degree of mind control and unwavering faith, your amazing brain will go to work and the dormant powers of your mind will become aroused. Your body's natural resources will become awakened. And, before long, you will find yourself empowered to perform such miracles as overcoming illness, recovering quickly from injuries, operating in a heightened state of health and wellness, and, according to multiple studies, even living longer.

*"There is power lying latent everywhere,*
*waiting for the observant mind to discover it."*
-Orison Swett Marden

Your mind is much more than a wrinkled mass of grey matter; it's a powerhouse of metaphysical resources, which, once brought under your control and set into motion on your behalf, enables you to begin achieving feats you once considered "impossible." What if I told you that performing the kinds of miracles we've discussed over past chapters was just the tip of iceberg?

What if I told you that you possess the ability to invent (or reinvent) yourself...at will? Would you be eager to begin the process of evolving—at a rate of speed you deem appropriate—into the much smarter, wholly energized, and limitlessly capable being you were meant to become?

If so, it's time to discover the principle of *Mental Identity...*

# 5

# Mental Identity

*Mastering the Principle of Self-invention*

*"Life is not about finding yourself; life is about creating yourself."*
-George Bernard Shaw

Arnold Schwarzenegger foresaw his Ultimate Identity with clairvoyant accuracy...

Born in 1947 and raised near Graz, Austria, Schwarzenegger was just 15 years old when he strolled into a local gym for the first time, gazed in captivation at a poster of "Mr. Universe" Reg Park, and prophesied, "I'm going to become the world's greatest body-builder, a millionaire, and a movie star!"

When Schwarzenegger made this declaration, he wasn't merely casting an idle wish into the air. He was scorching his mental blueprint for success into his neurology and verbalizing an agreement between the powers within himself and the Laws that govern Life.

Young Arnold was, at that very moment, activating the process of *Mental Identity.*

Schwarzenegger's father, a police chief in Austria, reportedly frowned upon body-building. And accusations that Arnold, 15, "borrowed" some of the gym's equipment so that he could lift weights around the clock certainly didn't help matters. Arnold redeemed himself, however, and won his father's respect in 1962 when—just four years after picking up his first barbell—he won the body-building contest that earned him the title, "Junior Mr. Universe."

After gaining notoriety among European weight-lifting circles, Arnold ventured to the United States where he dominated the stages of the IFBB in Venice, California, and beyond. At age 20, Arnold became "Mr. Universe"—the title formerly held by his idol, Reg Park.

Two years later, Schwarzenegger claimed the "Mr. Olympia" title, body-building's highest honor. Arnold would go to seize the Olympia title an unprecedented seven times, a feat never before accomplished!

Officially the *world's greatest body-builder* by age 22, Arnold was fast on his way to transforming his three-fold prophesy from mind to matter…

*"All evolution proceeds from within."*
-James Allen

By 1977, Schwarzenegger, 30, was already in the process of transforming himself from championship body-builder into legendary movie star with his debut appearance in the body-building documentary, "Pumping Iron." That brief on-screen appearance was just what Arnold needed to get himself on the radar of multiple Hollywood film producers.

Sure, Arnold never attended acting school, wasn't a U.S. citizen, and suffered the disadvantage of a thick, German accent, but none of that mattered. The detailed mental blueprint locked inside his head and designed around motion-picture fame provided Arnold with the ideas, strategies, smarts, energy, skills, and resources necessary to make his enormous dreams real, in spite of the steep odds against his success.

Arnold's next mission became one of establishing himself as a commercially viable Hollywood actor.

After proving to producers that a market existed for muscle-bound movie-stars by first appearing in low-budget films like "Hercules in New York," Arnold applied the combined force of his sculpted physique and his magnetic personality to land roles such as "Conan the Barbarian" in 1982 and as the unstoppable cyborg "Terminator" in the 1984 box-office smash which would shape Schwarzenegger's self-scripted destiny as Hollywood's #1 action hero.

It's difficult to say at what exact point Schwarzenegger realized he was living the life he'd set in motion at age 15. By age 35, however, Schwarzenegger found himself surrounded by the film crews, gunfire, and explosions of one Hollywood blockbuster after another. Making a fortune battling everything from bad guys to alien creatures, and earning the admiration of a global fan base in the process, the confident Austrian had, at last, transformed his childhood dream into its physical equivalent, with *scientific* precision.

Young boys around the world were now walking into the local gym or cinema house, gawking at posters of their hero, Arnold Schwarzenegger—the muscle-bound, millionaire movie-star—and wishing *they* were *him*.

Over the course of his willful evolution from body-builder, to movie-star, to politician, Arnold Schwarzenegger has proven himself more masterful at morphing into his choice of life-roles than the Predator itself. In his latest display of limitlessness, the 2-time Terminator reinvented himself as 2-time "Governator" of California—the very state where Arnold had staged his American body-building debut some 40 years earlier!

*"Everyone has it within them to say, 'This I am today, and that I will become tomorrow'."*
-Louis L'Amour

### You Possess the Power to Invent (and Reinvent) Yourself ...at Will!

Arnold Schwarzenegger's fascinating life illustrates one of the most important of all mind control techniques—*Mental Identity*. Mental Identity is the process by which you may invent (or reinvent) yourself according to your mental blueprint for the Ultimate Roles you wish to assume in your life, career, relationships, and finances.

This principle costs nothing to employ but can revolutionize your life, practically overnight. The first great step to applying this process to your life is to understand your dominant thinking pattern.

## Exposing Your Dominant Thinking Pattern

*"A man is what he thinks about all day long."*
-Ralph Waldo Emerson

Your destiny is forged and changes with your thoughts. And since your ability to evolve into a smarter, more energized, highly capable version of yourself will require the skill of forming and maintaining a mental blueprint of this Ultimate Identity, you'll need to understand what you think about, and what you think about most often.

To begin exposing your current *dominant thinking* pattern, ask yourself the following questions:

(1) What ***category*** could the majority of my thoughts be classified into? Work? Family? Relationships? Past failures? Recent successes? Perceived weaknesses? Definite strengths? Grievances? Blessings? What I *can't* do, or what I *can* do?

(2) Are my thoughts linked mostly to the past, present or future?

(3) What ***specific thoughts*** dominate my thinking?

(4) Do I think primarily in the ***context*** of image or message?

(5) Do the ***feelings*** I experience as a result of my dominant thoughts tend to hold me back or propel me forward?

(6) Are my dominant thoughts aligned with the ***spectacular results*** I want to see take place in my life?

(7) A final question: If your current dominant thinking pattern hasn't been facilitating the superior lifestyle you deserve, isn't it time for a change?

*"All that we are is the result of what we have thought. We alone are the makers of our own states of existence."*
-Ancient Indian Maxim

## Your Ability to Reinvent Yourself is Unlimited

One of the most inspiring facts of the 21st century is that we not only possess the ability to invent ourselves as fit, but to *reinvent* ourselves as many times as we wish. Don't like the "ordinary person" that small thinking has caused you to become? Reinvent yourself into an *extraordinary visionary* instead.

Not happy with your current job, boss or salary? Locate a better position, start your own business or make the financial investment necessary to open the door to greater earnings. And if your current level of fitness keeps you locked in a pattern of low self-esteem, break the chains. Form an image in your mind of the Fit You, and then join a gym and begin the process of building your ideal body.

Perhaps you're thinking: *I'm too far along in age to reinvent myself.* Sorry, our story of Arnold Schwarzenegger debunks this myth. Schwarzenegger did begin mapping out his legendary journey as a teenager. However, the Austrian native transformed himself from world-class body-builder into professional actor at age 30, and then reinvented himself as an American citizen at age 36. During his 40's, Arnold took on a political role as President Bush's Chairman of the Council on Physical Fitness. Then the Terminator reinvented himself again as the "Governator" of California at age 56. Finally, in his 60's, Schwarzenegger morphed back into a Hollywood action hero with a return to the Terminator series.

The only thing more inspiring about Arnold's ability to cast himself into the personal and professional roles of his choosing is this: *You* can do the same!

Your ability to reinvent yourself into new, expanded, and more satisfying roles resides within you right now, and is not limited by your age, race, gender, current income or educational background. The only requirements for initiating the process of Mental Identity are that you refuse to allow the tides of chance to dictate your course in life; that you develop a mental blueprint for the Ultimate Roles you wish to assume in your life, career, relationships, and finances; and that you demonstrate the force of will it takes to keep that blueprint locked inside your Mental Theater until your desired evolution is complete.

*"Compared with what we ought to be,*
*we are only half awake."*
-Dr. William James

**GURU'S TIP**: The fact is that *you* are the architect who designs your Future Self with the blueprint of today's thoughts, beliefs, hopes, desires, ambitions, philosophies, expectations, dreams, plans, and projections. The process of designing your Future Self through the principle of Mental Identity is reliable, powerful, and inevitable. You will—either by default or design—determine the person you become in the weeks, months, and years to come.

Want to redefine your current "identity?" Wish to reinvent yourself? Start by determining what Ultimate Roles you wish to assume in life and business. The evolution you seek will begin taking place, virtually overnight.

## The Overnight Transformation of Bing Crosby

In the early 20th century, New York's finest clubs hosted the miraculous transformation of a "hopeless lush" of a lounge singer whose antics included vomiting on members of his front row audience after taking to the stage under the spell of his dear friend, alcohol. That singer was Bing Crosby.

During the 1920s, few entertainers were in greater demand than Bing Crosby. Club owners sought him. Men wanted to be him. And women wanted to be with him. Bing had enormous talent and the potential for greatness, and everybody knew it, except him. Crosby's narrow focus and poor self-image kept his mouth glued to a bottle, preventing him from seeing the legendary destiny that awaited him beyond his current, self-imposed limitations.

It was during one of Crosby's shows that something life-changing took place. Bing's interests shifted from alcohol to the wealthy socialites who came to watch him perform. The singer was fascinated by the way his well-dressed fans enjoyed themselves, handled their liquor, and mingled comfortably with one another after his shows. Bing imagined himself in a similar role. Hard to believe, isn't it? The star of the show was gazing out into his audience and wishing *he* could be like *them!*

Ironically, it would be Crosby's aspiration to become a member of high society that would activate the principle of Mental Identity on his behalf, shatter the distorted prism through which he saw himself, and break the spell of the bottle, forever.

Shortly after developing the mental image of his ritzy "Socialite Self," Crosby found the courage to begin mingling with the prominent members of his audience—his adoring fans. He accepted invitations to parties after shows, where he made friends. Trading his intoxicated isolation for social interaction, Bing told funny stories, sung songs, and became the life of the party everywhere he went.

Then, one self-defining night, while mingling and laughing among the guarded circles of New York's high society, Bing Crosby, beaming with newfound confidence and joy, arrived at the wondrous realization that he had, in fact, become the Happy Socialite of his former, mental projections.

*"You will become as small as your controlling desire, as large as your dominant aspiration."*
-James Allen

Embracing his *new identity* and evolving beyond it, Bing Crosby the once seemingly hopeless alcoholic reinvented himself as a responsible drinker, cut his first solo record in 1927, and then transformed himself from lounge singer to Hollywood actor in 1933. Crosby would go on to play party host to some of the most influential figures of his day, date some of Hollywood's biggest actresses, and woo directors after landing his dream role in the 1956 film titled—almost unbelievably—*High Society.*

The secret to Crosby's amazing turnaround? Mental Identity.

Not until Bing visualized himself in an expanded, more satisfying role was he able to break the chains of alcohol, awaken his dormant potential, and fulfill his Ultimate Identity as the enormously talented singer, song-writer, and actor the world has come to know him as today.

*"No one need to live another moment as they are,*
*because the Creator has endowed us*
*with the ability to change ourselves."*
-Orison Swett Marden

## The Art of "Self-estimation"

*Recalculating Your Personal Value*

*"Self-image sets the boundaries*
*of individual accomplishment."*
-Dr. Maxwell Maltz

Aspiring to great heights—and to rewarding roles—becomes much easier once you begin to grasp what you're already worth.

Have you ever considered how valuable your skills, time, energy, and companionship truly are? Well, before you do place a price-tag on your head, consider this:

• According to Einstein's E=MC2, a kilogram of mass (about equal to a single bone of your pinky finger) could be converted into 25 billion kilowatts of electricity. That's enough raw energy to supply New York's power needs for about 3 months. There's literally *millions* of dollars' worth of energy stored inside your pinky finger alone. Your "energy value" as a person calculates into the billions!

• The average blue collar worker earns about $1 million over his or her career, but carries a whopping, lifetime revenue value of about *$5 million* for the organization for which he or she works. Perhaps it's time to go into business for yourself.

- Your *creative potential* represents a cash value of millions (or even billions) of dollars, depending on how you use it. What's more, you may begin converting your creative potential into the ideas and plans that generate cash at any time you choose.

- Genetic science has shown that, in the entire world, there is no one exactly like *you.* In fact, your uniqueness began before birth. After all, the odds against *you* having been the lucky sperm that reached the egg were literally *billions* to one. Think about that: You're better than 1-in-a-million; you're *1-in-many-billions!*

- Finally, if you possessed $100 billion would you not trade it for the chance to live life again? Of course, you would. Well, if your life is worth $100 billion, every hour of your life—whether sleeping or awake—is worth a staggering $158,548. This is something to consider before ascribing yourself a worldly value!

### Understanding the Power of *Self-pricing*

How important is the *right price?* Donald Trump once had a group of properties that simply wasn't selling. However, after market analysis later revealed that Trump's properties were priced comparative to the similar units of a nearby competitor, Donald made a genius decision. He *raised* the price of the slow-selling units. As expected, orders began pouring in for the higher-priced properties. The reason? People want what they perceived as the "best available."

The *principle of self-pricing* works the same way. Employers, partners, associates, employees, customers, and members of the opposite sex will value you according to your own estimation of who you are, what you deserve, and how you should be treated.

Your mental valuation of yourself causes you to carry yourself in a certain manner, thus projecting a correlating physical presentation to others as you move about your world on a daily basis. Think of yourself as someone of immense value and others will unfailingly perceive you as someone worth hiring, doing business with, befriending, working for, buying from, and loving.

Do you believe you are worthy of the *best that life has to offer?* If not, start believing as much. A low estimation of yourself will cause you to settle for much less than you deserve. It is only when you become certain you're meant to enjoy the "good life" that you will say and do the things that *make* the good life possible.

*"What a man thinks about himself,*
*that is what determines, or rather indicates, his fate."*
-Henry David Thoreau

**The Self-pricing Challenge**: Over the next 30 days, go about your day and interact with your world as if hanging around your neck is an imaginary "price-tag" representative of the full value of your greatest strengths, highest potential, explosive energies, forthcoming earnings, precious time, and future achievements.

And, as you do, expect three things to happen:

(1) You will begin to **feel** more energized and important.
(2) You will begin to **act** according to this *higher value*.
(3) The world will begin **buying into** your new, perceived (thus projected) worthiness.

**GURU'S TIP:** If you don't possess a high estimation of yourself, few others will either. Assign yourself the highest value.

## "Self-labeling"

*Source of Self-fulfilling Prophesy*

Similar to the value you place upon yourself, the *labels* you attach to yourself provide an accurate forecast of what decisions you will make, what types of people you will gravitate toward, what habits you will form, and what you will and will not do.

In other words, the labels we ascribe to ourselves (or allow others to thrust upon us) become self-fulfilling prophesies. It is for this reason that we must be extremely careful about the ways in which we define ourselves at work, home, and play.

If someone asked you to define yourself, what labels and definitions would come to mind? Would you define yourself based on what you do for a living? Are you a business person, civil servant, homemaker or student? Would your professional "title" enter the picture? How about your earning bracket?

Do you label yourself according to your preferences? Are you a dog or cat person? A Ford or Chevy man? A slave to fashion? Are you an animal lover, people person or environmentalist? Would your zodiac sign, nationality or political affiliation enter your mind? Do you favor geographical definitions, such as "proud New Yorker?" Do your habits define you? Are you an early bird or night owl? A shopaholic? A couch potato or fitness buff? Are you a prisoner to defeating labels like clumsy, lazy, depressed or dimwitted? Or do you benefit from empowering labels like dynamo, genius, optimist or attractive? Are you "stuck in a dead end job" or a "star on the rise?"

Think carefully about the way in which you define yourself, and whether these labels and definitions inhibit or empower you.

*"Life has a way of becoming a self-fulfilling prophesy."*
-Pat Croche

It's easy to fall victim to *labels* that serve no purpose of good, and which are based on false or outdated information. For instance, I wasted years telling myself "I suck at math" based on a perception I'd formed…in grade school! Truth was, my own outdated labeling kept me from even applying myself to mathematics. It was only later in life, after I broke into a profession that required the use of financial ratio analysis that I discovered that I'm not only good at math, but actually *enjoy* it!

The labels you ascribe to hold tremendous influence over the way you think, feel, and act. Define yourself as inferior, lazy or a failure and you will find that you never quite measure up, that you lack the energy to overcome your circumstances, and that you drop the ball during each important play of your life. On the other hand, if you label yourself a born winner, a world-class professional or a millionaire-in-the-making (and buy into your prophesies,) you will find yourself delivering more gold medal performances, regularly outshining your coworkers, and becoming regularly inspired with bright money-making ideas by which to pave your path to riches.

**GURU'S TIP:** Self-labeling is a strong regulator of the personal power that will become available to you today, and represents an accurate forecast of how you will perform in the future. Do yourself a favor and start referring to yourself as the predestined celebrity, world-class business leader, wealth magnet, or high class individual you aspire to become. To make your descriptions more authentic, simply follow your ideal terms with the catch phrase, "in the making." Use only the most uplifting and motivating labels and definitions to describe *you!*

## The Principle of "Self-projection"

*It's What Puts the* Magic *into Mental Identity*

Self-estimation and self-labeling are important cogs in the machine of "self-creation." But without adding *self-projection*—the act of visualizing the expanded roles you will play and the better person you will become tomorrow—to the process of Mental Identity, the process offers no real, evolutionary power.

The following story illustrates the vital role self-projection plays when in the process of Mental Identity...

### The Story of the Magical Statue

There once was a powerful CEO whose elderly mother contracted a rare, spinal disease which left the woman disfigured and unable to care for herself. Over the next years, after taking his mother in and providing her with the finest nurses, the CEO scoured the nation in search of a surgeon who could help make the woman's back straight. But her condition, said the country's foremost medical men, was "hopelessly incurable." The woman was destined to spend the rest of her life confined to a wheelchair.

For his mother's 70th birthday, the CEO threw an extravagant party in the courtyard of his mansion. When it came time to cut the cake, the son wheeled his mother through the garden and past the live entertainment to a banquet table where a delicious birthday cake was waiting. A crowd of family and friends gathered around as the CEO urged his mother to blow out the candles and make a wish.

"Whatsoever you desire, mother," offered the businessman, "speak it aloud and it shall be yours."

The woman, badly hunch-backed, struggled to blow out the candles, and then gazed up at her CEO son and requested, "Son, I would like a life-sized statue…of myself."

The crowd gasped. The music stopped.

"A…*statue?*" asked the executive, realizing what an awkward position he was in. After all, was he to present his poor, disfigured mother with a permanent reminder of her incurable condition?

"Yes, son," said the knowing, old woman. "However, the statue need not reflect my current, limited condition. Rather, the sculpture should portray what I will look like after I conquer my illness. For then my back will again become straight and I can leave this horrible, old wheelchair behind."

The brokenhearted businessman pitied his mother's naivety.

"Also, son," added the woman, pointing a shaky finger across the courtyard, "I would like the statue to be placed just outside my bedroom terrace, so that I can study it daily."

"As you wish, mother," agreed the CEO. "As you wish."

*"It is a fact that you project what you are."*
-Norman Vincent Peale

A short time later, a life-sized, marble statue was delivered to the mansion and positioned outside the woman's bedroom. Each morning, the woman eagerly wheeled herself onto the terrace, where she studiously absorbed the image of her healthier, stronger self for hours on end. Days became weeks and weeks became months, but the fiery glow of optimistic expectancy in the woman's eyes never dimmed. And as the woman continued to focus all of her aspirations, faith, and power onto the energizing image of her Ultimate Self, something magical happened—she began to *evolve*. In almost undetectable increments, the woman's horribly crooked spine began to adjust itself, like a flower reaching and stretching toward sunlight, to the image of her daily, mental obsession. Against all logic, the woman's "incurable condition" began to improve.

It was three years later that another celebration was held. Guests, food, and entertainment again filled the mansion courtyard. And a crowd eagerly awaited the woman's entrance for her 73rd birthday. To the guests' amazement, the CEO escorted his mother into the courtyard not in her wheelchair, but by the strength of her own, two feet. The woman, beaming with newfound vigor and joy, was a perfect reflection of her flawless, marble statue—the energizing image she'd kept locked in her sights since the day her transformational journey of "Mental Identity" had begun!

**GURU'S TIP:** The evolutionary powers of the mother in the fairy tale above are not so far from reality. In fact, these powers reside within you now. You may take on a desired trait, improve your reputation, assume a new personal or professional role or reinvent yourself from the ground up by using the principle of Mental Identity to design, and assume, your Ideal Identity.

Below, you will find the simple formula for activating the desired evolutionary transformation of your choosing.

*"The mold of a man's fate is in his hands."*
-Francis Bacon

## Activating the Process of Mental Identity

*Opening the Door to Your "Ultimate Identity"*

What's your "Ultimate Identity?" Your *Ultimate Identity* is that smarter, richer, more energized, limitlessly capable, and otherwise perfected version of yourself which appears in your grandest dreams and represents your greatest potential.

Below, are four simple mind control principles you can use to activate the process of Mental Identity and begin evolving in the direction of the Ultimate You.

(1) **Master Your Dominant Thinking Pattern:** Remember, the content and quality of your regular mental focus determines how much power and energy will become available to you as you move through life. Don't squander your resources by focusing on your flaws, dislikes or on what you *can't* do. Instead, concentrate your powers on what you *can* do, *want* to experience, and *aspire* to become.

Today's dominant thoughts are the seedlings of tomorrow's reality. Plant your thoughts with extreme caution!

(2) **Assign Yourself the Highest Price-tag:** Bing Crosby's narrow focus and low estimation of himself kept him chained to a bottle and trapped inside the limited role of an alcoholic lounge singer. Only after recalibrating his mental horizon did Crosby discover the authority to overcome his problems, infiltrate New York's high society, and fulfill his destiny as one of Hollywood's biggest stars.

Your ability to assume expanded roles in life and business is directly related to your own self-worth. Assign yourself the highest price-tag. If *you* don't, who will?

(3) **Label Yourself Wisely:** Arnold Schwarzenegger insisted that he was "destined for great things" and referred to himself as "a winner." It is by no coincidence that Arnold won the Mr. Universe contest 5 times, the Mr. Olympia 7 times, the California gubernatorial elections twice, and forged a living legacy as the greatest action hero of the 20th century.

*Self-labeling* is dependably prophetic. Never accept a label that makes you feel bad or keeps you from performing your best. Define yourself strictly in ways that benefit and empower you.

(4) **Start Foreseeing the Ultimate You!** You are today the physical manifestation of yesterday's mental operations. Likewise, your *identity* of tomorrow will be based largely on what you focus on today.

Take control of your destiny by beginning to *see yourself* not "as you are" now, but as the Ultimate Person you aspire to become. What spectacular personal and professional roles do you plan on playing? Practice projecting yourself into these roles by way of the *viewing screen* within your Mental Theater. Forge the habit of bringing these energizing images to mind often as you go about your day.

As you do, the *magic* of Mental Identity will take over, and your desired evolution will begin.

**GURU'S TIP:** Projecting your Ultimate Self onto the viewing screen in your Mental Theater acts a clear mental directive that tells your mind, "This is who I want to become—make it happen!" The more you project the image, the clearer the directive; the clearer the directive, the faster your desired evolution will occur.

Using intelligent self-labeling and possessing a high estimation of yourself further accelerate the transition between *who you are now* and the Ultimate Person you shall, at last, unveil.

## Inventing (or Reinventing) Yourself is as Easy as 1, 2, 3…4

(1) Master Your "Dominant Thinking" Pattern
(2) Assign Yourself the Highest Price-tag
(3) Label Yourself Wisely
(4) Start Foreseeing Your Ultimate Self!

*"It's never too late to become what you might have been."*
-George Eliot

You've learned the secrets of *Mental Identity*, the process by which you may invent or reinvent yourself, and which opens the door to the Ultimate Identity of your choosing.

The deepest mysteries of your mind, however, have yet to be revealed.

Right now, you are standing on the threshold of a whole new world; a world in which *you* are the master of your fate, and your mind and the Universe cooperate; a world in which circumstances conform to your plans, fortune favors your endeavors, and every good thing that you seek becomes yours…

# 6

# The Mind/Reality Relationship

*Cooperative Agreement between Your Mind and World*

*"The Universe constantly and obediently answers to our conceptions."*
-Henry David Thoreau

We humans are the only living creatures endowed with the unique ability to change our own circumstances and alter the world around us. For proof of this fact, you need only open the nearest history book. The chronicles of history represent a centuries-long study guide of fascinating success stories which demonstrate what can happen when one dares to imagine what *can be* or dreams of *changing the world*, and then exercises one's will in the quest to transform possibilities into actualities.

The lofty dreams that have been so skillfully realized by the greatest peak performers of yesterday and today stand to teach all people a valuable lesson about the power of "mind over matter." That lesson is this: We, too, can change our lives, forge a new and better reality, fulfill our dreams or even change the world, if only we will dare to begin moving in the direction of our desired ends.

You see, when you set out in pursuit of a dream, strange things begin to happen. Your senses about what actions to take and premonitions about what's to come become supernaturally acute. The ideas, strategies, smarts, energy, skills, and resources necessary to transform your dreams into reality become available to you at just the right time. Helpful people begin to align themselves to your objectives. Things begin to "fall into place" like the pieces of some grand, cosmic puzzle. The Forces of Heaven and Earth, it seems, begin to cooperate with your purpose. And the Universe, you come to realize, is irreversibly designed to assist you in reaching your chosen destinations.

*Mind Contrology*® refers to this thought-activated matrix as the "Mind/Reality Relationship." And there has been perhaps no greater master of the MRR than Abraham Lincoln...

## Abe Lincoln: 19th Century Mind Contrologist

*How an Illiterate, Destitute Farm Boy Mastered the "Mind/Reality Relationship"*

In 1809, lil' Abe Lincoln tumbled into the world by way of the dirt floor of an 18' x 20' cabin in the Kentucky wilderness.

Because the Lincolns depended on their fledgling farm for food and income, Abe was forced by age seven to become the family's full-time farmhand, instead of attending school. Due to a diseased irrigation system, Abe had to trudge miles each day (carrying pales and wearing tree-bark shoes) in order to fetch clean water for his illiterate parents and siblings. Never seeming to catch a break, Abe's mother died when he was just nine years old. To make matters worse, the brokenhearted youngster barely had time to grieve before his father remarried and moved the woman's children into the Lincoln cabin. Eight Lincolns in all shared a single, cramped shack!

Ridiculed for wearing rags, embarrassed about his inability to read, and fed up with his being worked like a plow horse, Abe, 12, made a genius decision. Refusing to allow his unfortunate circumstances to define him, the proud southerner took his destiny into his own hands by way of *self-education.*

"The things I want to know are in books," realized Abe. So, while other kids his age spent their mornings in school and their afternoons swimming in the local pond, Abe could be found from sunrise to sunset, sitting against a tree behind his father's cabin, eating apples, and teaching himself to read. First, Abe learned Bible verses and read them to his folks. Then he began devouring books about Ben Franklin and George Washington. Lincoln's studies of Ben and George—men who'd triumphed over many hardships along their journeys to riches, fame, and power—convinced the boy that anything was possible and motivated young Lincoln into action.

In 1821, on a quest to forge a better reality, Abe Lincoln began a 20-mile trek to borrow a book on the topic of his growing fascination—law.

*"Conditions and events are not to be fled from, nor passively acquiesced to; they are to be utilized and directed."*
-John Dewey

Continuing to be overworked and "loaned out" to neighbors by his father, Abe the indentured farmhand envisioned himself becoming a lawyer. It was a ridiculous dream for a boy who possessed a total of one year of schooling, no connections, and no feasible way to finance an education. But Abe, wholly focused on his ideal career, forced his mind to produce a strategy by which to set his future in motion.

Between the ages of 12 and 15, Abe ditched his chores and journeyed daily to the courthouse in the next town where he sat in the courtroom learning law and studying the lingo and maneuverings of those who were already living the lifestyle he himself aspired to one day enjoy—lawyers. It was while hanging around the courthouse, absorbing the legal culture, and befriending the attorneys who sported the snazziest duds and rode the finest horses that Abraham realized, "That some folks are rich shows that others may become rich, and is just encouragement to become industrious and enterprising."

Smitten with the prospect of prosperity, young Abe's proclamation soon became, "I desire to live. I desire place and distinction!" Before long, Abe's optimism, faith, and preparation would coax Life into providing him a perfectly timed miracle…

Throughout his teens and into his 20's, Lincoln held jobs as a ferry boy, lumberjack, bargeman (for $10 a month,) clerk, surveyor, militiaman, and mill foreman, all of which reinforced his distaste for manual labor. At age 22, Lincoln landed a cushy job as post master. The position paid well and offered prestige, but to Abe the job was merely a steppingstone to his Ultimate Destination. Refusing to surrender his dream of becoming a lawyer, Abe continued studying law, networking with attorneys, and dazzling members of the highly-educated Barrister Group (a group of high-level lawyers who controlled the legal profession in Illinois) with his vast, homegrown knowledge of the constitution.

Lincoln was at his desk at the post office, buried behind a mountain of law books when the Great Force of Life—cooperating with Abe's unobstructed vision for his future—delivered him, by way of a lowly postman, the U.S. parcel that would revolutionize his reality. The letter stated that the Barrister Group was willing to overlook Abe's lack of schooling and grant him "license to practice."

Abraham Lincoln was just 25 in 1834 when, against *impossible* odds, he found himself living his dream as a lawyer in Springfield.

*The people who get on in this world are those who get up*
*and look for the circumstances they want,*
*and if they can't find them—they make them!"*
-George Bernard Shaw

Lincoln's triumph over poverty, ignorance, and grunt work awakened within him the understanding that "visions upon which your thoughts and feelings concentrate" could influence the otherwise unforeseeable future, a principle Abe would use to help win himself a seat in the Illinois House of Representatives later that same year.

Tall, gaunt, dreary-eyed, and almost entirely self-educated, Lincoln quickly proved himself a good steward of his burgeoning mental powers by using his license to practice to fight for the rights of the downtrodden. After taking on the cases of mistreated locals who could not afford to pay him for his services, Lincoln won a series of landmark rulings and acquired the nickname, "Honest Abe."

Into the 1840's, after spending much of his 30's conquering the courtroom, Lincoln's ambitions soared and he began to *concentrate his thoughts and feelings* on a seat in Congress. Abe's intentions were brought to light one decisive night in 1845 while attending a town hall meeting hosted by the county preacher. As the preacher led a discussion on the topic of the "afterlife," Abe slouched into his chair and began daydreaming about his next, great achievement. Attempting to rustle the good lawyer from his daze, the preacher bellowed out, "Mr. Lincoln, do you care to tell the congregation where it is you think *you'll* be going?"

Lincoln rose from his seat, straightened his suit, and prophesied, "I'm going to Congress." In 1847, just two years after his bold declaration of destiny, Abraham Lincoln, 38, was a United States Congressman…

*"Our soul contains the events that shall befall us;*
*for the event is only the actualization of our thoughts."*
-Ralph Waldo Emerson

During the 1850's, continuing to operate from an office on Capitol Hill, Washington's newest big-shot soon discovered that he lacked the political insight to speak intelligently on the critical matters of the day. So, on a quest to increase his body of knowledge and expand his personal influence, Lincoln again turned to self-education as the primary vehicle for advancement. Abe read Congressional journals and newspapers to shape his political perspective and gained a reputation for using the Library of Congress more than any other Congressman on the Hill.

"I do the very best I know how," once admitted Lincoln, whose study habits and superior degree of mind control became the subject matter of those closest to him. One aide close to Lincoln observed, "The enduring power of Mr. Lincoln's brain is wonderful. He can sit and think without any food or drink longer than anyone I know."

It was during those rigorous sessions of mental exercise that Congressman Lincoln began *concentrating his thoughts and feelings* on the Ultimate Identity which would become his legacy.

It was 1858, during the swelling debate over slavery that Abraham Lincoln, 49, gazed from his office window in Washington, D.C. upon a group of protesting abolitionists. Following a premonition about what dream he was destined to fulfill next, Lincoln turned to his aide and announced, "I admit that I am ambitious, and would like to run for the presidency." And the rest, as they say, would become history.

*"I have no better expression than 'religious' for this confidence in the rational nature of reality to be accessible to some degree, to human reason."*
-Albert Einstein

## The Lincolnesque Mental Outlook

*Your Edge Over Circumstance*

*Mind Contrology* ® defines a "Mind Contrologist" as one who is in charge of one's life, career, relationships, and finances.

Among the greatest *Mind Contrologists* of the 19th century, Abraham Lincoln represents a true testament of every human being's God-given right to take the life we've been given—regardless of our current conditions—and mold and shape it into something better, something great, even something legendary, by simply redirecting our focus and energies away from the struggles, "limitations," and defeats of yesterday and toward the desired realities we want to fill our world with *tomorrow*. We'll refer to this mindset of mind-over-circumstance as a "Lincolnesque Mental Outlook."

Lincoln was a master at maintaining the caliber of focus and quality of attitude that heightens one's powers and transcends one's environment. A similar conscious direction of focus and positive expectations must become a daily priority for anyone who wishes to replicate Abe's effectiveness in forging ideal circumstances or fulfilling dreams. In other words, you must possess a *Lincolnesque Mental Outlook*.

Would it surprise you to learn that you create your own luck, determine how others will treat you, and regulate how much favor Life Itself will show you? It shouldn't.

After all, you've been manufacturing your daily realities (for better or worse) for most of your life.

Consider your own experiences. Surely you've had a day when, for one reason or another, you woke up on the wrong side of the bed. Isn't it *strange* how that's *also* the day you stub your toe on the dresser, your friend decides to borrow your last $20 dollars, and your car blows a flat…on the highway…in the rain?

Now consider those days when, by accident or design, you woke in the morning with a fabulous mental outlook—a Lincolnesque Mental Outlook. These are the days you smile more, work seems easier, people are friendlier, and the sun seems to shine just a little bit brighter. Your "luck" takes a turn for the better, but you fail to realize that you are the maker of your *own* good fortune!

*"Man is not a creature of circumstances;*
*circumstances are the creatures of man."*
-Benjamin Disraeli

As sure as the sun will rise, you will continue to fashion your own quality of reality over the days, weeks, and months ahead.

So, remember, you can think little of yourself and expect the worst in every situation. You can believe that a *black cloud of doom* shadows your every footstep and that you're susceptible to every germ and virus under the sun. You can complain that God has written you off and that it's just "not in the cards you've been dealt" to become wealthy. View life through this distorted prism, and your existence will be one marred by unnecessary mental, emotional, physical, spiritual, and financial difficulties.

On the other hand, you can be sure that you're smart and capable, and that God is on your side. You can be grateful for what you've got and expect *more* good fortune tomorrow. You can anticipate the help of others and open your eyes to the abundant resources at your disposal. You can dream big, proclaim, *"Yes, I can,"* and take bold action! Do this, and your circumstances will mold and conform themselves to the designs and dimensions of your superior mental viewfinder.

Maintaining a Lincolnesque Mental Outlook has a funny way of placing the entire Universe on *your* side!

*"Events and circumstance have their origins in ourselves; they spring from the seeds which we have sown."*
-Henry David Thoreau

So, what important lessons can we learn from Abe Lincoln, a poor, illiterate farm boy who recalibrated his mental horizons, changed his "luck" from bad to good, and not only envisioned but, in fact, orchestrated, every step of his remarkable journey to the Executive Mansion?

- We are the *makers* of our circumstances.
- We may invent (or reinvent) ourselves at any time we see fit.
- Adopting a *Lincolnesque Mental Outlook* has a way of increasing our good fortune.
- Commit to a dream and the Universe will come to your aide, courtesy of the "Mind/Reality Relationship!"

**GURU'S TIP:** The Mind/Reality Relationship may be defined as an interactive, thought-activated matrix which has been woven into the fabric of the Universe at the dawn of time. This relationship between your mind and your world exists for your benefit.

A growing mastery of the MRR will enable you to exercise exceptional control over your life, career, relationships, finances, and, as Abe Lincoln would put it, *otherwise unforeseeable events.*

Your God-given capacity for directing circumstances to your advantage is perhaps the most intriguing, misunderstood, and underutilized of all man's powers.

Fortunately for you, the nature and extent of your existence-altering capabilities will become much easier to grasp, and to use, as we continue to unravel the mysteries of the Mind/Reality Relationship…

## Henry Tudor

*How One Disgruntled Outcast Used the Mind/Reality Relationship To Crown Himself King of England...*

*"The foundations which we would dig about and find are within us, like the Kingdom of Heaven, not without."*
-Samuel Butler

In the summer of 1485, a young Englishman named Henry Tudor was exiled from his hometown by King Richard III for making the dreadful mistake of falling in love with the king's niece. Unable to return home, the 28 year-old Tudor spent the next days wandering the hillsides of England and imagining the impossible. Specifically, Tudor dreamed of overthrowing King Richard, winning back the love of his life, and making the king's palace...*his own.*

Among Tudor's obstacles were the facts that he was homeless, jobless, penniless, and alone. Refusing to dismiss his dream as unachievable, however, Henry scorched his vision into his brain and energized it with obsession.

Over the coming weeks, strange things began to happen.

Tudor's hopeless condition began to improve as Life provided him with everything he needed in order to begin working his *desired reality* into existence. Suddenly filled with bright ideas and confidence, Tudor—a peasant with no prior battle experience—began organizing a ragtag militia of Scottish, Welsh, and French wanderers, all of whom had emerged in unexplainable, growing numbers. Next, Henry practiced riding horseback, jousting, and fencing, and worked with his militia to produce a massive arsenal of homemade weapons. After each day spent preparing for battle, Tudor and his men gathered around an evening bonfire, where they devised battle strategies with the help of elderly vagrants who claimed to have fought valiantly in wars long ago.

By summer's end, surrounded by the people and conditions that he had summoned into existence courtesy of the working relationship between his mind and his world, Henry Tudor was prepared to set out in search of the favorable event with which to make history. And, once again, Life would *not* disappoint.

*"Kingdoms lay inside each man's mind."*
-T. E. Lawrence

On August 22, 1485, Henry Tudor and his army of 4,000 disgruntled vagrants advanced on King Richard's castle. King Richard, having heard rumors of Tudor's plot, laughed off Henry's scheme as the impossible dream of a lad who posed no real threat. However, when Tudor arrived, charging on horseback with sword in hand at the head of his large army of outcasts, the king suddenly realized that he was in trouble.

After hours of battle on Bosworth Field, the king's army—realizing that Tudor's army would stop at nothing to reign victorious—began to defect in growing numbers to Tudor's side. By day's end, what was left of Richard's army was forced to retreat by Tudor's mob, never to be heard from again.

As the sun descended on the king's castle that night, Henry Tudor was seated upon his throne. His desired circumstances had come to fruition. Surrounded by the luxuries of royalty, reunited with the woman he loved, and in charge of his new kingdom, Henry Tudor, the 28 year-old ruler of his own, self-generated empire, selected a more fitting title—that of King Henry VII!

*"He who fits himself for a king*
*will see kingdoms delivered into his hands."*
-Paul Brunton

Henry Tudor's ability to transform himself from homeless outcast to king of England in three, short months can be attributed largely to (1) his decision to cast his focus beyond his unacceptable, present circumstances to the superior reality of his choosing, (2) his stubbornness in not surrendering to the "thoughts of doubt" and fear of failure that surely entered his mind during the weeks he spent planning his coup, and (3) his persistence in pursuing his dream fiercely enough and long enough to allow Life to assist him in forging fantasy into fact.

Simply put, Henry Tudor's genius was in unwittingly mastering the Mind/Reality Relationship.

## Your *Mind* Creates Your "Reality"

*The Inextricable Link between Your Mind and Your World*

Dr. William James once observed that, "Genius is little more than perceiving in an unhabitual way." Are you ready to exercise your genius by interpreting your existence in a bold new way, a way which could revolutionize your life, multiply your force of influence, and increase your ability to master your world, virtually overnight?

If so, allow me to introduce you to a revolutionary concept. That is, "reality" is a state and product of mind; yes, *your* mind!

You see, *reality* is not a fixed existence. It is an *experience* which appears in as many varying forms as there are human beings on Earth to interpret it. In other words, *your* reality isn't *everyone else's* reality. Your reality is exclusive to you—a 3-dimensional reflection of your own thoughts, ideas, views, beliefs, philosophies, expectations, and dreams. And because reality shapes and molds itself to the perceptions and projections of the individual, you—a human being of Divine Dominion who possesses the ability to control your thinking—are in a privileged position to manipulate your circumstances to your benefit, in much the same way that Michelangelo hammers away at a blank slate of marble until the sculpture imagined within his mind emerges in physical form.

*"Life is formed from the inside out."*
-Dr. William Hornaday

Just as Henry Tudor's kingdom existed in his mind before it existed in stone and gold, the desired realities of your choosing exist inside your mind, waiting to be summoned forth. And just as Tudor transformed himself from homeless outcast into king of England in a few short months, you possess the phenomenal force of mind and being to give your life, career, relationships, and finances a complete make-over, almost overnight, by mastering the relationship between your thoughts and your world.

Ask yourself: Has the "reality" I've created become an unwelcome montage of undesirable circumstances for which I never bargained? If so, exercise your uniquely human ability to coerce into your life a more satisfying and rewarding existence. Your ideal reality, you will find, has been eagerly awaiting your cue.

## Demystifying the Mind/Reality Relationship

*More on the Interactive Relationship between Your Mind and Your World*

Maybe you're having a hard time wrapping your head around this bold, new concept. Perhaps you're thinking, "How could this be…*reality* responds to *my* thoughts, philosophies, beliefs, and aspirations?"

Well, let me explain this miraculous phenomenon in terms that are easy to understand. Just as scientists can send a rocket into space and (by nature of the laws of physics) predict with certainty where that rocket will land, you can (by design of the laws of the Nature) predict with certainty that the Universe will respond to the mental blueprint you carry in your head on a regular basis. This interactive relationship between your mind and world is the heart and soul of the Mind/Reality Relationship.

The Mind/Reality Relationship is the metaphysical framework by which Abe Lincoln transformed his presidential aspirations into reality without having completed a single year of schooling, and by which Henry Tudor acquired the abundant, timely resources to transform himself from outcast to king over the course of a summer.

When you master the Mind/Reality Relationship, you effectively place the laws of the Universe at your disposal.

The cycle diagram below illustrates how the Mind/Reality Relationship works, and what benefits and advantages you can expect to receive by mastering it.

*"A single idea from the human mind can build cities. An idea can transform the world and change all the rules."*
-Leonardo DiCaprio

**The Cycle of the Mind/Reality Relationship**

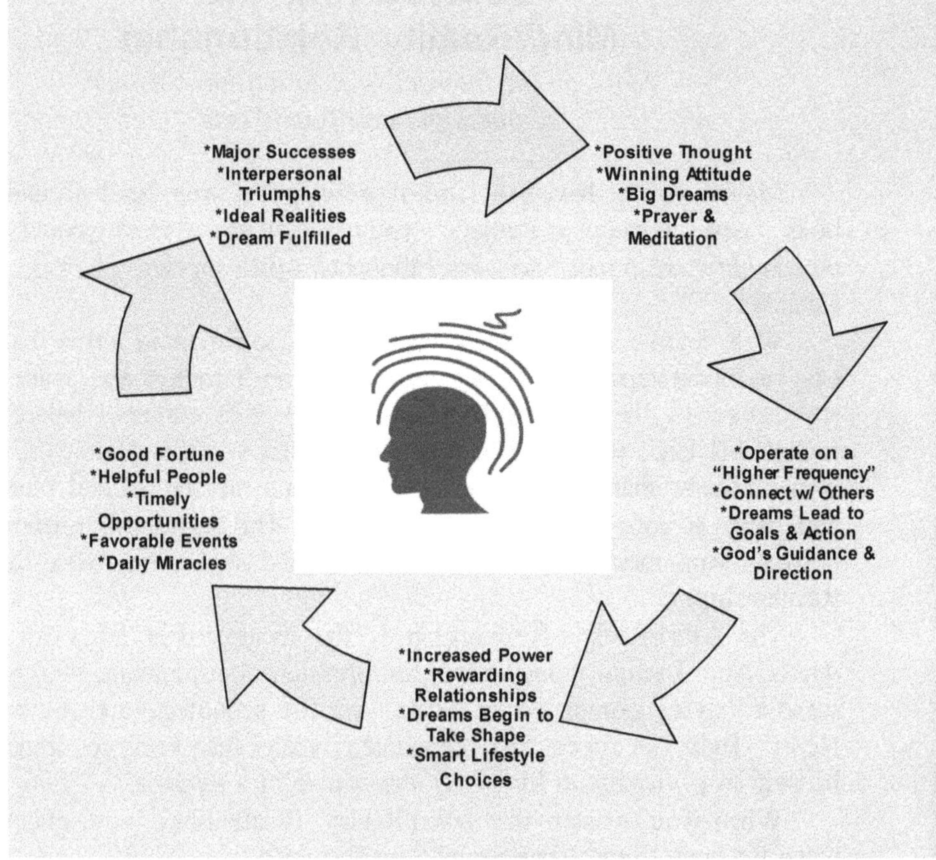


*"All that is comes from the mind;*
*it is based on the mind;*
*it is fashioned by the mind."*
-Ancient Indian Canon

The Mind/Reality Relationship is also the source of the promptings and warnings that have a funny way of prefiguring actual events.

Early in my career, I was hired by a company to turn around a $12 million subsidiary which had become unprofitable. During my initial assessment of the subsidiary, I met with the current president. My *instincts* immediately told me to "beware."

Later that night, I clearly foresaw a chain of events which were about to take place, including this president's abrupt ousting, an extensive regime change, and the appointment of an associate of mine to a key position. Although there were no current plans to remove the president or any logical reason to "beware of him," my prior experiences with the Mind/Reality Relationship instilled me with enough confidence in my premonition to begin assembling a team capable of supporting my associate once the president was removed.

In coming weeks, while conducting internal interviews at the company and gathering intel from the field, I discovered this president's secretive misappropriation of company resources. As if playing out the sequences of a pre-rehearsed dream, I was called to a private meeting at the parent company's corporate headquarters to discuss the subsidiary's future. It was during this meeting that the president's fate was decided. The president was subsequently removed, a new regime was put into place, and my associate assumed the position I had been preparing him to undertake for weeks in advance.

So, how did I *know* this company president was "up to no good" the moment I laid eyes on him? How was I able to *foresee* an entire string of events which were hinged on a discovery I hadn't yet made? Well, here we see the flipside (or receiving end) of the Mind/Reality Relationship.

Like any relationship, the alliance between your mind and world is a matter of give and take. Just as there are times in which you initiate the commands and Life responds, there are instances when Life initiates the communication—most often in the form of promptings and warnings—and it is up to *you* to decipher the message and act accordingly.

Evidence of the cooperative relationship between your mind and world exists all around you. Following are a few examples of this mysterious relationship.

- You *sense* someone is looking at you while your back is turned. You then turn around and discover you were correct!
- You visualize the face of an old friend whom you haven't seen in months or years. Then, only days or hours later, this person telephones you or happens across your path
- You correctly read the character of a total stranger
- You get a "bad feeling" or "good feeling" about someone or something which proves mathematically accurate
- Helpful people cross your path at just the right time
- "Signs" (designed to guide you) become increasingly apparent to you along your chosen path of success
- A critical resource becomes available to you just when you need
- You receive advice from a friend (or even a stranger) which leads to some key opportunity or result

*"Some physicists, among them myself, cannot believe that we must accept the view of events in nature as being analogous to a game of chance"*
-Albert Einstein

**GURU'S TIP:** In order to experience the true wonder of the Mind/Reality Relationship, you must become aware that it exists.

Start by paying attention to your thinking, and to how your thoughts, views, ideas, beliefs, philosophies, expectations, and dreams influence the content and quality of your daily life, for better or worse.

Once you begin to grasp the extent of the powers and forces within you, and of the willingness of Life to respond to you, you will find it increasingly easier to influence your circumstances and surroundings, to identify new opportunities, and to increase your exposure to favorable events.

With a little faith and a few initial experiences with the Mind/Reality Relationship, you will soon discover that this thought-activated matrix has been woven into the fabric of the Universe precisely so that you can begin bringing the furthest extents of your imagination into the palms of your hands.

*"The actuality of thought is life."*
-Aristotle

## The Universe of Thought

*How to Think the Physical Realm into Existence*

"Ideas are the archetypes of reality," taught Greek philosopher Plato. Look around you and you will discover overwhelming evidence that you indeed live in a world constructed by thought.

For instance, you rise each morning, brush your teeth, and dress for work never considering the fact that your bed, toothbrush, and clothing were conceived in the minds of craftsmen, inventors, and fashion designers. You then leave your home (which began as an architect's exercise in imagination,) and get into your vehicle. Of course, the car you drive was dreamed-up and designed by a team of automotive executives and engineers, shuttled through an assembly line (invented by Henry Ford in 1913,) and put together by robots, which also were created by engineers.

Then, on your way to work, you drive over roads and bridges, pass by traffic signals and local businesses, and breeze by billboards; all of which were brainstormed, designed, and organized in the brains of the civil engineers, architects, builders, landscapers, marketers, technology experts, and entrepreneurs.

Direct from the human imagination springs forth everything from the airplanes soaring over your head and to the house you live in, to the clothes on your back and the cell phone you use every day. Even the piece of furniture you're positioned on right now is a byproduct of human creativity.

Ours is indeed a thought-generated Universe.

*"The Universe begins to look more like a great thought than a great machine."*
-Sir James Jean

So, how does all of this benefit *you?* Let's start with this one, inspiring fact: You possess the power and authority to *think* the physical realm into existence! In the words of Plato, "Beholding beauty with the eye of the mind, one will be enabled to bring forth, not images, but realities."

So, the question is: What represents "beauty" to you? Is it living life your own way, in your own time, on your own terms? It is overcoming some psychogenic disorder like poverty, self-defeatism or addiction? Is it a satisfying career, loving relationships or wealth beyond measure? Is it starting a business or charity? Writing a book? Or do you see *beauty* in changing the world in some legendary way?

Consider what your ideal realities may be. As you continue reading, you'll learn numerous ways to begin cooperating with Life in bringing them to fruition.

**GURU'S TIP:** Tomorrow's existence will appear in shocking resemblance to the content and quality of today's thoughts, perceptions, and projections. The world becomes a vast playground of unlimited opportunities for the man or woman who arrives at the realization that the catalyst for everything we could ever hope for or dream of begins within the depths of our own, limitless *mind.*

## Thomas Edison

*How a Home-schooled Paperboy Used the Mind's Powers To Manufacture an Empire and Redefine Civilization*

Born in 1847, Thomas Alva Edison spent just three months in school before he was labeled "problematic" by his teachers because of his insatiable curiosity and non-stop inquiries. Quickly realizing that the public education system could not quell her son's inquisitiveness, Thomas' mother withdrew her son from school and devoted herself to home-schooling the boy instead. By age 10, Thomas, eager to earn a day's wage, began spending his days selling newspapers to passersby on street corners and, later, at the Port Huron railway station in Ohio.

Who could've known, as they hustled by the young entrepreneur waving newspapers and yelling, "Get your daily copy, here!" that Thomas Edison would go on to revolutionize civilization and become a legend.

*"You can chisel out your own existence by the thoughts you constantly project every moment of your life."*
-Anthony Robbins

By 1875, after discovering the "secret to success," Edison, 28, would launch an unceasing stream of genius inventions while working by lamplight inside his unassuming, stone-built laboratory in Orange, New Jersey. First, in 1877, came the phonograph, the world's first machine capable of recording and playing back a human voice. Two years later, at age 32, Edison (in the wake of thousands of failed experiments,) at last, perfected a product which channeled electricity through a glass bulb by way of a thin filament. Edison called his invention—which produced 13 hours of manmade daylight—the *light bulb.* Later, after developing a method for increasing burn time in his light bulbs, Edison founded Edison Electric Light Company through which the young CEO began mass producing light bulbs, sparking a chain reaction which would render lanterns obsolete first in New Jersey, then across the east coast, and finally, throughout America. Before long, electric light would become the measure of progress for civilized societies around the world.

Edison's imaginative faculties and reservoirs of energy seemed only to grow stronger and sharper with age.

In 1896, Edison, 49, created the world's first motion pictures. Then, in 1910, the scientist devised a method for adding voice-overs to film. After such films were adopted by cinema houses nationwide, audiences across America sat captivated by the sights and sounds of the first-ever "talking movies."

Continuing to forge his legendary destiny well into his 80's, Edison would lay claim to 1,300 inventions and over 1,000 patents, and would enjoy creative alliances with the likes of Andrew Carnegie, George Eastman, Henry Ford, Walt Disney, and Teddy Roosevelt.

As a CEO, Edison cultivated the careers of countless associates and apprentices and became one of the wealthiest businessmen in New Jersey. And, let's not forget that Edison's little lighting company, EELC, would go on to become America's largest manufacturer, General Electric!

*"If you chance to live and move and have your being in that thin stratum in which the events that make the news transpire, then these things will fill the world for you."*
-Henry David Thoreau

Thomas Edison is arguably the most accomplished and beloved scientist who ever lived. So, what was the *secret of success* by which Edison was able to launch the lifelong series of genius inventions, famous alliances, financial windfalls, and enduring business ventures that enabled the scientist to redefine civilization and become a legend without having completed a single year of formal schooling?

An Edison associate attributed the scientist's success to his deep understanding that "the human mind can achieve anything it can conceive." Edison was a *Mind Contrologist* who demonstrated exceptional skill in using the Mind/Reality Relationship to make the world a better place for himself and others.

Edison's empire was not built upon a series of lucky breaks or random events. Edison himself revealed that, "I never did anything by accident, nor did my inventions come by coincidence." To the contrary, the Great Inventor consciously and deliberately coerced his *ideal realities* into existence through a combination of the mind control principles you will find in this book, tons of resultant creative energy, and the proverbial hard day's work.

*"The Universe spins upon the axis of each man's mind."*
-John Echols

Looking back on the extraordinary existence he had summoned forth from the depths of his own limitless being, an elderly Edison insisted, "If we did all the things we are capable of doing we would literally astound ourselves."

So, what does it take to begin forging an Edisonian existence, an existence in which your mind is wholly under your command, your world is largely under your control, and every good thing that you seek becomes *yours?*

## How to Begin Generating an "Edisonian Existence"

*7 Steps to the Superior Reality of Your Choosing*

Below, are seven steps you can take to begin dematerializing your current, undesirable circumstances and replacing them with the richer, more enjoyable, and thoroughly satisfying life experiences you truly want and deserve.

(1) **Know How Your Mind Works:** Congratulations, you probably now know more about how your mind operates than your doctor and 99.9% of the population!

(2) **Take-on a "Lincolnesque Mental Outlook:"** The quality of your life will generally reflect your own dominant thoughts, views, ideas, beliefs, ambitions, expectations, and dreams. To improve your *external* circumstances and conditions, first improve your *internal* perceptions and projections.

(3) **Apply the Genius of Henry Tudor**: Exert authority over circumstance by projecting your mental focus beyond any current, undesirable conditions to the ideal outcomes, experiences, associations, and events you *do want* to fill your life.

The superior mental practices of achievers like Lincoln, Tudor, and Edison teach us that an ability to see beyond the present represents a key step in the materialization process by which, in due time, our dreams are transformed into reality.

(4) **Fiercely Guard Your Focus**: Distractions derail dreams and thwart goals. It is your discipline in *maintaining* strict focus on what you want that will determine your success in bringing your ideal realities into fruition *over the long run.*

(5) **Revise Your Philosophy**: Ascribe to this dogma. "Today is going to be magical; anything that can go right, will; I'm more capable than I know; God loves me more than I realize; and happiness and good fortune will find me wherever I go!"

(6) **Master the "Mind/Reality Relationship:"** Pay close attention to how your thoughts affect your personal well-being, the quality of your relationships, your "luck" (for better or worse,) your access to opportunities and resources, and your exposure to favorable events. Also, take heed of the promptings and warnings Life seems to be sending you.

(7) **Follow Edison's Lead:** Develop the legendary skill of using your mental powers and physical capabilities to make the world a better place for yourself and others, too! Remember, your new "superior reality" is eagerly awaiting *your* cue.

*"I marvel when I see your Heavens, the work of Your Fingers, the moon and the stars You have set in place. And yet, You are mindful of man. You care for him. You have made him little less than a god, crowned him with glory and honor, and placed all things at his feet."*

-Psalms 8:47

## The Mind/Reality Relationship

*A Final Word*

In this chapter, you've discovered The *Mind/Reality Relationship*: the thought-activated matrix that enables you to communicate with, and influence, reality. The relationship between your mind and world is scientific, predictable, and designed for you to use for your benefit.

You're now ready to learn about an unfailing law of progress which could forever change the way you think about your world and open the door to possibilities which you have not yet dared to consider…

# 7

# The Universal Law of Open Doors

*When one door closes, another opens; and it's always a bigger and better door*

*"I have learned over the years that when one door seemingly closes, another door opens."*
-Jack Canfield

*God opens doors*. How do I know this? Through a lifetime of personal experiences and research of more than 500 of the world's most fascinating Mind Contrologists. In order to fully experience this unfailing Law of the Universe, however, you've got know where you're going. Experience has taught me that once you've determined your chosen destinations in life and business, the "doors" you want and need to step through will be opened to you at just the right time.

Take Thomas Edison for instance.

In the fall of 1862, Thomas Edison, 15, was working on the Grand Trunk Railway, selling newspapers, cigars, and candy to passengers on their way to work. Naturally ambitious, Thomas already had his eye on where he wanted to take his career next. He had become fascinated with the budding field of telegraphy after discovering the miles of telephone poles and wires that were being constructed along the rail route.

While peddling his goods in the aisles of the rail cars, Thomas found himself staring out the windows with childlike curiosity about the underlying sciences that enabled this complex infrastructure of poles and wires to transmit messages across Ohio. Before long, the teenager decided to trade his job as a newsboy for a "more important" role at one of the area's emerging telegraph stations. And why wouldn't he want to make the change? As a telegraph operator, Edison would enjoy an office job, better pay, and the opportunity for advancement in a fast-growing field which he truly enjoyed. Of course, Thomas would first have to learn enough about telegraphy to make himself worth hiring.

Soon after considering a career move, the stars became magically aligned in Tom's favor. At the Port Huron Train Station, Station Chief J. MacKensie was in the process of seeing his wife and three year-old son off on a trip when Edison began grilling the chief with questions about telegraphy. MacKensie, an important man who had little time for Tom's inquiry, became aggravated by the intrusion.

That all changed, however, when MacKensie's son wandered into the path of an oncoming train. Alerted to the drama by the blood-curdling screams of MacKensie's wife, young Tom darted to the tracks and rescued the boy without a moment to spare! A tattered Tom gleamed with pride as he returned the boy to his grateful parents. Placing a hand on Edison's shoulder, MacKensie said, "Telegraphy—is that your interest? Then step into my office and I shall teach you everything you wish to learn." Following several weeks of after-work tutorials, a well-informed Thomas Edison ditched his job as newsboy for a dream position at Western Union.

Edison's story demonstrates how the "doors of opportunity" on which we knock readily swing open to us, often in the most mysterious of ways, once we determine where it is we want to go. As Christ has promised, "Seek, and ye shall find; ask, and ye shall receive; knock, and the door shall be opened unto you."

However, what if a door of opportunity we're attempting to step through appears to *close* on us for any number of reasons? Ah, this brings us to what I refer to as the *Universal Law of Open Doors*.

That is, when one door closes, another opens—and it's always a bigger and better door.

*"The Rule of Life is to be found with yourself."*
-Confucius

One of my first vivid experiences with the Universal Law of Open Doors occurred when I was in my early 20's.

I was really into high-performance sports bikes. I loved everything about them. The looks. The sound. The speed. I'd set my sights on owning one: a brand new CBR 900 RR. I learned the specs: 919 CCs and a top speed of 200 MPH. I picked out a color: Ferrari red. I even made regular trips to the dealership to sit on a CBR, and then studied the brochure for hours after returning home.

Living paycheck to paycheck, however, I lacked one important thing: the $10,000 ticket price.

As is always the case, my dominant thoughts about owning a CBR triggered a couple of ideas about how to generate the $10,000. First, I tried a loan through the dealership, but the loan officer informed me that I lacked sufficient credit history. Undeterred, I reasoned that the credit union I belonged to might help. After all, they'd already extended me a loan of $5,000. But again my request was denied.

With two doors slammed in my face, I could've given up. Instead, I chose to believe that there had to be a way to acquire that bike. I went back to studying my brochure and awaited another idea. That's when help arrived, not in the form of an idea, but in the form of an unexpected offer. After hearing through the grapevine that I'd been turned down for multiple loans, my favorite aunt, Cindy, offered to cosign for the $10,000.

I learned two important things that day: no one could ever take the place of Aunt Cindy—and *when one door closes, another opens….*

Over the years, the Universal Law of Open Doors has made many glorious appearances in my life, career, relationships, and finances.

For instance, some years ago, I was in the market for a company car. Following weeks of research, I located what I thought to be the perfect car at a faraway dealership. It was the model and color I wanted at a price I was willing to pay. I traveled to the dealership with my daughter, but when we arrived, I noticed a "sold" sign on the vehicle. When I confronted the salesman—who just hours before had assured me that the car was available—he informed me that a customer had arrived shortly after my call and plunked down a large cash deposit.

Although I was disappointed, experience had taught me that *when one door closes, another opens—and it's always a bigger and better door.*

Encouraged by this unfailing Law of the Universe, I resumed my search for the perfect company car. This time, the Chevy Cruze caught my eye. Bold design. Great gas mileage. And incredibly safe. Based on the MSRP, I came up with a monthly payment I was willing to pay: $275. Later at the dealership, my wife and I test drove a black Cruze with the right options. However, the saleswoman assured me that the monthly payment I had in mind was "impossible." Whenever I'm told that something is impossible, I look for an opportunity to disprove it. So, I stood my ground and was prepared to walk out of the dealership when the saleswoman decided to speak to the GM. After searching the dealership database, the GM located a "preferred buyer" discount reserved for my father by Chevy. The GM offered to extend that discount to me, reducing the monthly payment to the *exact* amount I was willing to pay: $275.

That's where the story gets interesting…

While the paperwork was being processed, I realized that by paying off the Cruze over the next 36 months, I would have the perfect gift for my daughter (who was 13) for her 16$^{th}$ birthday. After sharing this plan with my wife, Denise called our daughter to inform her that we were at the dealership and would be home for dinner. My daughter—who had no idea what car I'd bought—said to her mother, "Please tell me it's a black Chevy Cruze…" Apparently, the Cruze was my daughter's favorite car.

Suddenly, the vehicle that had been sold out from under me days before seemed little more than a small piece of a bigger, more perfect plan!

*"Keep going and the chances are that you will stumble upon something, perhaps when you are least expecting it."*
-Scientist Charles Kettering

Here's another, larger scale, illustration of the Universal Law of Open Doors...

During my 30's, I somehow managed to ascend the corporate ladder with half my brain tied behind my back. That is, I'd been fighting an on-again-off-again battle with chemical abuse. In the end, this battle left me virtually homeless, penniless, and on the brink of insanity.

At the lowest point of my life, I scoured the shelves of the local bookstore for a book which could help me understand the human mind and provide me with the inspiration necessary to get back in the game. What I discovered was this: a handful of antiquated mind science and personal development best-sellers, and a ton of PhD-penned neuroscience books which were either too technical to appeal to average Joes and Janes or failed to teach me how to *use* my mind to live more successfully.

Ironically, my thinking suddenly crystallized: If I was going to find a masterwork capable of deciphering the mysteries of mind science and personal development for average Joes and Janes, I would have to author it *myself.*

That moment sparked my unyielding quest to decode the mysteries of mentality and peak performance, a quest upon which *Mind Contrology®* would be engineered. In the meantime, however, I had to rebuild my life and career.

At the time, my Ultimate Professional Goal was to become CEO or COO of a thriving national company. So, while continuing to pen *Mind Contrology®*, I reached out to a network of executive recruiters in an attempt to secure my next dream position. Initially, it appeared that my efforts had fallen on poor timing. With the economic recession looming in America, many large companies had placed a freeze on hiring. Undeterred, I pressed forward. And after speaking with the CEOs of several target firms, I received a truly exciting offer. The

CEO of a Virginia-based national service firm offered me a position as COO in the salary range of $250k, plus bonuses and a relocation package.

This appeared to be the dream position I'd been working toward all my life. With my wife entrenched in her career and my daughter recently enrolled at one of the best charter schools in the country, however, relocating my family at the time proved impractical.

Very regrettably, I was forced to decline the offer.

Continuing to operate according to the Universal Law of Open Doors, I accepted a contract assignment to assist the CEO of a fast-growing company in Pennsylvania. Although the position was not what I had in mind, the challenge of managing a start-up would allow me to sharpen my management skillset. More importantly, the assignment enabled me to apply to the company's CEO and management team some pioneering coaching techniques I was in the process of developing.

*"A thorough understanding of the Great Law which permeates the Universe leads to the acquirement of that state of mind known as obedience."*
-James Allen

While the CEO for whom I was working had ideas of us working together for years to come, I did not share his sentiments. Although I applied 100% of my efforts to the assignment, I continued to keep my eyes open for the bigger and better opportunity I was sure would present itself at just the right time. What I could not have imagined, however, was the life-altering conversation I would have with the CEO's wife, who was also the company's CFO.

It was while teaching Mary, the CFO, a new ratio analysis program I was installing that the conversation shifted from financial analysis to tax strategy. Out of the blue, she proposed, "John, why don't *you* incorporate? As president and CEO of your own management consultancy, you can write-off your expenses and substantially reduce your tax rate."

*Humm, President and CEO of my own management consultancy*, I thought. I have long believed that God speaks through people. And that day, the Great God spoke to me quite clearly through the helpful CFO who had been placed in my path.

Suddenly, the road ahead seemed so clear.

I would launch my own firm and deliver top-flight coaching and consulting to midsize firms at a rate of $250 per hour. As president of my own consultancy, I could provide meaningful employment to a team of sales executives and consultants who would help me grow my business just as I had helped CEOs of companies across the country grow theirs. While running my own consultancy, I could focus more on coaching clients in using the mind control principles and *Peak Performance Technologies (PPT)* I'd been developing through my work in the fields of mind science and personal development. Plus, setting my own schedule would enable me to complete and publish the *Mind Contrology* ® series—three books through which I could begin moving from mind to matter my expanded vision of ushering the fields of mind science and personal development into the 21st century.

And that was just the beginning…

*"When one door closes, another one opens."*
-Super Salesman Joe Girard

Since the time I launched Mindbiz Coaching & Consulting, Inc., I have developed our *Bizology Management Science System (MSS)*—a revolutionary executive training framework which combines the fundamentals of strategic management and the latest business sciences with proprietary "business psychology" principles. The development of this framework has enabled me and my team to teach many small business CEOs how to think, lead, and mange like Fortune-level CEOs, and my work at the firm has earned me invitations to speak at business colleges and professional organizations.

Meanwhile, authoring the *Mind Contrology* ® series has brought me into contact with my intellectual hero and iconic professor, Dr. Fred R. David, as well as with personal development legends such as Dr. Dennis Kimbro and Dr. Karyl McBride, fascinating and wonderful individuals who have long inspired me in life and business.

Finally, building my business, delivering speeches, and publishing the *Mind Contrology®* series have collectively amounted to a quantum leap in my mission of helping others master their minds and fulfill their dreams.

Through the years, God has opened many doors on my behalf.

I often think back to the time I was forced to decline the offer to become COO of a well-known national firm. It was by operating according to the Universal Law of Open Doors that one seemingly closed door eventually led me to the much bigger and better opportunities ahead. Moreover, my long-held dream of becoming CEO or COO of a thriving national company has since become realized beyond my wildest dreams. Most importantly, that firm is, in fact, my *own.*

The Great God is always ready to open another door for you, no matter how many opportunities you may have missed out on in the past. But first, you've got to determine where it is you wish to go in your life, career, relationships, and finances.

Perhaps you've suffered a recent setback or continue to kick yourself over a "missed opportunity" which you thought was your only shot. If so, establish (or reestablish) a vision for your future. Then, trust in God, and believe in the *Universal Law of Open Doors.*

Remember: **When one door closes, another opens—and it's always a bigger and better door!**

*"God has opened many doors of opportunity throughout my lifetime..."*
-Ben Carson

## How to Get Your Foot in the Doors You Wish to Step Through

Nothing opens the doors you wish to step through faster than choosing your desired destinations in life and business, and then preparing in advance for the opportunities you expect to encounter.

Following are some suggestions for how to prepare for your *next* opportunity of a lifetime.

- Begin studying the field(s) you wish to master, even if you're currently working in a different field altogether
- Prepare your "elevator pitch" or presentation
- Learn the *industry lingo* specific to your target field or dream job
- Take a dance or music lesson
- Master a specific software program
- Develop an expanded list of contacts through social media
- Get professional "headshots"
- Attend a seminar or workshop to gain key knowledge
- Stage an "accidental meeting" with someone important
- Go back to school and earn a degree
- Practice interviewing for an upcoming *media appearance*
- Join a gym or hire a trainer
- Earn a pilot's license
- Master an instrument and produce a demo
- Join Toastmaster's International and practice your speech
- Take an etiquette class
- Attend a trade show or industry conference
- Rebrand your business to target a fast-growing market

*"When one door closes, another opens; but we often look so long and regretfully upon the closed door that we do not see the one which has opened for us."*
-Alexander Graham Bell

Now, you know about the *Universal Law of Open Doors* and have a list of ways to get your foot in any door you wish to step through.

Next, let's delve into the *"7 Pillars of Mind Control"*—a set of mind control principles and applications you can use to boost your brain power, gain greater control over your life and destiny, and begin attracting into your days the personal, professional, and financial rewards reserved for those choosing today to become the *Mind Contrologist*s of tomorrow…

# 8
# The 7 Pillars of Mind Control!

*How to Become a 21st Century Mind Controlologist*

*"You either control your mind, or your mind controls you."*
-Dr. Napoleon Hill

Want "mind control?" Here's lesson #1: *Mind control* isn't about brain-bending spoons; it's about masterminding your ideal reality. And because your thoughts lay the foundation for everything that you will do, have, and become in life, your destiny is constantly being scripted, either by the tides of chance or according to the intelligent designs of a mind brought under conscious control.

So, you're now faced with two important choices. You can allow your mind to operate as it always has, leaving much of your destiny-defining powers unrealized. Or you can maximize your potential in life and business by undertaking a regimen of conscious mental programming through the "7 Pillars of Mind Control."

**What are the "7 Pillars of Mind Control?"** The *7 Pillars of Mind Control* are a set of principles and strategies designed to help you:

- Master your focus—and maximize your mental powers
- *Redirect* misguided energies into more productive and satisfying outlets

- Exploit the IQ-boosting benefits and far-reaching rewards of organized mental exercise
- Tune into the positive and develop a can-do attitude!
- Learn the ancient secret of finding good fortune, and discover the magic of forward thinking
- Increase your mastery of the *Mind/Reality Relationship*

Let's begin sharpening your mental mastery skills with a lesson on "mastery of focus"—the holy grail of mind control...

The 1st Pillar of Mind Control

## Mastery of Focus

*The Holy Grail of Mind Control*

*"There is power under your control that is greater than the lack of education, greater than all of your fears and superstitions combined. It is the power to take possession of your mind and direct it toward whatever ends you may desire."*

-Andrew Carnegie

The secret to unlocking (and ultimately mastering) your mind can be reduced to one simple, critical skill: *mastery of focus*. And one of the history's greatest masters of concentration was famous financier, Jay Gould.

Born in 1836, Jay Gould grew up on a farm in upstate New York. Not a fan of milking cows and fertilizing soil, Gould was still in grade school when he decided on a career in the city. Studiously preparing himself for his chosen destiny, Jay, 12, taught himself mathematics, chemistry, and surveying. He then used what he'd learned to open a tannery on his father's farm, ingeniously transforming hemlock trees into supplemental income for his family.

Gould saved every penny he earned with a glorious future in mind.

During his teens, Jay's interest shifted to finance and to how commerce and investing drove the economy. Before long, he realized that if the field of high finance was to become his destination, then Wall Street should be where he was focusing his energies and attention. Jay began making friends with investors and, like most smart would-be tycoons, he soon found himself a mentor.

"Uncle Dan" Drew (Cornelius Vanderbilt's arch rival in stock market speculation) took a liking to young Gould and spent the next years not only teaching Jason the ins-and-outs of trading, but plugging him into the guarded circles of Wall Street. Still in his 20's, Jason Gould was already living his big city dream. Jay, however, immediately set his sights on the next world he wished to conquer.

Putting their heads together, Gould and Drew hatched a creative plan to get rich quick. Gould quickly began scouring New York to raise investor capital which he then used to buy large chunks of stock in the Erie Railroad, the chief transportation route between New York and its surrounding regions. Sensing that Drew and Gould were out to seize control of New York's commercial commerce route, Vanderbilt, who was heavily invested in the railroad, predictably entered the fray, and the war over the Erie Railroad ensued. What Vanderbilt did not know, however, was that the railroad war was a masterful ploy designed to outsmart the aging investor.

Once Vanderbilt became committed to gaining total control of the Erie Railroad, Drew and Gould sold their interests in the railroad to Vanderbilt for a handsome, overnight fortune. Although Vanderbilt thought he'd gotten over on Drew and Gould, Uncle Dan and Jay were the real winners. You see, Vanderbilt's new investments in the rail road rendered the aging magnate financially incapable of thwarting the *true plans* of Drew and Gould to conquer the stock market.

At last, while Vanderbilt's capital was tied-up in The Erie, Drew and Gould began investing, without contest, in a commodity whose profits eclipsed those of Vanderbilt's aging railroad—*gold.* Newly focused on controlling Wall Street's gold futures, Jay Gould began orchestrating lucrative trades of up to $200 million in a single day!

Gould later served as an advisor to U.S. presidents on matters of finance and would amass a fortune rivaling those of Andrew Carnegie and J.D. Rockefeller. So, what was the secret to Jay Gould's success? A Gould friend and associate explained, "When intensely interested in a matter, Mr. Gould devotes his whole concentration of thought to that one thing."

In other words, Gould's secret was *mastery of focus.*

*"Seldom can success be achieved without an almost complete and universal focus on what it is you're trying to accomplish."*
-Donald Trump

The art of attention is much more than what you're looking at from moment to moment. *Focus* is what you're concentrating on with your mind and what you're devoting your energies towards. It's what "mental directives" you're programming into your brain, what powers and capabilities you're currently making available to yourself, and what caliber of existence you're in the process of generating for yourself tomorrow.

And when it comes to mastering your life, career, relationships, and finances, the misdirected focus of an unconditioned mind can bring the entire process of dream acquisition to a screeching halt.

## Rogue and Random Thoughts
*The Antitheses of Mind Control*

You experience approximately 60,000 to 100,000 discernable thoughts each day.

Due to the sheer volume of the daily thoughts that pass through your cognitive loop during any given 24-hour period, it is of monumental importance that you learn not only to maintain a strict and constant focus on what it is you wish to accomplish, but to mitigate those instances of distraction which inevitably occur as a result of what I refer to as rogue and random thoughts.

While the person who possesses dreams, goals, priorities, and responsibilities also possesses built-in defenses against distraction, even top peak performers run the risk of becoming derailed from their important purposes, if they're not careful. So, obviously, the odds of becoming distracted increase exponentially for the person who suffers from limited mental conditioning.

Since rogue and random thinking is the antithesis of "mind control," it's important to know how to recognize and mitigate these destroyers of destinies.

## How to Regulate Rogue and Random Thoughts

Make sure you don't fall victim to derailing distractions by taking heed of the following facts and guidelines.

(1) Thoughts, your mind's energy, can and will occur at random. However, the frequency with which you experience rouge and random thoughts generally decreases as your degree of mental mastery *increases.*

(2) You are *not* obligated to focus on, or act upon, every thought that passes through your cognitive loop. Simply dismiss unwanted or unworthy thoughts as "unwelcome intruders," and then shift your attention to more important matters.

(3) Focus and act strictly upon those thoughts that are *consciously conceived* in your own best interests.

*"Concentrate your thoughts, your energies."*
-Andrew Carnegie

**GURU'S TIP:** An exceptional degree of mental focus is the fundamental underpinning of mind control.

If it's mind control you seek, strive always to maintain conscious, disciplined direction of your thoughts. Developing an unswayable focus on what it is you wish to achieve enables you to concentrate your resources in the direction of your chosen pursuits and endeavors, helps you to minimize the occasional distractions which could otherwise derail your dreams, and allows you to maximize the far-reaching benefits of the Mind/Reality Relationship.

Simply put, *mastery of focus* is the holy grail of mind control!

The 2nd Pillar of Mind Control

## Harness the Power of Redirection!

*"Don't be afraid to replace the way things were with the way they should be."*
-Super CEO Al Dunlap

What's "Redirection?" *Redirection* is a mind control principle which allows you to effortlessly rechannel current energy expenditures (especially those that are producing undesirable results in your life) into more rewarding outlets.

### Habits: Application of Neutral Energy

Human beings are creatures of habit, and habits (whether productive or destructive) are expenditures of our own precious energies. Our most demanding habits require our constant attention and draw from us the physical and spiritual resources necessary to "keep them going." However, the energy we use to drive our habits is neither good nor bad; it's just *energy.* It's the "outlet"—the activity we choose to channel our energies into—that makes our habits either the worst of masters or the best of servants.

So, why do people have such a hard time overcoming their addictions? For starters, the entire "rehabilitation industry" is occupied by unwitting psychologists and addiction counselors who are trained to get the patient talking about their problem, expressing feelings about their problem, and attending groups centered on their problem. Unfortunately, focusing on and talking about a problem rarely leads to a solution, only to a bigger, more intimidating problem.

This kind of misdirection of energy and resources, however unintentional, is the very reason why prevailing methods of drug and alcohol treatment in America have such horrifyingly low success rates.

That's where the *Principle of Redirection* comes in...

*"Your life changes the moment you make a new, congruent, and committed decision."*
-Anthony Robbins

## An Inspiring Story of Redirection

Dale was a "hopeless" drug addict who lived in his truck and breathed for his next fix. Then something changed.

By the time Dale was 35, he had been homeless for four years and had a hard time remembering what it felt like to be clean from drugs.

All of that changed one day when Dale, gazing at the world from behind the dirty windshield of the pick-up truck that had become his home, began to envy other men his age, men who had houses, families, careers...lives. Suddenly craving a better existence for himself, Dale's focus shifted from chasing drugs to becoming a respectable person. And that higher purpose *redirected* the silent but unstoppable forces within him.

In coming weeks, Dale began to channel the energies he once used to chase drugs into a new outlet—a career. Dale scraped together some tools and some customers, cleaned up the truck he'd been living in, and went into business. Dale never quite realized, as his business grew and his new, professional identity began to emerge, that the very same passions that had once fueled his addiction were now driving his overnight success.

Dale is not a fictional character. He's president of a multimillion dollar development firm, owns a fleet of trucks, and lives in a mansion the size of a small hotel!

*"Since everything is a reflection of the mind, everything can be changed by the mind."*
-Ancient Indian Canon

## How to Put Redirection to Work for You

Redirection works. Two of the smartest and wealthiest people I know—an ex-heroin addict and a former problem drinker—are self-made multimillionaires who overcame their "bad habits" on their own by redirecting their energies into more productive outlets.

Overcoming bad habits such as smoking, drinking or over-eating becomes much easier when you put the Principle of Redirection to work in your life. Here's how…

(1) **Change your Perspective**: *No one* is "hopeless," and *all* bad habits can be exchanged for better ones.

Remember, all habits (whether productive or destructive) are fueled by harmless, human energy. Furthermore, it takes no more effort to fuel a lifestyle of wealth and fitness than it does to sustain an addiction to food or chemicals. Taking this perspective, it's easy to see how redirecting one's energies into new, improved outlets often transforms seemingly hopeless individuals into amazing, overnight success stories.

(2) **Choose New "Outlets:"** Pattern energy expenditures (like those used to fuel addictions) do not simply *die out* overnight because one tires of being addicted and decides to change one's life. This is why replacing destructive habits like smoking with more productive interests and activities, like working-out for example, is such an effective method for conquering bad habits.

Redirection allows you to rechannel the *same* energies into a new and better "outlet!"

(3) **Give Redirection Time to Work:** Although forging the new, neural pathways by which good habits are formed requires doing something just once, doing something for about 30 days is the key to making a new habit permanent.

Rigorously engage in your newly chosen outlets for at least 30 days. Once you begin to feel *drawn into* your new habit(s) as if operating on auto-pilot, you can rest assured that the Principle of Redirection is at work on your behalf.

*"You can make a positive out of most any negative if you work hard enough at it."*
-Sam Walton

**GURU'S TIP:** Remember, every bad habit carries within it the makings of more rewarding interests and activities.

Got anger issues...mad at the world? Hate *losing* instead. Then teach the world a lesson about *winning.* Addicted to smoking or eating? Trade up to an addiction to money, and then become a charity junkie. Got OCD? Terrific, *obsession* is exactly what it takes to achieve greatness!

How do you spell "overnight success?" R-E-D-I-R-E-C-T-I-O-N!

The 3rd Pillar of Mind Control

## Exercise Your Mind

*"Strength of mind is exercise, not rest."*
-Alexander Pope

You've already learned that your cerebrum and cerebral cortex represent your rational, learning brain. What you may not know, however, is that stimulating your cerebrum through a program of "mental exercise" (including reading, analyzing, discovering, studying, memorizing, learning, and, yes, doing) *turns on* your neurological components, builds stronger or entirely new synaptic bridges and neural superhighways, and keeps your brain young, healthy and sharp.

### Choosing a Program of Mental Exercise

*Mental exercise* should be both functional and fun. This isn't difficult to accomplish since there are so many ways to challenge and exercise your brain. To exercise your brain, you might: devour literature, do crossword or jigsaw puzzles, solve brainteasers, play chess, try Scrabble or Pictionary, study a new language, learn a new software program, conduct research, take on a home improvement project, do some math, help your child with homework, take a business or art class, write an essay or poem, engage in an intellectual conversation, or delve into any hobby which requires *thought,* as well as action.

## The Benefits and Advantages of Mental Exercise

Modern behavioral science has shown that simply wanting to achieve a goal is perhaps the single most important factor in attaining one's desired result. And since the speed and accuracy by which you may sharpen your mind is largely determined by your desire to do so, you will surely benefit from some added incentive.

Below, are a few of the benefits and advantages you can expect to gain by challenging your cerebrum through a program of mental exercise.

(1) **Mind Muscle!** Mental exercise stimulates your neurology, builds synaptic bridges, strengthens your sensory data receptors, and builds cerebral muscle.

(2) **The Reader's Edge:** Reading newspapers, magazines, and trade journals is a great way to stay up to date on current events, business trends, political issues, and the economic climate.

Reading books written by experts in your current or target field is a fabulous way to become an "expert" yourself. Reading just two industry-related books per month can place you in the top 25% of experts in your field within 12 months.

Reading is among the most effective methods of mental exercise.

(3) **An "Affordable Education:"** Many of the world's top peak performers—from George Washington to Donald Trump—have been avid self-educators.

Educating yourself according to your long-range and short-term goals provides focused learning without the "filler materials" upon which most formal education curricula are based. What's more, self-education costs nothing more than the price of an internet subscription, library card or your choice of books.

Want to build brain power, avoid the ridiculous costs of formal education, and become better prepared for a successful life? Become a *self-educator.*

(4) **A Higher IQ:** Challenging your intellect through a comprehensive mental fitness program that incorporates information gathering, problem-solving, vocabulary and communication building, and the use of imagination has been shown to boost one's IQ up to 25 points!

(5) **The Professional Advantage**: The professional who takes a *cerebral* approach to the workplace typically makes smart decisions, demonstrates keen insight, remains informed, and exhibits competence and expertise. Coincidentally, the professional who possesses these traits also tends to ascend the ranks the fastest and commands a higher income than those who are *not* mental fitness buffs.

Reap the rewards of becoming a "cerebral" professional.

(6) **Street Wisdom:** Weak-mindedness creates susceptibility to the scams of criminals and marketers. On the other hand, being alert and informed acts as a barrier against both being *had* and being *sold.*

A razor sharp mentality means never having to play the sucker.

(7) **An Ageless Mind:** Keeping your brain busy has been shown to combat mental decline well beyond one's golden years. For instance, Dr. Fred Gage of the Salk Institute in Switzerland recently observed new neurons being formed in the minds of patients aged 50-70.

Want the benefits of regenerative brain cells and the advantages of neural youthfulness for years, or even decades, to come? Exercise your mind!

*"Great care is due to the mind and soul; for they,*
*like lamps, grow dim over time unless*
*we keep them supplied with oil.*
*Intellectual activity gives buoyancy to the mind."*
-Cicero

**GURU'S TIP:** Building your lifestyle around a program of daily mental exercise promotes a supercharged mentality and leads to increased control over your personal and professional affairs.

The 4th Pillar of Mind Control

## Tune into the Positive

*"No pessimist has ever discovered the secrets to the stars, or sailed to an unchartered land, or opened a new Heaven to the human spirit."*
-Helen Keller

There is perhaps no better way to employ your powers of attention than to purposely and habitually *tune into* all that is wonderful in your life and world. The desirable effects that positive thinking has on everything from your cells and heart to your mood and relationships are well documented.

Unfortunately, for most people, the focus is on all the *wrong* things.

As an executive coach and management consultant, one of my jobs is to prepare CEOs and key executives for the next level of performance by helping them improve their mindsets and skillsets. During my firm's *Bizology Management Science* seminars, I sometimes rely on an exercise based on mastery of focus and positive thinking. Standing at the head of a conference room filled with ambitious executives, I hold up a beautiful plaque engraved with the affirmation, ***"You will leave here today knowing more abutt growing revenues, reducing cost, boosting employee productivity, and enhancing your bottom line than you ever dreamed possible."***

"Tell me what you see," I say to the group. Hands quickly shoot into the air across the room. The answer is invariably the same—the word *"about"* is misspelled.

"What a shame," I reply, shaking my head in pity. "The beautiful plaque. The inspiring message. It all goes unnoticed in light of a single mistake which represents *less than 1%* of the total picture!"

*"Creation widens to our view."*
-Henry David Thoreau

Many of us have been conditioned by our families or communities to see the worst in ourselves, to find reasons why we *can't* do or acquire something, to seek in the name of humility the bare minimum we need to "get by," and, perhaps, even to expect to receive the short end of the stick in every situation. Mental habits like these cause us to miss out on the beauty and wonder that Life presents to us at the dawn of each new day.

Maybe you are among those who have failed to make the best of too many sunrises. Perhaps you have foregone much of the beauty and wonder of Life because you have been "tuned into" the *few* unlikable people and undesirable circumstances in your life.

Fortunately, you need only recognize your blindness in order to begin to see rightly. And you are free to begin enjoying the miracle of each day on Earth simply by lifting your thoughts above and beyond the herd of mediocrity.

## Thinking *Above* the Herd of Mediocrity

Every day, intelligent and highly capable individuals unwittingly derive their thoughts and opinions from second-rate sources such as CNN, negative family members and coworkers, and the local, nightly news. I refer to these unworthy sources of information (along with those foolish enough to relinquish their minds to them) as the "herd of mediocrity."

Have you been busy keeping with the herd by *tuning into* headlines that assure you that the economy is doomed…the job market impenetrable? Have you fallen for the self-limiting mantras of those who tell you, *It can't be done*, *It takes money to make money* or *Life sucks and then you die?* Have you allowed the nightly news to infect your being with a level of doom and gloom that would drive Jesus Christ to antidepressants?

Well, here's good news.

No matter how long you've been tuned into the wrong things, no matter what dismal circumstances your negative thinking has conjured up in your life, you may begin to forge a better set of circumstances by refocusing your mind's-eye on the positive results and desired outcomes you now seek.

Is it difficult to dream big, think positive, and remain driven while surrounded by others who have no dreams, spew negativity, and have no specific purpose in life? Perhaps. However, it is only by having the discipline to think *above* naysayers and statistics, to believe *beyond* the media's agenda and current economic conditions, that you will find freedom from *what is* and the authority to dictate what *can be*.

It is up to you, a human being of freewill, to transcend the herd of mediocrity by tuning into and believing in only that which allows you the greatest use of your power and potential.

*"Man, being a thinking creature,*
*there is nothing more worthy of his being*
*than the right direction and employment of his thoughts."*
-William Penn

**GURU'S TIP:** Today's thoughts—positive or negative—are the building blocks of tomorrow's reality. These building blocks will continue to work their architectural magic, methodically constructing your destiny, with each passing moment. Strive to construct a superior existence built upon a foundation of elevated thoughts and empowering beliefs, kind words and contagious smiles, good deeds and premium associations. Exercise your God-given right to transcend the herd of mediocrity. Tune into the positive!

The 5th Pillar of Mind Control

## Develop a "Can-do Attitude!"

*"Where the willingness is great,*
*the difficulties cannot be great."*
-Niccolo Machiavelli

During the 1980s, President Ronald Wilson Regan saw America through one of the most volatile eras in recent history—the Cold War. Regan's road to victory, however, was one paved with obstacles.

In 1981, Regan entered the White House amidst a global environment fear-stricken by threats of nuclear annihilation. Strained relations between the U.S. and Soviet Russia fueled an arms race with no end in sight. And, further complicating matters, the 70 year-old Regan faced fierce opposition from bipartisan detractors who labeled the president a Hollywood actor who lacked the mental acuity to lead the country through a crisis.

It was in 1987, after peace talks with Russia broke down, that Ronald Regan made a decision which would later prove legendary. Seeking an edge in the tense nuclear standoff, Regan assembled a team of military strategists and scientists tasked with rethinking national security and designing an impenetrable defense network based in space. Then came the dream—a futuristic, intercontinental missile-defense system, later dubbed "Star Wars" by program critic, Ted Kennedy.

Controversy over Star Wars ensued. Detractors argued that a global defense system capable of deflecting a nuclear attack from space was *impossible.* Star Wars, naysayers argued, was too sophisticated to be transitioned from mind to matter. So, burdened with ensuring the safety of millions and armed with his "*can-do* attitude," the president and his team descended into a bunker beneath the White House on a quest to conquer the impossible task of satellite, missile defense…

In 2008, in response to aggressive nuclear capable missile testing initiated by North Korea, a U.S. naval battle group was commissioned to conduct war games off the coast of Korea. Put to the test for the first time since its conception, the Star Wars system successfully intercepted its test target just above the Earth's atmosphere.

On Ronald Reagan's desk in the Oval Office during the 1980s could be found a plaque bearing the inscription, **"IT CAN BE DONE!"**

*"Every obstacle yields to firm resolve."*
-Leonardo da Vinci

Research has shown that what you believe you can accomplish accurately regulates your ability to succeed. Convince yourself that all possible objections must be considered before launching some worthwhile endeavor and you'll never begin a single, exhilarating venture. Believe that your Maker shortchanged you on courage and you will lack the guts to take risks and shrivel at first signs of a challenge.

On the other hand, you can be *sure* you've got what it takes—whatever the mission—and your eyes will become open to ideas, strategies, energy, skills, and resources not readily visible to those who are blinded by doubt. You can *believe* that you were born with the force of will and strength of being to beat steep odds and overcome difficult obstacles. Take this attitude, and you will rise to every challenge, transcend all barriers, and silence the naysayers by achieving all that you dare to imagine, and more.

*"Accept the challenges*
*so that you may feel*
*the exhilaration of victory."*
-George S. Patton

**GURU'S TIP:** The world's *can-do* artists have long been devising ways and means to accomplish feats labeled "impossible" by doubters, and you can, too.

Got stuff that needs doing? An envelope that needs pushing? A mountain that requires moving? Develop the belief that *it can be done* and that you're the one who's going to do it.

Difficult circumstances bow down in submission to the man or woman who lives by the philosophy, "Yes, I *can!*"

The 6th Pillar of Mind Control

## Seek & Find Good Fortune

*"Seek, and ye shall find;*
*ask, and ye shall receive;*
*knock, and the door shall be opened unto you."*
-Jesus Christ

You are the author of the story of your life and the maker of your own fortune. The freedom to script your own destiny—or freewill—is a Divine Inheritance so sacred that your Creator Himself refuses to violate it. Ancient Hebrew Scriptures assure us that we will *find* those things we *seek* on a regular basis. This is more than religious doctrine; it is a living promise, a long-proven guideline for effective living and for making the most out of this one, blessed lifetime.

Unfortunately, the time with which you have to generate superior circumstances is *not* unlimited. The average lifespan equals about 28,470 days. By age 39, approximately only 14,235 days are left.

The clock is ticking. And since Life willingly grants us what we seek on a daily basis, isn't it time you start *actively seeking* things like personal power, financial freedom, knowledge, wisdom, health, fitness, expertise, excellence, rewarding relationships, authority over reality, an abundance of every good thing, and the life you've always dreamed about?

*"Learn to seek good fortune,*
*for good fortune's always here."*
-Johann Von Goethe

### 7 Ways to "Seek & Find" Good Fortune

Below, are seven measures you can take to begin increasing your good fortune, virtually overnight:

(1) Start each day by contemplating what you're grateful for, happy about, proud of, and looking forward to.

(2) Every day, congratulate yourself for something you've done well. Did you close a tough sale? Stick to your diet? Live a smoke-free day? Help someone in need? Did your cost-effective shopping lead to great values for you and your family? Reward yourself with a small, meaningful purchase, candlelit bubble bath or by looking into the mirror and declaring yourself a "winner!"

(3) Every day, compliment *someone else* for any reason you choose. Start with your loved ones.

(4) Learn something new each day that will give you a personal or professional edge.

(5) Live by this rule: "I will become the *best in the world* at how I earn a living!"

(6) Dream impossibly big. Spend time each day considering what you'd do with your life if you had unlimited resources. By reading this book, you'll discover that this mental exercise has preceded the rises to prominence of history's greatest figures.

(7) End each night by counting current blessings and anticipating *more* good fortune tomorrow!

*"We make our own fortune and call it destiny."*
-Benjamin Disraeli

Your ability to "seek and find" what you're looking for is the oldest known, most widely used, of all mental principles. It is also the fundamental underpinning of the Mind/Reality Relationship. There is perhaps no more effective method for mastering the construct of reality than *actively seeking* all the wonderful things you wish to find, or want to find you. So, ask yourself: What do I want? What do you really desire on both personal and professional levels? What level of wealth do you want to retire with? What would you like to experience, acquire, accomplish, become, learn, share, and give over the next 10 years? 5 years? 12 months? 6 months? 90 days? In what special ways will you enrich the lives of your loved ones? And how will this world have become a better place for having hosted the marvelous years of your life?

Search your mind and heart for the answers. And as you do, forget about obstacles and limitations, as these generally exist to the degree to which you acknowledge them. Instead, consider only the forthcoming fortune and abundance that awaits you in the years, months, weeks, and days ahead.

The 7th Pillar of Mind Control

## Master the Magic of Forward Thinking

*"Those who look only to the past or present are certain to miss the future."*
-John F. Kennedy

What's "forward thinking?" *Forward thinking* is the skill of disengaging yourself from what's going on around you and directing your mind's-eye to the dreams, goals, expectations, opportunities, and possibilities upon the horizon.

In 1880, opportunity knocked on the door of New York's George Eastman, a grade school dropout who held jobs throughout his teens and 20's that included messenger boy and office clerk for an insurance company. Until that year, photography was largely the craft of "skilled lensmen," professional photographers who traveled door to door, hauling their bulky cameras and tripods, and taking pictures of individuals and families in the most intrusive way possible. Each photo also produced a dangerous powder flash. "Say, *cheese*"...POOF!

That's where George Eastman took over.

Eastman was 33 years old, and working as a bookkeeper at the Rochester Savings Bank, when he overheard the grumblings of townspeople who'd become fed up with the costly hassle of hiring traveling lensmen to take their pictures. Perceiving that a lucrative opportunity existed in solving the lensmen crisis, Eastman's wheels began spinning. So, while the locals remained consumed with the *problems* of picture taking, Eastman began envisioning a *solution.* George imagined a reality in which ordinary people could take their own pictures, at their own leisure, and at an affordable price.

In pursuit of the dream that would shape his destiny, George quit his job at the bank and invested every dollar he possessed to open the Eastman Dry Plate and Film Company. Then, off went George Eastman, into business in an industry that did not yet exist…

*"Look before or you will find yourself behind."*
-Ben Franklin

After opening a second shop in 1887, Eastman put lensmen out of business by inventing hand-held cameras and "roll film," a product that accelerated exposure curing time and made possible the sale of film to the public. 24 months later, in 1889, Eastman teamed up with Thomas Edison to create 35mm film, giving way to motion pictures. Then, in 1890, Eastman struck gold when he invented the "Brownie," the world's first pre-loaded, snap-shot camera. Pricing his Brownies at just $1, Eastman sold 250,000 of his practical, affordable marvels of photography in the first 12 months alone! George Eastman's little company, Kodak, would evolve into a billion dollar empire which would dominate the snap-shot camera market for the next 100 years straight. Forward thinkers, you will find, run the world.

## Discovering Your Primary Reference of Thought

Everyone approaches life primarily through one of three "references of thought," past-, current- or future-reference. Although we may shift from one reference to another as often as from one moment to the next, we all have our favorite reference.

Scan the list below to determine which reference of thought *you* favor most.

(1) **Past-reference Thinkers:** These are the folks who can't seem to break ties with the past, always either reveling in the "glory days" or wasting energy worrying about what *might have been.*

These poor souls spend their entire lives staring into the rearview.

(2) **Current-reference Thinkers:** Concerned less with the past or future, current reference thinkers absorb themselves in the issues of the day. These folks tend to lead "normal lives." They work decent jobs, pay their bills on time, and take vacations during their two weeks off each year. Because current reference thinkers rarely visualize the future, however, they rarely harbor dreams; thus, they progress through life in increments far beneath their greatest potential.

The middleclass is built on current reference thinking.

(3) **Future-reference Thinkers**: These are the Eastmans, Kellers, and Schwarzeneggers of the world, visionaries who see themselves and their world not as they *are*, but as they *could be.* These forward lookers are prone to dream, create, produce, climb, reach, lead, and regularly achieve the "impossible." Comfortable visualizing and planning for the future, future-reference thinkers tend to accomplish more in a few short years than past- and current-reference thinkers do in a decade.

*Forward thinkers* display an uncanny knack for transforming dreams into reality.

*"There is no incentive so great, no tonic so powerful, as the expectations of tomorrow."*
-Orison Swett Marden

## Only About 10% of the Population are Forward Thinkers

Are you among the 10% of the world's *forward thinkers?* If someone asked you, "What's your next, big move?" "What excites you about your future?" or "What are you destined to achieve?" how would you answer? Have you even *considered* your future? If not, be patient. We'll make a visionary out of you in coming chapters.

In the meantime, practice focusing your mind's-eye on tomorrow's possibilities. After all, you can't enjoy freedom and power if you're consumed by the issues of years gone by. It's hard to build wealth or achieve anything spectacular if all your energies are being exhausted "getting by" over the next 24 hours. And ascending the workplace ladder is a hopeless endeavor if you're too shortsighted to *see* the next rung.

Embracing the future will help you to unlock your mind, to enjoy a continuum of personal power, and to open your eyes to a whole new realm of possibilities.

Tomorrow is the storehouse of unlimited opportunities.

## The 7 Pillars of Mind Control

*A Quick* Review

Let's recap the *7 Pillars of Mind Control:*

The 1st Pillar: **Master Your Focus**
The 2nd Pillar: **Harness the Power of Redirection!**
The 3rd Pillar: **Exercise Your Mind**
The 4th Pillar: **Tune into the Positive**
The 5th Pillar: **Develop a "Can-do Attitude!"**
The 6th Pillar: **Seek and Find Good Fortune**
The 7th Pillar: **Master the Magic of Forward Thinking**

**GURU'S TIP:** *Master Your Mind* is the "precursor" to the Dream Acquisition Formula (DAF) found exclusively in *Mind Contrology* ®.

Over the past chapters, you've learned more about mental mastery than any aspiring mastermind ever has. You've learned about your amazing brain and discovered your Mental Theater. You know how to use the principle of Mental Identity to begin evolving into the Ultimate Person you've always wanted to be. And you've been introduced to the Mind/Reality Relationship, a thought-activated relationship between you and your world.

You've also learned more about "mind control," and how to use your mind's powers to your benefit, than most PhDs and 99.9% of the population. You're fast on your way to becoming a *Mind Contrologist.*

*"He who decodes the mysteries of the mind,*
*unlocks the door to the Universe."*
-John Echols

Now that we've thoroughly covered the "precursor" to DAF, you're well prepared to move onto the 1st Element of the Dream Acquisition Formula.

It's time to *awaken your imagination...*

# Awaken Your Imagination

*The 1st Element of the Dream Acquisition Formula (DAF)*

# 9

# Awaken Your Imagination

*How to "Flip the Switch" on your Machine of Ideas*

*"Imagination is more important than knowledge. Knowledge is limited, whereas imagination embraces the entire world."*
-Albert Einstein

What if I told you that you're not only capable of improving your circumstances by changing your thoughts and attitude, but that you also possess the distinct capability to think "physical objects" into existence with roughly the same precision by which a manufacturing plant cranks out consumer goods? Well, it's true. And those who've mastered this secret over the centuries have revolutionized their lives, and often our world, in the process.

For instance, automobiles took the place of carriages after Henry Ford imagined man being pulled across town by an engine instead of a horse. Oil lanterns were rendered obsolete as a result of Thomas Edison's intuition in channeling an electrical current through a filament. And manual typewriters were still standard equipment in the average American household until a college dropout named Bill Gates invented a "digital language" which allowed computers and humans to communicate freely. Gates' idea gave birth to software goliath Microsoft and spawned the Age of Information.

These men provide proof to the world at large about what can be accomplished when a human being "flips the switch" on his or her imagination and gets down to the business of moving ideas from mind to matter.

Of course, this gift of creative genius is not exclusive to *Mind Contrologists* like Ford, Edison and Gates. You, too, are endowed with God-given creative powers by which to manufacture *tangible assets* such as a business or a better body, money or a career, luxury items or a book, or even personal relationships. In fact, you already use this creative process quite frequently in your daily life.

For instance, surely you've been at work when suddenly into your head pops the thought of a few groceries you're running low on at home. You take out a pen and make a quick list (an initial step in transforming thoughts, your mind's energy, into reality.) Then, on your way home, you pick up milk, bread, and eggs, and then store them away in your kitchen cabinets without ever having given much thought to where those *physical items* actually came from—the "Machine of Ideas" inside your head!

*"The human race is governed by its imagination."*
-Napoleon Bonaparte

If you're like most people, you tend to engage the creative process *passively*. A thought pops into your head, and you react. The entire process is so mundane that you hardly even realize it's taking place.

However, once you understand how your "Machine of Ideas" actually works—by discovering the schematic for the creative faculties inside your head—your ability to transform ideas into the physical assets which represent your ideal lifestyle becomes multiplied to infinity. You see, once you gain the knowledge required to take charge of the creative process, once you begin to exchange passive creativity for the habit of *proactive imagination*, you will have discovered one of the great secrets of exerting the power of mind over matter, and no object under the sun will be beyond your reach.

Whether you dream about defining the next era of human existence, or simply redefining your life, it all begins as an exercise in imagination...

## How Henry Ford Transformed a Dream Into an Automotive Empire

Henry Ford was a sixth grade dropout who transformed himself from a factory worker and part-time auto mechanic to the CEO of the Ford Motor Company. Then, after reinventing himself through an active application of the principle of Mental Identity, Ford would go on to single-handedly redefine the automotive industry, again and again, through the advent of a series of complex manufacturing processes, automotive dealerships, and high-tech automotive components which would earn his automotive dynasty a top market position that still exists today.

Ford produced more in a lifetime than 100 average men combined. The secret to his success? Ford manufactured his empire with the building blocks of *proactive imagination*, a can-do attitude, and an ever-increasing mastery of the Mind/Reality Relationship…

Detroit's Henry Ford was 30 years old when he designed and built his first "motorized carriage" in 1893. The excitement of transforming a crazy idea into a crude vehicle sparked within Ford the dream that would become his legacy. Henry imagined starting a company by which to sell affordable, motorized vehicles to the masses.

Over the next decade, Henry built and sold his motor carriages just as fast as his hands and financial resources would allow him. By 1903, however, demand for Ford's "motorcars" outgrew his capacity for building them.

Financially strapped, Henry turned to local lenders for the capital he needed to expand and legitimize his operation. He didn't have much luck. While pitching his vision of launching an unheard of motorcar factory to a series of prospective lenders, banker after banker gazed through the window at the horses and buggies creeping slowly down the street, and then quickly deemed Ford's idea as impossible before laughing the 40 year-old grade school dropout out of their establishment.

Undeterred by the rejection, Henry tapped into the ingenuity that would make him famous and borrowed $30,000 from a handful of back-alley investors. Then, guided by the mental blueprint for the automotive factory he would methodically summon into existence, he opened a small storefront business where he and his small team of employees worked from sunrise to sunset building and selling Ford Motor Company's first marketable "Quadracycles," 8 horse-power vehicles with 2 cylinders.

As Ford began cruising around town in Detroit's first automobile, people began to talk. Word that the era of the horse-and-buggy was over quickly spread from one end of town to the other. And demand for Henry's vehicles went through the roof.

*"Physical concepts are nothing more than free creations of the human mind, and are not, however it may seem, uniquely determined by the external world."*
-Albert Einstein

Previous to 1908, Ford's motorcars were labor intensive and comparatively expensive. However, all of that changed with the introduction of the Model T.

Henry's "motorcar for the multitudes" was an $850 car with no frills and no color. Despite the Model T's 4,830 components, Ford's clever cost-cutting solutions and willingness to accept a slim profit margin allowed him to sell his cars at 57% less than the sticker price of the similar vehicles of emerging competitors. At such a bargain, Henry's little company needed to expand to keep up with demand.

Eager to cash in on Ford's ingenuity, Detroit businessmen dove headlong into the motorcar market. However, before the competition could begin producing automobiles which were as well-built and as sought-after as Henry's Model T, the self-taught engineer was already in the process of transforming his *next* industry-shaping idea into existence—the "automotive assembly line."

Launched in 1913, Ford's assembly line was an innovative 84-step manufacturing process by which cars were assembled along a 250-foot lane manned by a series of workers each assigned to their own specific task. It was there, standing in the middle of the physical world of machinery, workers, and vehicles that he had created, that Ford could be found studying the line, coaching his employees, and figuring out ways to make the process faster and better. And the more hours Henry spent cranking up the power on his Machine of Ideas, the more productivity *soared.* In less than twelve months, Ford reduced the time it took to build the chassis from 12.5 hours to 1.5 hours. Next, Henry shrunk per-car assembly time from 24 hours to 2.5 hours. By 1914, Ford's specialized labor initiative had rocketed automobile output 400%, from 200 per year to 1000. And before long, Ford Motor Company was churning out 100,000 cars per year!

Ford never stopped *foreseeing* his next move, never tired of *imagining, creating, inventing, designing and building.* And as a result, Henry always managed to outperform the competition when it came to pioneering the products and processes by which the automotive industry in Detroit, and eventually the world, would be measured.

Between 1915 and the early 1920s, Ford's vast array of pioneering innovations included everything from the foresight to pay his workers $5 per day (rightly predicting that larger paychecks would create happier employees and more internal customers;) to the introduction of an electric starter, inflated rubber tires and windshield wipers for the Model T; to the advent of "dealerships" and stock parts which made vehicle purchases and repairs more convenient and affordable for Henry's customers.

Before long, the bankers who'd denied Ford's requests for financing were noticing the town's horse-drawn carriages being increasingly replaced by the motorized vehicles being produced by the man they'd mistaken for a fool. Everyone wanted to own a motorcar, and Henry Ford was busy satisfying the demand and getting rich in the process.

By 1924, Ford Motor Company was churning out a staggering 1.8 million automobiles annually and had become the largest automobile company in America. And its founder, Henry Ford, had become one of the wealthiest men in the country!

*"What is now proved was once only imagined."*
-William Blake

**GURU'S TIP:** Few men have harnessed the power of the imagination like Henry Ford. By forging the habit of *proactive imagination,* Ford invented the motorcar and the assembly line, created jobs for thousands of workers, and manufactured a real-life empire out of the raw mental material of dreams and ideas.

Proactive imagination is the skill of consciously using your imaginative faculties and creative capacities to make the world a better place for you, your family, and your fellows. Developing this skill is a prerequisite to mastering the process of manufacturing the raw mental material of dreams and ideas into "physical products," such as a business or a better body, money or a career, luxury items or a book, or even personal relationships.

Henry Ford was a master at converting dreams and ideas into tangible realities. And you, too, can bring ideas to life, ideas as grand and as plentiful as your imagination can muster. You may begin by gaining a deeper understanding of how the creative process works and how to put your imagination to the best possible use.

The following chapter is designed to help you "flip the switch" on your Machine of Ideas…

# 10

# Commanding the Creating Process

*Learning to "Flip the Switch" on your Machine of Ideas*

*"Tis wise to learn;*
*tis Godlike to create."*
-John Godfrey Sax

The "creative process"—or the process by which you *imagine, create, design, invent, build, and produce*—can involve one or some combination of several creative faculties, at any given time, depending on what it is you're trying to achieve. These faculties include logic and reasoning, insight and intuition, and mastery of focus and visualization.

If you want to command the creative process, it helps to develop a working knowledge of the components and nuances specific to this process.

Following are a series of "Creative Muscle-building" exercises designed to familiarize you with your imaginative faculties and supply you with specific methods by which you may strengthen these faculties independently or *pump-up* your creative musculature as a whole.

## Creative Muscle-building Methodology

### Creative Muscle-builder #1) **Targeting Logic and Reason**

*Logic* and *reason* are important components of your creative process. Often referred to as the "rational mind," logic and reason represent the intellectual operations which lead you to bright ideas, smart solutions, and brilliant strategies.

To understand how your mind tends to produce ideas, solutions, and strategies, and to gauge the speed and accuracy by which you apply logic and reason to everyday situations, try the following exercise.

*"Only the human can think, and therefore create."*
-Albert Einstein

**Exercise:** You've got a problem. You're driving along a highway at 8 am, on your way to an interview for a job that pays *double* your current salary, when suddenly your car dies! You coast to the side of the road and try starting the engine but nothing happens. Your interview is at 9 am. But you're 10 miles from your destination.

Take a moment to brainstorm several ways you can still land the job. Then review the follow-up section below.

**Follow-up:** Identify what methodologies your brain favored in producing your answers. Did you rely on similar past experiences for ideas? Or did you *visualize* yourself on the highway and go from there? Do you produce solutions rapidly or take a slower, more methodical approach to problem-solving?

Did you choose to rely solely on personal resources, such as your cell phone or mechanical inclination? Or did you choose to rely on others by hitching a ride or flagging a cab? Did you bring math into the equation (dividing 60 minutes and 10 miles by 10) to arrive at the speed necessary to reach your destination on foot?

Just how *creative* were your ideas, solutions, and strategies? Did you consider calling your interviewer for a ride?

> *"Woe to him that would ascribe something like reason to chance, and then make a religion of surrendering to it."*
> -Johann von Goethe

**GURU'S TIP:** Creative genius often relies on logic and reasoning. For instance, Thomas Edison waded through nearly 10,000 systematic experiments, methodically building upon each step, on his way to inventing the light bulb.

Begin to pay attention to how you use logic and reason in your approach to daily life. And as your prevailing patterns emerge, expand upon them. Boost your resourcefulness by adding mathematics, diagrams, research, and brainstorming to your repertoire. Doing so will help build both your cerebral and creative muscles.

## Creative Muscle-builder #2) **Targeting Insight and Intuition**

*Insight* and *intuition* are the heart and soul of the creative process.

Henry Ford's *insightfulness* was what empowered him to exploit all available resources (such as his mechanical inclination, enterprise financing, and employees) in creating his motorcars, his factory, and his assembly line. However, it was Ford's *intuition* that allowed him to keep his finger on the pulse of his customer's tastes and to consistently remain several steps ahead of the competition, long before market research and competitive intelligence became common tools of executive managers.

"Insight" may be defined as one's capacity to assess a situation based on knowledge or similar experiences. "Intuition," however, needs no comparisons. Operating beyond the restrictions of facts and stored memories, the intuitive mind is to the creative process what the spirit is to man.

Below, you'll find a few exercises for sharpening your powers of perception and strengthening your instincts.

## Building Insight

Because your degree of insightfulness is largely based on your knowledge and experience with comparable situations, a lack of insight in areas in which you are familiar and experienced is often a result of (1) a lack of self-confidence, or (2) an over-reliance on the input of those around you.

Unfortunately, mental habits such as these tarnish your effectiveness in accessing stored knowledge and cause your powers of penetration to atrophy.

Becoming more insightful begins by learning to trust yourself and view yourself as a knowledgeable and competent individual. Start by realizing that cataloged within your expansive mental library is practically every unit of pertinent data you have ever seen, heard, read, or experienced. You're not "short on knowledge," you simply need to practice *accessing* your semantic memory and *applying* this body of knowledge more assertively to your personal and business affairs.

*"Thinking is the hardest work a man can do,*
*that is probably why so few engage in it."*
-Henry Ford

**Exercise in Insight:** Take more "silent guesses" about how to solve a problem at work or improve a relationship at home. Gradually turn these inner guesses into confident opinions. Then practice expressing your *insights* to others.

Try solving your favorite detective shows or mystery novels before they end.

Or, next time you make a smart decision, dissect the decision-making process. What approaches, information or experiences did you rely on to arrive at this decision? Strive to replicate this process when faced with future decisions. Then reward yourself for every wise decision you make.

Practice the above, and you'll soon enjoy greater confidence, better decision-making skills, and sharper insights.

## Building Intuition

Intuition has a lot to do with your ability to "interpret" your environment, as well as the signals your body is sending you. With honed intuition comes a heightened ability to make good use of the promptings and warnings initiated by the Higher Forces of the Mind/Reality Relationship.

*"The intuitive mind is a sacred gift."*
-Albert Einstein

**Exercise in Intuition:** Want to become more "intuitive," more *instinctive?* Here are a few tips...

Next time you walk into a business office, a friend's home or any neighborhood establishment, attempt to "interpret the atmosphere" the moment you arrive. Is it a *professional* office? A *happy* home? A *respectable* establishment? What about your surroundings gives you this hunch?

Take more walks in Nature. And as you do, dissect the scenery around you. Discern the sounds you hear, the rustling of leaves, chirping of birds, etc. Detect any odors and the direction from which they are coming. Tune into temperature, wind speed, and even gravity. Notice how these elements of Nature affect your body and being.

Also, conduct an occasional "feelings check." Pay attention to your physical being and become more attuned to signals your body is trying to send you. Heightened awareness of the relationship between incoming sensory data and your body's natural responses is the underpinning of powerful intuition.

Strive to become more in tune with the communication between your physiology and your environment.

**GURU'S TIP:** Whip your insight and intuition muscles into shape by exercising your powers of perception and flexing your instincts.

To become more *insightful,* read often, gather information from reliable resources, offer more of your *own* thoughts and opinions, and be absolutely certain about the depth and accuracy of your semantic memory.

A couple of ways to strengthen your *instincts* include learning to "read your environment" (by relying more on sensory perception) and becoming attuned to the signals your body is sending you.

Remember, insightfulness and intuition grow stronger with use. And as these faculties mature, so will your command of the creative process.

## Creative Muscle-builder #3) **Targeting Mastery of Focus**

Loss of focus is the #1 cause of abandoned dreams.

While your visualized desires act as powerful mental directives which enable you to transform energy (such as dreams and ideas) into matter (such as material possessions, rewarding relationships, and more,) your guiding purposes must be vigilantly visualized with your mind's-eye and constantly nurtured with optimistic expectation until the manufacturing process is complete. If not, your important dreams and intentions can lose their "transformational potential" either amidst the 60,000 to 100,000 thoughts that pass through your head each day or among any number of distractions you may encounter as time passes and life happens on your way to your chosen destinations.

Simply put, transforming dreams and ideas into their real-life equivalent requires exceptional *mastery of focus.*

The following exercise is designed to introduce you to your "Inner Optical Mechanism" and help you begin developing 20/20 vision of the mind.

## The Mental Focus Builder

**Exercise:** In a comfortable place of limited distraction, close your eyes and visit your Mental Theater. Then follow these three simple steps.

**Step #1)** *Envision* something or someone that you find particularly pleasing: the face of a loved one, your dream home or vacation spot, a pyramid of cold hard cash, or a candle burning peacefully on a mantle.
Take your time bringing this image into sharp focus.

**Step #2)** Once you've projected this image onto the viewing screen in your Mental Theater, *hold it* until you become aware that another thought or image has dominated your mind.

**Step #3)** Once you become aware of this intrusive thought or image, note the *time* it took to "lose focus" on the original image. Was it 3 minutes? 30 seconds? 3 seconds?

After noting the time it took you to lose focus, dismiss the intrusive image then repeat the process. Attempt to gradually increase the timeframe in which you are able to focus on any image you so choose.

**What purpose does the *Mental Focus Builder* serve?**

- The MFB exercises the "Inner Optical Mechanism" of your Mental Theater—or your *mind's-eye.*
- The MFB reveals your current *mastery of focus.*
- The MFB represents a method by which to improve your mental eyesight and mastery of focus.

*"Praised be the human mind,*
*which sees more clearly than does the human eye."*
-Aaron Bernstein

**GURU'S TIP:** Using the Mental Focus Builder for just 5-15 minutes a day is an effective method for improving your skills of focus and concentration.

Using a stopwatch to note increases in "time in focus" is an excellent way to measure progressive mastery of focus.

Remember: the more you flex your inner optical muscle, the stronger your mental vision and creative powers will become.

## Creative Muscle-builder #4) **Targeting Your Visionary Skills**

Aren't mental focus and visualization the same thing? Not exactly.

Whereas mental focus relates to your ability to control your attention, "visualization" is a broader form of mind control which incorporates all three of the components of your Mental Theater that relate to internal audio-animation: mental imagery, your Internal Messaging System (IMS,) and the bodily sensations generated by your limbic system.

Visualization plays a major role in the creative process. In order to manufacture high-grade physical products (like your dream home, ideal career, or first or next $1 million) in the shortest time possible, you've got to foresee these realities—pre-experience them—in your Mental Theater.

The problem? The average person consciously engages his or her imagination fewer times per month than *Mind Contrologists* like Edison, Disney, and Gates might during a typical hour! As a result, the creative process coasts along in neutral, our powers of visualization go sadly to waste, and we find ourselves operating within a physical reality formed more as a game of chance than a product of design.

The following exercises will familiarize you with the visualization process, expose you to the correlation between visualization and *peak performance,* and increase your level of control over the creative process.

## The Art of Visualization

**Exercise #1)** Call to mind something you do well and enjoy. Perhaps "your thing" relates to work, school, music, technology, sports, art, parenting, etc.

Next, summon "your thing" to the viewing screen within your Mental Theater. Except, don't access an actual memory. Instead, construct a Mental Movie of yourself engaged in this activity sometime in the near future.

Spend 15 minutes tuning into the details of your visualization. Identify your surroundings. Are you indoors or out? Is it daytime or night? Are you alone or are others present? Is your vision black and white, or color? What conversations are taking place? What background noises can be heard? Tune into what you are "seeing and hearing" not with your eyes and ears, but with your *mind.*

Next, identify—and this might take some concentration—whether your vision is 2-dimensional (as if you're watching a movie) or 3-dimensional (as if you're *starring* in a movie.) The former represents a "disassociated" visualization. The latter represents what we'll call "self-projection," or the skill of experiencing anticipated events through the eyes and skin of your Future Self.

Finally, what *feelings* does engaging in "your thing" give you in real life? Joy? Excitement? Confidence? Satisfaction? Have you managed to *trick* your limbic system into replicating these sensations through your visualization?

*"Without this playing with fantasy, no creative work has ever yet come to birth. The debt we owe to this play of imagination is incalculable."*
-Carl Jung

Tinker with the exercise above. The objective is to familiarize yourself with the audio-animation features of your Mental Theater, and to get comfortable with engaging your imagination.

**Exercise #2)** By visualizing future performances, you can improve your ability to perform these imagined activities. Let me show you what I mean.

Take out a piece of paper and write your first name, but use the *opposite* of the hand that you usually write with.

Next, take hold of your pen or pencil, again using your non-dominant hand. This time, with your paper in front of you and your writing instrument in hand, close your eyes and *imagine* yourself writing your name again. "See" the letters flowing effortlessly and accurately from your hand. You may find your hand and fingers *automatically adjusting* more naturally to your pen or pencil. Spend a minute or two concentrating on improving, then go ahead and write your name again.

Did your skill improve? Vastly improve? If so, you now understand how imagined performances affect actual performances.

**GURU'S TIP:** Practice visualizing the things you want, and want to do better. Produce, direct, and star strictly in Mental Movies which serve you well. Expand upon your "ordinary roles" by seeing yourself as the hero, expert or giver more often. Also, move from disassociated visualizations to *3-dimensional self-projection.*

Apply your visualization skills to various real-life scenarios, tasks, and goals. And as you do, be aware of how proactive imagination leads you to brighter ideas, sharper insights, boosted confidence, honed skills, better performances, and more successes in your everyday life.

*"Imagination, not invention, is the supreme master of life."*
-Joseph Conrad

Okay, you've "flipped the switch" on your Machine of Ideas, and learned that your creative faculties include logic and reason, insight and intuition, and mastery of focus and visualization. You also know that *proactive imagination*—the secret of inventive geniuses like Ford, Edison, and Gates—is the Big Bang of the creative process.

Imagining is far from child's play.

Are you ready to stop using your Machine of Ideas *passively* to produce grocery lists and create excuses for why you can't achieve great things? Are you eager to begin using your imagination to manufacture the tangible assets that make the world a better place for you, your family, and your fellows?

If so, it's time to become an *Idea Engineer*…

# 11

# Idea Engineering

*Manufacturing Tangible Assets through the Mind/Reality Relationship*

*"The supreme fact that I have discovered is that, it is not willpower, but imagination that creates. Imagination creates reality."*
-Richard Wagner

Although your cerebrum houses the neurological components of your Machine of Ideas, your creative powers extend far beyond your skull. It is exactly because of this reach of creativity that we humans are able to transform our current ideas into the life-enhancing, tangible assets of tomorrow. In fact, converting mental material into tangible assets is as much a science as chemical engineering.

Just as a chemical engineer combines chemicals and mathematics to produce high-grade products for his or her company, the "Idea Engineer" combines the base ingredient of proactive imagination with the element of an energizing purpose, and then infuses it with the higher properties of the Mind/Reality Relationship in order to manufacture high-grade tangible assets—such as a business or a better body, money or a career, luxury items or a book, or even personal relationships.

Transitioning dreams and ideas into tangible assets is the essence of the mental manufacturing process.

Following are seven material outcomes you can manufacture with your mind, as demonstrated by *Idea Engineers* who've mastered the process of asserting mind over matter. Study their methods, and make them your own by putting them into practice in your quest to construct your ideal reality...

## 7 Tangible Assets You Can Convert from Mind to Matter

### Tangible Asset #1) **Your Own Business**

A *single idea* often contains within it a level of transformational energy capable of producing an explosion of physical results which materialize so quickly, and are so far-reaching, that we fail to recognize them, even though we are standing at the center of our own, self-generated mini-universe.

Take the *Ben & Jerry's* ice cream company for example.

Ben and Jerry's didn't exist until two aging free spirits named Ben Cohen and Jerry Greenfield came up with the *idea* to spend $5 on a mail-order ice cream making kit. Adding their unique flair and select ingredients to the basic recipe, the two buddies from grade-school began churning out delicious pints of gourmet ice cream—their *physical products.*

Expanding their mental horizons to include a storefront property, Ben and Jerry, combined their savings of $6,000, bought a broken-down gas station, and then converted it into an ice cream parlor.

Ben and Jerry's ice cream soon became so popular that the frozen treats duo was forced to expand again in order to quench the appetites of their growing market. After investing in a small factory in Vermont, and then a second plant, Ben and Jerry's operation grew so large, so quickly, that Ben and Jerry were credited with helping jump-start Vermont's sluggish economy through the company's enormous dairy purchases and the creation of hundreds of jobs.

Now, did either Ben or Jerry, who toured their production facility daily in order to ensure the highest quality products, ever stop, gaze around at their machinery, workers, and endless pints of gourmet ice cream and think, "Hey, this wonderful, profitable physical reality grew from the single idea to spend $5 on a mail-order ice cream making kit?"

Who knows? What we do know, however, is that mental manufacturing processes just like this are available to you, too—if you will but activate your mental machinery, give birth to an idea, and then nurture that idea into physical maturity by way of conscious effort.

*"The hero is the one with the ideas."*
-Dr. Jack Welch

Do you dream about owning your own business, but aren't sure what business or how to go about getting started? Initiate the mental manufacturing process by thinking outside the parameters of your current professional role—*way* outside, in fact—with the help of the following exercise.

## Awaking Your Inner-Consultant

**Exercise:** Imagine that you are the highly-paid consultant for a fledgling client-firm which is trying to open up a new, unexplored market.

Knowing what you know about your own tastes and needs, and what you believe about emerging potential market trends, what product or service would you advise your young CEO client to invest his or her resources into pursuing?

What methods would you recommend your client use to *promote* this product or service? A public speaking tour? YouTube videos featuring your client's company? A late-night infomercial? Radio spots? An in-store sweepstakes to get people talking?

What hiring priorities, financing options, operating strategies, and distribution channels would you recommend?

Finally, ask yourself: Is this business venture something I could begin pursuing *myself?* Perhaps even in my spare time? If so, do it!

Keep in mind, Steve Jobs built Apple's first computers with his bare hands in his parents' garage. Three years later, Apple was worth $1 billion!

*"You see things and say, Why?*
*But I dream of things that never were and say, Why not?"*
-George Bernard Shaw

**GURU'S TIP:** Remember, every business that exists began in the *mind* of its founder. Only after Ben Cohen and Jerry Greenfield acted on their simple idea to start making ice cream was the rest of their success story able to unfold—converting the gas station into an ice cream parlor, hiring the employees, and purchasing the factory which enabled Ben & Jerry's ice cream to reach a national market.

If you've ever considered owning your own storefront shop, internet business or a global corporation, *now* is the time to get started! And everything you need to get your venture off the ground lies under the rim of your hat.

## Tangible Asset #2) **A Better Body**

You've already learned that your mind influences your health and wellbeing, but it doesn't end there.

Research has shown that the mind has a hard time deciphering the difference between real and imagined events. This is why athletes who visualize their performances beforehand—a common practice among today's top Olympic stars and pro athletes—tend to dominate the competition come contest time. Likewise, *foreseeing* yourself in possession of your ideal physique and performance levels—including toned arms, sculpted abs, and tight glutes; or even heightened abilities and energy levels—makes producing these results in real life a much more accurate and rapid process.

For instance, during his days as a competitive bodybuilder, Arnold Schwarzenegger used his Machine of Ideas to help manufacture his legendary physique. Arnold admitted visualizing his biceps as "volcanoes exploding" during each repetition of his intense biceps routine. Is it merely a coincidence that Schwarzenegger is famed for having built the *tallest biceps peak* in the history of bodybuilding?

Olympic diver Greg Louganis practiced his gold metal dives in his Mental Theater before climbing the platform. And Michael Jordan's secret to athletic performance which often appeared to defy the laws of physics? The famed basket baller once revealed, "I visualized where I wanted to go…and focused on getting there."

Maybe you're a science buff who's wondering *how* visualizing your desired figure, musculature, and performance levels leads to increased control over your physical being and to improvements in your performance?

The answer is the *Principle of Destinational Relativity.*

## The Principle of Destinational Relativity

The "Principle of Destinational Relativity" states: If you've been there in *mind*, you can go there in *body.*

It works like this…

Have you ever driven to an unfamiliar destination, someplace you've never been to before? Notice how that first journey *seems* to take much longer than the second, third or fourth trip? The miles traveled haven't changed, so what makes successive trips *seem* so much shorter and faster? Your mind becomes used to the territory. Familiarity builds neurological connections and personal confidence. Before long, you could find your destination blindfolded—the route becomes second nature.

That's *Destinational Relativity*, and the same principle governs the relationship between the outcomes you repeatedly imagine in your Mental Theater and the results you produce in real life.

Visualizing your ideal physique and performance levels not only coaxes your brain into producing ideas, strategies, smarts, energy, skills, and resources by which to achieve your desired ends, it actually tricks your subconscious mind into thinking that you've already been there and done that.

This primes your neural circuits and interconnected musculature by forging the electrochemical roadmap by which you may reach your destination in the flesh with the ease and familiarity of having *been there before.* If you've been there in *mind*, you can go there in *body.*

*"We are such stuff as dreams are made of."*
-William Shakespeare

**GURU'S TIP**: Looking for a better body—a fabulous physique? Visualize your Ideal Self in graphic detail. If you want sculpted abs and muscular arms, *see yourself* with sculpted abs and muscular arms.

Close your eyes and get to know your future Fit Self. *Imagine* the personal and social rewards of your showcase physique. Foresee the benefits of improved cardiovascular fitness. Study up on health and fitness, use your new insights to create a workout routine and diet regiment, and then see yourself following this regiment to the trim, muscular physique you've been dreaming about. Pre-experience in your Mental Theater the peak performance improvements you've not yet dared to consider until now.

The more you practice visualizing the Ultimate You, the faster and easier you will evolve into the eyes and skin of your Ultimate Self.

## Tangible Asset #3) **Money**

There are three ways you can initiate the money manufacturing process.

(1) **You can make *money* your primary goal**: An example of this is deciding on a specific financial goal like, "I'm going to retire at 45 with $5,000,000 in the bank."

(2) **You can trade *service* for *income:*** Here, your primary goal is to provide a service of value for a company or customer base, and earn income as a result.

(3) **You can *do what you love*—and let riches follow!**

By making any one of these methods your primary conduit for manufacturing money, you will soon find yourself in possession of the ideas, strategies, smarts, energy, skills, and resources with which to begin moving money from *mind to matter*. However, making your living by doing that for which you are best suited and that which you thoroughly enjoy is without a doubt the most satisfying of all the ways to transform dreams and ideas about financial freedom into cash, and eventually, wealth.

Babe Ruth is a prime example of how to manufacture riches by doing what one loves…

## George Ruth's Story of Rags to Riches

Born in 1895, Baltimore's George Herman Ruth hated school and did largely whatever he wanted. With George's parents unable to tame him, the boy soon graduated from back-talking and truancy to fist fights and a growing rebellion against authority. Ruth was eventually labeled "incorrigible." As a result, George ended up spending most of his years between ages 7 and 19 locked away in St. Mary's Industrial School, a reform school which doubles as an orphanage.

It's hard to say exactly when it happened, but at some point between the ages of 10 and his early teens, while assigned to the chores of cleaning the dugout and raking the diamond of St. Mary's ball field, George developed an affinity for the game by which he would forge his own legendary destiny.

Fascinated with baseball, Ruth imagined becoming a rich and famous Major League star, employed by the Boston Red Sox. And he didn't care that his keepers or circumstances might have predicted otherwise.

*"The lively power of his mind prevailed as he traversed the Universe in thought and imagination."*
-Titus Lucretius Carus

Moving fantasy one step closer to fact, George joined St. Mary's baseball league. Throughout his teens, he juggled the positions of catcher and pitcher, and honed his skills at bat.

Each night, after the game, George went to his room, lay in bed and reviewed the day's performance. He also foresaw tomorrow's improvements and became adept at transitioning his plans from his mind to the field. Season after season, he pitched into the "strike zone" a little faster, smashed the ball just a little bit harder, and became increasingly confident about securing the luxury items that he'd assured his teammates he would one day purchase with his fat, Major League paycheck.

It was during Ruth's late teens, while dominating St. Mary's field like a pro in training, that another piece of his dream materialized. Sitting in the stands during the school's baseball season in 1914 was a scout for the minors. And his eye was on Ruth.

Call it a miracle. Call it reality responding to the designs of Ruth's mental blueprint. However, just one week after George's 20$^{th}$ birthday, Life presented him with a gift he would never forget—a $600 season-long contract to play for the Baltimore minors. It was the first of many payments which would fill Ruth's bursting bank account.

Once rescued from St. Mary's, George Herman Ruth would spend the rest of his life revolutionizing the Major Leagues—and getting *rich* doing it. After just six months in the minors, Ruth, 20, was drafted by the Boston Red Sox (the team of Ruth's imaginings) and won the World Series later that same year! Affectionately nicknamed "Babe" by his older teammates, Ruth used the speed-pitching and power-hitting skills he'd developed while at St. Mary's to earn the best pitching record in baseball and to smash a homerun in every major city in the league (a new Major League record) by the age of 24. Ruth later joined the New York Yankees, hitting 54 home runs in 1919 (another record) and winning national acclaim as the league's youngest MVP.

In 1930, George Ruth took the money manufacturing process to a new personal height of operation when, after selling the Yankees ownership on his inflated *ideas* about what he was worth, Ruth commanded the unprecedented annual salary of $75,000.

Babe's contract made him the highest-paid player in baseball, at a level of income equal to that of then-President J. Edgar Hoover!

*"The resourceful and aggressive man who wants to get rich will find the field wide open, provided he is willing to heed and act upon his imagination."*
-J. Paul Getty

Self-made riches begin as an exercise in imagination.

Not until George Ruth dared to imagine becoming a rich and famous baseball player did he open the door to the *idea* of joining St. Mary's ball club, to the *skill* with which he mastered multiple positions (which played a key role in his Major League success,) and to the *energy* to play his heart out at the industrial school (which attracted the baseball scout who helped George get into the minors, and eventually, the big leagues.)

By *foreseeing* himself as a well-paid ball player, Ruth unknowingly set the gears of the mental manufacturing process into motion, the process by which his dreams and ideas of fame and wealth were converted into the *actual roles* and *financial fortunes* he would come to enjoy in real life.

Want more *money*—a tangible asset? Here are three tips:

• Imagine the *amount* of money you're after. Then pay attention to your thoughts and environment for ideas about generating that level of income. Your own business? A smart, real estate investment? A well-selling book, perhaps?

• Boost your "Demand Factor." Increase your ability to command a larger income by increasing your value to a company or customer base. Start by becoming better at whatever it is you do.

• Devise an actionable strategy for earning a living *doing what you love*. Wealth and happiness most certainly will follow!

## Tangible Asset #4) **A Career**

Want a better career, and all the material, financial, and interpersonal perks that come with it? Well, would it surprise you to learn that your ability—or inability—to begin manufacturing your dream career depends almost entirely upon the direction and speed at which the gears of your Machine of Ideas are currently spinning? Consider the following…

### Your Machine of Ideas

*Source of Action and Inaction*

Japan's Shigeru Miyamoto was just a small boy in Japan in the 1960s when he began using his vivid imagination to manufacture the job of his dreams. Fascinated with cartoons, Shigeru spent hours parked in front of the television in his parents' living room sketching his favorite superheroes. Before long, Shigeru was even creating his *own* characters. Shigeru envisioned a future in which he could earn a living sketching cartoons nonstop.

Remaining faithful to his dream, Shigeru began pursuing a career in computer graphics while he was still in high school. What happened next is representative of the *timely miracles* reserved for those who dare to choose their destiny, and then pursue their vision with faith and persistence.

Guided by the mental blueprint for the kind of career that would make him most happy, Shigeru's "intuition" led him to Nintendo, a small playing card company with plans on breaking into the blossoming video game industry. Shigeru was just 17 years old when Nintendo bosses brought him aboard as a creative programmer. Still a teenager, Miyamoto was already enjoying the dream job he'd converted into reality through his Machine of Ideas.

Since 1977, Shigeru Miyamoto's presence at Nintendo has played a critical role in the company's domination of the global gaming industry. Among Miyamoto's creations are "Donkey Kong" and "Super Mario Brothers," games which sold more than 100 million copies by the year 2000!

*"What each man does is based*
*not on direct and certain knowledge,*
*but on pictures made by himself...*
*The way in which the world is imagined determines,*
*at any particular moment,*
*what he will do."*
-Journalist Walter Lippmann

For some, like Shigeru Miyamoto, the imagination provides rich, visual inspiration by which to foresee one's next great move, or series of moves. For countless others, however, it's a rusty *unused* Machine of Ideas that keeps them shackled to the unrewarding jobs, relationships, and habits that prevent them from realizing their truest potential.

For instance, reflecting back on his legendary career in his captivating book, *Iacocca*, Super-CEO Lee Iacocca revealed the trials of his turbulent years at Ford Motor Company. Working under a tyrannical boss with whom he could not see eye to eye, Iacocca was under constant stress and wondered just how much more he could take. Lee, an educated executive, could've contacted a headhunter and found a better job. He could've gone anywhere; yet, he stayed.

So, what kept him chained to a boss he could no longer stand and a job he no longer enjoyed?

"Why did I stay?" posed Iacocca in afterthought. "Because I couldn't imagine working anywhere else."

Only after Lee began *entertaining the idea* of moving on to another company was he able to assume his Ultimate Role as chief executive and savior of Chrysler during the 1980s.

## Doing What You Love

*Life's Sweetest Reward*

Thomas Edison once said, "Find your living doing what you love and you'll never have to work a day in your life." Simply put, making money doing what you *enjoy* doing is one of life's sweetest rewards.

Unfortunately, the large majority of the population is in the wrong line of work. A recent study found that as many as 8 out of 10 people are *not* in the career field of their choice. Part of the problem is that more people "fall into" their careers haphazardly, compared to those that design their ideal professional roles in advance.

Are *you* in the right line of work? To find out, answer the following question:

- If you won the lottery or your rich Uncle Wall Street passed and left you a multimillion dollar inheritance—and you no longer *had* to work—what you do simply because you *love* doing it?

If your answer coincides with your current professional parameters, you're a shoulder above the herd. If not, perhaps it's time to make the switch to a career that's more aligned with your heart's desires.

**GURU'S TIP:** Later, we'll focus on designing your mental blueprint for your professional future.

In the meantime, take a moment to "flip the switch" on your Machine of Ideas and brainstorm some ways to *set the stage* for a potential career move. What books or trade journals could you read, or classes or seminars could you attend, to gain an edge in your current or target career field? Could you conduct informational interviews with people in your target industry, or join an online networking group, in order to gain valuable insights or forge contacts? Could you use your creative resources to put together a stellar resume or business plan?

Henry Ford insisted that, "Before anything else, getting ready is the secret to success." Decide how you can prepare *now* for tomorrow's advancement opportunities.

And remember, your ability—or inability—to manufacture the career of your dreams is hinged largely upon what ideas and possibilities may be swirling around inside your head at this very moment.

## Tangible Asset #5) **Luxury Items**

My best friend, Mike Girm, shatters many of the myths about successful people. He wasn't born into money and never attended college. Yet, in spite of his humble beginnings, Mike is a brilliant businessman who enjoys a net worth of about $10 million. And contrary to popular belief among the masses of mediocrity, Mike's riches have *not* spoiled him. He is a charitable giver who loves helping others. Mike also knows how to have fun and enjoy the finer things in life. Some years ago, Mike and I were driving through the middleclass neighborhood in which we grew up. As if sparked by the memory of our meager upbringing, Mike produced a canary-eating smile.

"What?" I coached.

His grin widened. "Johnny, I bought a Ferrari."

Mike had purchased this dream vehicle through a combination of proactive imagination, hard work, and a series of smart investments. I'd never seen him quite so happy.

You, too, can acquire the luxury items you dream about possessing.

Generating big ticket items through the creative process is so simple even a child can do it. In fact, there are no greater masters of imagination than the children we see around us every day. These miniature *Mind Contrologists* spend their days dreaming about "what could be," aspiring to become their favorite heroes, and immersing themselves in a world of cardboard forts, two-story sandcastles, and elaborate tea parties.

Sure, there are those, like Shigeru Myamoto and my friend Mike, who, through some apparent predisposition to superior mental programming, manage to maintain their childlike imagination and make the transition from forts, sandcastles, and tea parties to building businesses, erecting empires, and purchasing luxury items. For most of us, however, the story plays out a little differently. We may start out with our bold dreams and aspirations, but then we "mature." Adult logic takes the place of imagination and passion. Then life happens. We find a job that *pays the bills*, buy a home *within our price range,* and drive a car that *gets the best gas mileage*. And before we know it, we have abandoned our dreams, surrendered our aspirations, and have little idea about what truly makes us happy.

Fortunately, there is a way to rekindle lost dreams, to recapture the wonder of your youth, and to begin filling your world with the toys that make life much more enjoyable. And it starts by closing your eyes, flipping the switch on your Machine of Ideas, and tapping into the power that has been lying dormant inside you since the days of your youth—the power to *imagine* with no regard for logic or limitation.

*"Great is he who does not lose his child's heart."*
-Mencius

## Bargaining with a Genie

When you were a kid, life was fun and exciting, and anything was possible. Recapture that childlike wonder now by answering the question below.

If a genie gave you three *purely material* wishes, what would they be?

(1)
(2)
(3)

**The Rules:** Place no restrictions on your wishes. Be totally honest with yourself. And don't cheat by asking for more wishes!

**GURU'S TIP:** Taking this exercise seriously will help get the gears of your Machine of Ideas spinning and help you discover (or rediscover) the deepest desires of your heart. And remember, imagining what you want is the first great step in transforming these desires from mind to matter.

## Tangible Asset #6) **A Book**

Writing a novel or non-fiction book is a fantastic way to convert your thoughts, ideas, and creative juices into a valuable, physical product.

And why *not* write a book? Much (or all) of the "mental material" you need to get the manufacturing process underway lies inside your head already in the form of stored information and experiences. Plus, writing a book is convenient. You can put together a novel in your spare time over the course of several months, or exploit the internet to compile research for a business or educational book based on your unique knowledge and expertise. What's more, lay-offs, maternity leave, and retirement are all great opportunities to launch a literary project which could potentially reach the hands of millions of people.

Some 60 years ago, a young shipmate named Herman Melville engaged his Machine of Ideas and produced one of the greatest literary classics of all time, in 12 short months…

Born in New York in 1819, Herman Melville spent much of his childhood sitting on the wharf by the Hudson River watching ships come and go, and wishing he was on them. Herman loved the sea.

When Melville was 13, his father died and the family business folded. Herman, his mother, and his siblings were left struggling to make ends meet. Before long, the Melvilles' financial woes forced the family to sell their furniture to stay afloat. Seeking to lighten his mother's burden, Herman set off to make his own way in the world. He found enough work to pay tuition at a local academy and earned an engineering degree. However, after failing to find a job in his field of study, Herman instead signed on as a cabin boy with the merchant marine then drifted out to sea. He was 20 years old.

In 1847, after eight years at sea, Melville washed ashore in Boston, married his sweetheart, and bought a small farm nearby the home of famous writer, Nathaniel Hawthorne. Melville, 28, became fascinated with the fine living and local celebrity Hawthorne enjoyed as a writer. While befriending the 43 year-old Hawthorne over the next three years, Melville came to the realization that his older neighbor, though talented and dedicated to his craft, was not a literary god but a mere mortal made of flesh and blood, and of replicable skill.

So, not to be outdone by his mentor, Melville devoted himself to the purpose of writing a book of his own.

In 1851, using the mental material of his own sea-faring adventures for inspiration, Herman Melville, 32, churned out his legendary classic, Moby Dick, in just 12 short months!

*"Happiness lies in the joy achievement, and the thrill of creative power."*
-Franklin Delano Roosevelt

**GURU'S TIP:** Looking for a superb way to shift your mental machinery into high gear? Write a book. A writing project is an excellent way to express yourself creatively, to gain valuable research and organizational skills, and to potentially touch the lives of thousands—even millions—of people in a positive way.

Everybody's got a story to tell. What's *your* story?

## Tangible Asset #7) **Personal Relationships**

The Mind/Reality Relationship is nothing short of miraculous. Because of the interactive relationship between your mind and world, the creative process can have a far-reaching impact on your life in terms of the quantity and quality of personal relationships you are able to *manufacture into existence* according to the specific designs of your own mental blueprint. It can be a hard concept to get your mind around—the ability to *think* people into your own, personal universe.

However, if you'll quiet that inner-voice of doubt which may be contesting, "That's impossible," I'll do my best to explain.

*"The primary imagination I hold to be*
*the living power and prime agent."*
-Samuel Coleridge

I've used the Mind/Reality Relationship for many purposes over the years, but I'll never forget the first time I experienced its influence in summoning *strangers* to my cause…

I was perhaps 20 years old and in the market of a wristwatch of a specific brand and design—a gift for someone special. Soon afterward, an unrelated personal matter summoned me to Center City Philadelphia. Since the kind of watch I was after was sometimes sold by street vendors in town, I handled my business, and then set out in search of the item I had in mind. Unable to find what I was after, my search appeared to be a fruitless one; that is, until my "intuition" led me to an untraveled street between a pair of office buildings. While walking down the sidewalk, I was approached by a mysterious man who asked, "Looking for a watch?" The hair on the back of my neck stood on end at the *coincidence.*

"Yes," I said, "I am." (This was a time when I dared the risk of such encounters.) The man pulled from his jacket a watch. "Close," I said. "Right brand. Wrong design."

I was about to walk off when the man asked what design I was looking for. After receiving my order, the man walked off and returned less than 5 minutes later. He opened the case, and there was the exact watch I had imagined—delivered to me by the *human hands* of my mysterious watch salesman!

Of course, the Mind/Reality Relationship is a two-way street. Not only is the creative process a great way to do for yourself through others, it's a conduit to do for others through *you.*

More recently, my company engineered a course-correction strategy for a national service chain.

Over a period of years, this chain had suffered declining sales, rising cost, and high employee turnover. Based upon our ongoing work with this client, my team and I were able to help ownership devise a long-term strategy and build a team of industry-leading professionals to carry it out. Our solutions not only helped to keep the company's doors open, but salvaged numerous careers, and led to the delight of countless satisfied customers. Moreover, keeping our client in business will ensure that the chain continues making supply chain and equipment purchases totaling millions of dollars each year from suppliers across the country. This impacts the bottom lines of our client's suppliers and helps pay the paychecks of *their* employees. Finally, all of this activity helps to drive the economy in the various regions in which our client operates.

My intentions were simply to do right by my client. However, through my firm's work, literally millions of lives will be positively affected, all as a result of our *proactive imagination* in designing a turnaround strategy for a struggling company.

*"Imagination is man's power over nature."*
–Wallace Stevens

The creative process can greatly influence your ability to generate new relationships or improve existing ones.

It was Thomas Edison's *ideas* and *inventions* that brought him into acquaintance with millionaires and presidents, and enabled him to "shed light" on people the world over. It was by *building* his motorcar factory and *designing* the automotive assembly line that Henry Ford revolutionized transportation and created jobs for thousands of workers. Babe Ruth's Major League dreams led to the speed-pitching and power-hitting that drew a minor league scout to his games at St. Mary's. Furthermore, Ruth's professional career later brought joy to countless baseball fans. And it's the *visionary skills* of today's corporate strategists that support the businesses that drive local economies around the globe.

Remember: God works through people—including *you!* Although our Creator holds the patent to the laws that govern the Mind/Reality Relationship and make the mental manufacturing process possible, you are free to use these universal conduits of embetterment to locate a trusted business partner, to attract your soul mate, or to help others in ways that only you can.

Experiment with the creative process as it relates to personal relationships. Give the process *time* to work its magic. And see just how far you can expand, and improve upon, your sphere of influence.

*"To know is nothing at all; to imagine is everything."*
-Anatole France

Remember, *one single idea* holds the potential to produce results so far-reaching that they become difficult to recognize. Become an "Idea Engineer" by using your creative capacities to manufacture high-grade tangible assets like a business or a better body, money or a career, luxury items or a book, or even your choice of personal relationships. And as you do, observe the mental manufacturing process with a careful eye…you just may be standing at the center of your own, self-generated reality.

Okay, you've learned that "proactive imagination" is the timeless secret to mastering the creative process. And you know that you may use your Machine of Ideas to manufacture all sorts of tangible assets. Next, you're going to learn to expand your scope of imagination; use it to create an all-encompassing mental blueprint for everything you want to do, have, and become in life; and then direct the whole of your powers and energies toward the future.

It's time to *become a visionary…*

# Become a Visionary

The 2nd Element of the Dream Acquisition Formula (DAF)

# 12

# Vision

*Facilitator of the Future*

*"The mind is capable of everything—because everything is in it; all of the past, as well as all of the future."*
-Miquel de Montaigne

Developing "vision"—or the skill of directing your imagination toward the future and anticipating, even *foreseeing,* what lies ahead for you in life—is the 2nd Element in the formula for transforming your wildest dreams into waking reality.

Scientifically speaking, the projection of your dreams, goals, and aspirations onto the viewing screen in your Mental Theater takes place in your prefrontal cortex. As you visualize forthcoming events, blood flow increases to your brain as glucose is converted into "visual images." Existing synaptic bridges are strengthened and new bridges are often built as your brain searches for the ways and means by which to begin bringing your mental directives to life.

This is your "Inner Optical Mechanism" hard at work.

Although neuroscientists have discovered that the miracle of internal eyesight is produced in your prefrontal cortex by a natural interplay between neurons and neurotransmitters, scientists and doctors remain confounded as to how images can be seen…while one's eyes are *closed.* The phenomenon of vision is indeed a miraculous neurological process. However, the most astounding fact about the mental operation we refer to as "vision" is that it is the primary facilitator of your future as you choose to define it.

When you envision your dreams, your mental horizons expand, your spirit soars, and you feel empowered. Your body becomes a circuit board of usable energy as your limbic system and nervous system exchange electrochemical signals, awakening your senses to a heightened state of performance and preparing your muscles to take action. With all this activity taking place, the Mind/Reality Relationship inevitably goes to work on your behalf. Your availability to the ideas, strategies, smarts, energy, skills, and resources necessary to realize your vision becomes increasingly more apparent. And, before long, the gap between today's *vision* and tomorrow's *reality* begins to merge, fusing mind and matter into one.

*"Vision is the art of seeing things invisible."*
-Jonathon Swift

## Charles Schultz: Boy Visionary

Charlie could *see* the future. Born in 1924, Charles Schultz grew up in St. Paul, Minnesota, where he attended Richards Gordon Elementary School. It was while sitting in class, learning the basics of math and science, that young Charles began exercising one of the greatest powers of the ages—the art of *seeing* one's future before it happens.

Schultz loved drawing and saw himself becoming a cartoonist. So, inspired by his vision, Charles convinced his parents to buy him a mail-order cartoon drawing kit, and then began sketching cartoons with utter faith in his ability to one day make a living out of it. It's hard to say if Charles realized that each cartoon he drew throughout his years in grade school—and then high school—was bringing him one step closer to vast wealth and international stardom. However, as Charles Schultz continued fine-tuning his craft, the process of transforming dreams into reality was undeniably underway…

In 1941, Schultz was drafted into the military where he was promoted to staff sergeant, met his first real girlfriend, and continued drawing. Each of Schultz's letters home revealed the sergeant's newest cartoon character, evidence that Charles' childhood vision was still driving his being. After his tour ended in 1945, Schultz returned home to St. Paul and landed a job as an art instructor.

The stage was being set according to Charles' mental blueprint.

With the art studio providing a platform for his imagination to run wild, Schultz morphed a fellow art instructor into the character, "Charlie Brown." Schultz's tomboy cousin became "Peppermint Patty." Charles then used the family beagle as a model for "Snoopy." At last, Schultz's signature cartoon strip was perfected. He called it, *"Peanuts."*

In 1950, Schultz, 26, unveiled *Peanuts* to the world and it became an instant hit. Fans lined up around corners at Schultz's appearances at bookstores. *Peanuts* appeared on lunch boxes and tee-shirts, then in magazines and on television. Newspapers fought to carry Shultz's cartoon strip, and Charlie Brown and the gang soon found their way onto the pages of 2,500 newspapers in 75 countries!

By 1990, Charles Shultz found himself sitting upon the throne of a multimedia empire which generated $1 billion in annual revenues. Reducing his skill in transforming dreams into reality to its simplest terms, the aging visionary once explained, "I wanted to be a cartoonist—period."

*"A man will never achieve anything great*
*without having dreamed it first."*
-Dr. William James

## From Confused Teenager to Visionary General

In the 1950's, while Charles Schultz's vision was being materialized, the mental blueprint for one young boy's legendary career was about to take shape in New York...

School was becoming a bore for the 12 year-old son of two Jamaican immigrants. Like many young boys, Colin wasn't thrilled about reading books or studying for tests. Colin's distaste for school work, however, placed him at an uncomfortable disadvantage to his academic superstar sister. She managed to get all the positive attention, what with her perfect grades and model behavior. Meanwhile, poor Colin seemed destined to remain in the background, simply getting by.

In 1950, Colin, 13, entered Morris High School where he attempted to find purpose in sports. Colin joined the track team, doing well enough to earn a letter—but lost interest after only one season. And later, after trying to make a name for himself on the basketball court, Colin ended up riding the bench more often than running the court. He soon quit the basketball team, too.

Hope came alive for the teen and his family when, after holding down a job unloading trucks between the ages of 14 and 16, Colin managed to graduate high school and coast into CCNY. Undecided as to what major to choose or what profession he was best suited for, Colin, perhaps for the first time, began seriously contemplating his place in the world. And that's when something magical took place.

It was in 1954, while walking around campus at CCNY, that Colin spotted a group of cadets in their crisp, paramilitary uniforms strutting to and from the ROTC building. It was during this encounter that Colin's confusion and indifference began to give way to clarity and enthusiasm. Colin, 17, joined the ROTC program at CCNY where he began assembling the mental blueprint for what he would do with the rest of his life. He was going to become a *soldier!*

Newly focused on a career in the military, Colin soon began earning A's in college and was awarded the honor of "Best Cadet, Company D" for his exceptional performance in the ROTC program. Colin's parents were thrilled when he earned his Bachelor's Degree before heading off to Ranger School in 1958.

*"Vision is the primal means to full understanding."*
-Leonardo da Vinci

Almost overnight, Colin was transformed from confused teen to aspiring military officer and academic peak performer. So, what accounted for Colin's sudden awakening of personal power?

By setting his sights on what excited him about his future, Colin opened the door to the ideas, strategies, energy, smarts, skills, and resources by which to begin mastering the affairs of the present on the way to his chosen destinations. Just like that, a life was forever changed for the better. However, that was only the beginning of Colin's amazing, true-life story of success.

Colin later served as field commander in Vietnam in the 60's, became a White House Fellow during the 70's, reinvented himself as President Reagan's national security advisor during the 80's, then masterminded the battle strategy for Desert Storm (the swiftest military victory in U.S. history) while serving as a general under President Bush during the 1990s.

Who was that confused teenager turned visionary? None other than legendary general and Secretary of State, Colin Powell!

## The National Lack of Vision

*"Where there is no vision, the people perish."*
-Proverbs 29:18

The habit of planning for the future is one of the key factors that separate the world's super-achievers from the rest of society. Deliberate future planning lays the foundation for fast, accurate success in your personal, business, and financial affairs. In fact, the habit of planning for the future (which we'll call *proactive foresight*) is the fundamental "investment management" secret of the mega wealthy—the top 1% of the population who control 50% of the nation's income.

Unfortunately, for most folks, the future represents a giant roulette wheel. For these folks, the Wheel of Fortune is left to spin on its own in a blur of countless variables which often have their way with those who fail to take a conscious and proactive approach to future planning.

The following statistics are representative of the gross lack of foresight and future planning among the masses of mediocrity.

- Millions of Americans are approaching retirement "under-invested." Sadly, these folks are depending on a Social Security system which economists say may become entirely bankrupt over the next 10 years.

- While the average blue-collar worker's annual salary rests in the 40k's, the annual income of the nation's top 100 CEO's (the business world's strategic visionaries) has reached a staggering 1000 times that of the average worker!

- As of 2016, credit card debt in America soared to $729 billion. Research also shows that while the average American earns less than $50k per year, he or she carries about $12k in monthly debt and lives paycheck to paycheck by operating according to the philosophy, "Buy *now*, the future will take care of itself."

- Over the seven-year period between 2008 and 2015, the wealth of the top 1% of earners in America increased 100%, while median family income has fallen $2,500 under the Obama Administration during this same period.

- A recent survey found that 82% of the nation's workforce is unhappy with their current job, boss or salary. The clincher? The same lack of future planning that landed these folks into their crummy jobs *keeps them from moving on*...in spite of their unhappiness!

*"The most pathetic person in the world*
*is someone with sight, but no vision."*
-Helen Keller

## The Link between Foresight and Earnings

*"We have to wager our salvation upon some prophesy."*
-Oliver Wendell Holmes, Jr.

There is a direct correlation between foresight and future planning, and *earnings*. For instance, during the late 1990s, the mega wealthy (the richest 1% of the population) accounted for about 5% of the America's wealth. By 2008, that same 1% represented 22.3% of the country's cash. In 2015, the 85 richest people in the country commanded a staggering 50% of the nation's wealth.

What's this trend mean? It means that the world's top visionaries have been getting increasingly richer. More specifically, it means that the world's wealthiest people—who happen to rely heavily on foresight and future planning—are progressively commanding larger salaries, making smarter investments, and growing their businesses, while the masses of mediocrity are falling deeper into debt and further into the shadows of obscurity.

If you find yourself on the wrong side of this trend, don't panic. There are several steps you can take to begin generating wealth and increasing your potential for total financial freedom over the weeks, months, and years to come.

## Combatting "Shrinkage of Income"

One initial step you can take in the direction of financial freedom is to better understand "shrinkage of income" and how to combat it.

To demonstrate the dynamic of income shrinkage, let's measure what you think you earn against what you *actually* earn.

Let's say you have an annual income of $50,000, taxed at 30%. After the government takes its share, you're already down to about $35,000 in "take-home" income. And, for anyone who doesn't own a business, take-home income is the only income that matters.

Now, let's say that half of your take-home income will be allocated to annual purchases made at a 6% sales tax.

That brings your actual annual income down to $32,900.

Next, let's consider inflation. Inflation rises an average of 4% each year. And as inflation rises, the value of your dollar *shrinks* in equal proportion. So, after deducting 4% for rising living costs, you're left with $31,584. Now, factor in the $12,000 in various debts the average person carries. Then let's say your annualized interest on this debt averages 3.5 %. At last, your $50,000 annual income has *shrunk* to $31,164—without a single item of value having ever reached your hands!

So, what can you do to begin offsetting this "shrinkage of earnings?" Here are three actionable strategies:

(1) **Earn a Larger Salary**: This may require negotiating a raise or higher sales commission, or making the move to a better paying field or company.

(2) **Create a Small Business Tax Shield:** Start a business and take advantage of government grants, tax write-offs, and green-energy incentives available only to small business owners.

(3) **Invest against Inflation, Taxes, and Interest**: Allocate a portion of your income to investments which earn a rate-of-return high enough to offset inflation and what you pay in taxes and interest each year.

Since real estate values double on average every 12 years, carefully researched real estate investment is a wise place to start.

Roth IRAs and other tax-deferred high-growth vehicles are also smart options.

*"Who is the wise man?*
*He who sees what is about to be born."*
-King Solomon

Foreseeing what glorious realities will take place in your life isn't about predicting the future, it's about *designing* your future.

Chinese philosopher Confucius taught, "If a man takes no thought about what is distant, he will soon find sorrow near at hand." Simply put, life holds little chance of advancement for past- and current-reference thinkers who fail—or refuse—to consider tomorrow.

The visionary, on the other hand, *sees* the future through 20/20 mental eyesight. Driven by the possibilities on the horizon, the man or woman who embraces tomorrow devotes considerable time and energy to designing and building the kind of life he or she wants on personal, interpersonal, professional, and financial levels. And, as a result, this forward thinking individual gets to confidently predetermine what horizons he or she will reach, horizons equal in dimension to the furthest stretches of his or her imagination.

Looking to the future and dreaming in focus makes *you* the architect of your destiny.

## Michelangelo Buonarroti

*Architect of Dreams*

Italy's Michelangelo Buonarroti was just 15 when he began studying sculpture at a small academy in the Garden of San Marco in 1490.

Michelangelo was convinced that a glorious legacy in the arts was his birthright. So, after informing his instructor that a fortunate alignment of the Heavens had graced him with the gift to create, build, and achieve, the headstrong Buonarroti manned his station among a dozen students, took hammer and chisel into hand, and then proceeded to carve out his destiny, one careful chip at a time.

During his two short years of study, Buonarroti's mastery of sculpture surpassed not only that of his fellow students, but also that of his instructor. Of course, this is no surprise since the Michelangelo never thought of himself as a novice sculptor. He viewed himself as a predestined master of his craft who was well on his way to fulfilling his Ultimate Role. Insisting that a crude slab of marble contains within it the finished masterpiece, the Italian confidently chiseled away the unnecessary stone with precision and excitedly imagined the crowds that would gasp in awe at his finished product, until, at last, the lifelike image trapped inside the slab emerged.

By school's end, Michelangelo's skills as a sculptor were arguably the best in Italy. The Italian was just 17 years old.

Between the ages of 19 and 21, Buonarroti opened a small shop in Bologna and earned a living selling artwork and producing public monuments. By 1496, however, Michelangelo's ambitions urged him to dream bigger. Guided by his overriding purpose of becoming, in his words, the "world's greatest artist," Buonarroti, 21, traveled to Rome where he negotiated a contract with the Vatican to produce the "Pieta." Committed to achieving his goal of high success in the arts, the young artist predicted in writing on his contract that the sculpture would be the *"most beautiful work in marble that Rome has ever seen."*

Michelangelo did not disappoint.

The "Pieta" was said to have taken the crowd's breath away upon its unveiling. Rome fell in love with Buonarroti and his creations. Back home, he became a celebrity. Almost overnight, Michelangelo's work had become the standard by which all European art was measured, and the Italian's dream of becoming the *world's greatest artist* was quickly beginning to materialize…

*"The destiny of each human being is decided by what goes on in his skull."*
-Dr. Eric Berne

During Buonarroti's 20's, Pope Julius II and the Vatican became the Italian's best customers. After earning a big payday for the 17' tall sculpture known as "David," Buonarroti was asked by Pope Julius II to build a papal tomb. This massive project was to pay Michelangelo 1,200 ducats per year (10 times the annual earnings of an average artist,) plus a payment of 10,000 ducats more upon completion.

In 1506, Buonarroti, 31, reinvented himself as a structural engineer after being contracted by Pope Julius to renovate the aging St. Peter's Basilica from the ground up. However, following a falling out with the Pope, Michelangelo abandoned his shop and tools in Santa Caterina, left behind 100 tons of marble, and fled Rome, swearing never to return.

Two years later, unable to cope without Michelangelo's unsurpassed expertise in architectural design, Pope Julius sent for Buonarroti and begged his help. Prompted perhaps by the higher calling of fame and glory in the fields of engineering and the arts, the Italian returned to Rome to head-up the renovation project on St. Peter's Basilica—and to begin writing the next chapter of his amazing story of legendary success.

It was in 1508 that the Vatican paid Buonarroti a small fortune of 3,000 ducats to begin the project that would enable him to fulfill his chosen destiny as the "world's greatest artist." After assembling a team and slapping together some primitive scaffolding, Michelangelo took brush and pallet into hand, and then spent the next seven years painting the vaulted ceiling of a massive church in Rome.

Perhaps you've heard of it—the Sistine Chapel!

Although internationally revered as one of the greatest artists and architects of all time, Michelangelo Buonarroti's most breath-taking masterpiece can be found in the deliberate design of his own, legendary destiny.

*"Your hopes, dreams and aspirations are legitimate.*
*They are trying to take you airborne,*
*above the clouds, if only you will let them."*
-Dr. William James

**GURU'S TIP:** 500 years ago, Michelangelo's mental blueprint for high success in the arts guided him toward a legacy in direct reflection to his own dreams and aspirations. Charles Schultz's vision of becoming a cartoonist was the driving force that led him to the Ultimate Role of his dreams, plus all the riches and fame he could handle. And it was a dream of a career in the military that transformed the Bronx's Colin Powell into one of the most accomplished generals in recent history.

So, what do you *see* in *your* future? What barriers will you overcome or "limitations" will you shatter? What will you experience, acquire, and become? What level of wealth will you attain? And what will you give back when all that you seek becomes yours?

Unlock your mind, and dream without restriction.

If you're ready to design the destiny of your choosing—as legends past and present themselves have done—then turn the page, and let's continue the exhilarating process of transforming your wildest dreams into your waking reality.

It's time to become a visionary…

# 13

# Engaging the Science of Dream Architecture

## *How to Design Your Destiny*

*"The whole secret to a meaningful life is to find out what it is one's destiny to do—and then do it."*
-Henry Ford

In order to qualify yourself as a "visionary," you've got to have a *vision.* But before we get down to the business of designing your chosen destiny, there are a few things you must do:

(1) Delete the words *impossible* and *can't* from your mentality.

(2) Disengage yourself from your present circumstances, and embrace the future.

(3) Believe that you absolutely have what it takes to fulfill your dreams—because you do.

(4) Decide now to commit to your vision for your future. Once you do, Life will commit to it, too!

If you agree to these terms and are ready to begin the process of transforming your wildest dreams into your waking reality, then you're ready to engage the *Science of Dream Architecture.*

## The Science of Dream Architecture

**What's "Dream Architecture?"** *Dream Architecture* is the life-altering process of designing the future you wish to create.

In this chapter, you will discover "possibility lists" for seven major life categories, including: professional, home/living, relationships, financial, travel & adventure, advance payment, and the Ultimate You.

**Your task is simple**: Cast your mind's eye to the horizon. Begin looking months, years, and even decades into your future and assemble a detailed vision of everything you want to do, have, share, give, and become. Use the "possibility lists" provided within each life category for ideas and inspiration. Then use the space below each list to capture all the exciting details of your ideal future.

As you construct your vision, know that you will be following in the footsteps of legends like Lincoln, Keller, Schwarzenegger, and Michelangelo, master visionaries who've proven beyond a doubt that one's destiny is entirely a matter of *choice.*

*"Every man is the architect of his own fortune."*
-Sallust

## Your Vision "Master List"

*Formulating Your Blueprint for the Life of Your Dreams*

(1) **Your *"Professional"* Vision**: What's your *professional* vision? Does your dream involve ditching your dead-end job for a more rewarding career? Do you see yourself ascending the ranks of your current organization? Becoming CEO of your *own* small company? Your own Fortune 500 company?

Will you write a best-seller, open a restaurant or break thoroughbreds for upscale clients? Is launching a clothing label or gourmet food chain in your future? Will you reinvent yourself as a business, fashion or security consultant? Do you imagine trading currencies, dealing in rare art or "shooting indies" for a living? Or is acting, singing or creating an animated sitcom more *your* goal?

Are you destined to become the next Trump, Oprah or Seinfeld? A future U.S. president? Will you create the world's first holographic TV or computer? Or will you simply become the best in the world at what you already do?

Whatever your dream is, take a moment to project yourself into that role *now*.

Foresee the details of your ideal professional situation. Will you spend your days selling products to consumers? Crunching numbers in a cubicle? Authoring books from your home office? Directing activities in the field? Negotiating deals from your executive suite? Hosting sold-out seminars in speaking venues across the country? Do you see yourself working with celebrities and Fortune 500 companies?

Will your office be located downtown? In Hong Kong? In your living room? Will you have a driver? A helicopter? A chartered jet?

What company will you keep as a professional? That of the major players in your field? Your own CFO and team of consultants? Politicians? Your family and dearest friends? Will you lead a team? A company? A technological *revolution?* Consider not only what your professional dream is, but *why* these objectives matter to you. And remember—if you can dream it, you can *achieve* it!

Spend some time constructing the roles, relationships, environment, and activities that represent your professional vision

Detail your ***professional*** objectives below:

(2) **Your *"Home/Living"* Vision:** What geographic areas, and types and sizes of homes, describe your ideal living situation?

Do you dream of living in a high-rise condo in Manhattan? A colonial mansion in the laid-back south? A cattle ranch in Montana? A log home in the mountains of Aspen? Would you move into a house boat on the bay? A bungalow in Europe, perhaps?

Is a Caribbean cottage or Italian villa in your future? Will you design your own home, a modern masterpiece to be featured in Architectural Digest? Will you manage a portfolio of properties around the country…around the world? Or will you redecorate and cherish the home you already have?

Go to your dream home *now.* Take a mental tour of your estate or property. Are you surrounded by Nature? Buildings? The ocean? Celebrity neighbors? Who greets you when you walk through the door? Your spouse, kids, and pets? Your concierge?

Go ahead, take a lap in your indoor pool or join the kids in the game room. Peruse your private library or tend to your garden. Cook a meal in your remodeled kitchen or enjoy the view from the marble balcony of your master bedroom suite.

Take some time to bask in the excitement and pleasure of your dream home and ideal living situation. Then capture the details of the lifestyle you wish to make real.

Detail your ***home/living*** objectives below:

(3) **Your *Relationships* Vision:** What's your vision for your family, romantic, social, and business relationships? Will you build a happy family by supplying a lifetime of love and encouragement? End a "toxic relationship" and find *true* love? Rekindle the romance in your marriage? Locate the ideal business partner?

Will you join a club, gym or trade association? Strengthen existing friendships by initiating phone calls, visits, and outings? Will you make a new best friend?

Will you expand your contact list (or customer base) by 100%? 1000%? Forge international alliances? Build a million-member following on Facebook or Twitter? Will your smart phone contain a long list of high-profile associates who depend on *you* for favors? Will you become a better parent, the "world's best" mom or dad? Become socially proactive? Master the art of communication or love-making?

Will you spend more time with loved ones? Find a mentor? *Become* a mentor?

Detail your ***relationships*** objectives below:

(4) **Your *Financial* Vision:** What's your financial destiny? Do you want to increase your income by 50%, 100% or 1000%? Will you join the top 1% of the nation's earners?

Will you make millions in stock options as a corporate turnaround expert? Develop a portfolio of investments in Dollars, Renminbi, and Euros? Will you get rich by investing in real estate, precious metals or timeless art?

Just how *wealthy* will you become? Will your finances require a team of accountants, and multiple domestic and off-shore accounts?

Engage your Mental Theater and assemble a meeting with your business partners, executive team, legal advisors, and/or accountants. Review your investment portfolio. Get updates on your finances and make a few decisions regarding your upcoming ventures. Spend some time in the exciting world of the new, Wealthy You!

Detail your ***financial*** objectives below:

(5) **Your *Travel & Adventure* Vision:** Seeing photographs of the Sistine Chapel or watching people vacationing on the Travel Channel is *not* the same as visiting the famous church or traveling the world *yourself.* A life lived fully will require seeing new places and experiencing new things.

Does your travel/adventure vision include visiting the Grand Canyon and Mount Rushmore? Going on an African safari? Climbing Machu Picchu in Peru? Seeing the Mona Lisa…face to face?

Do you dream of piloting a helicopter? Driving a Ferrari? Floating weightlessly in a space capsule? Attending private seminars with celebrities? How about flying a Russian war jet? Guess what. Classes or clubs exist to make all of these impossible dreams *real.*

Engage your imagination, cue your limbic system, and "pre-experience" your favorite scenarios. Do you see yourself riding horse-back on a Mexican beach or exploring the Australian Outback? Snorkeling in the Caribbean or taking an Alaskan cruise? Will you visit Disney, interact with dolphins, and jet ski the coast—all in the same week? Will you surf Hawaii or ski Aspen? Whale watch in Maine or hike the Appalachian Trails? Hunt sharks in the Atlantic or study martial arts in the Orient?

Will you enter a rodeo or marathon? Book a "paintball war" with friends or take your family camping? What about a trip to Mars? A Netherlands-based space travel company is currently taking applications for $38 (if accepted, you will be among a group whose historic trip will be the focus of a reality show.)

What countries, cultures, attractions, customs, foods, languages, thrills, and experiences will you come to know intimately during your one, blessed lifetime?

Detail your ***travel & adventure*** objectives below:

(6) **Your *"Advance Payment"* Vision**: Success creates the ability to give back and help others in special ways. Demonstrate your faith in your chosen destiny by determining *in advance* what you will give back when all that you seek becomes yours.

When your dream becomes real will you donate some of your fortune to a worthy cause like "Make-a-Wish" or the "Dream Works Project?" Will you start your *own* charitable foundation?

Will you mentor novices in the fields you have (or will have) mastered? Will you finance environmental research or open an endangered species rescue? Revitalize a blighted neighborhood or volunteer the expert services of your future company? Will you devote a portion of your fortune—or an organ—to science?

Now, ask yourself: How can I begin "making payments" *now* on my future success? Could you encourage your kids to succeed more regularly? Teach others how to master their minds? Come to the aid of a struggling friend? Deliver groceries to a lonely senior citizen? Buy a homeless person a meal? Adopt a needy animal? Offer free advice? Dispense more compliments? Give more love?

Determine *now* what you're committed to giving back—in the future and along the way—in exchange for the forthcoming realization of your dreams.

Draft your ***"advance payment contract"*** below:

- *When my dreams become real, I will give in these ways...*

- *Along the way to my destiny, I will give in these ways...*

(7) **Your *Ultimate You* Vision:** You may have decided on your purpose in life and your place in the world, but you've yet to put the principle of Mental Identity to work by constructing your vision for your Ultimate Self.

How would you *define* the Ultimate You? A young tycoon or wise elder? An elite mastermind or world-class expert? An educated intellectual or streetwise entrepreneur? A famous celebrity or legendary philanthropist? How about a devoted family man or woman?

What special skills, talents, abilities, and gifts will the Ultimate You possess?

What fields or endeavors will you have conquered, and what stamps will mark your passport? Will you possess an MBA or PhD, an Academy Award or Nobel Prize? Will you have added a magazine cover to your credits? What about clubs or directorships? Will you reserve a seat in the Young Presidents Club, the result of your $8,000,000 or more in annual revenues?

Finally, how will you think, look, speak, dress, act, and communicate? Will you possess an ageless brain; a lean, muscular body; and endless energy—the rewards of rigorous daily exercise and smart eating habits? How will you *manage* your power, wealth, and notoriety? And how will you honor your family, friends, partners, employees, and, perhaps, your fans?

Detail your ***Ultimate You*** objectives below:

**GURU'S TIP:** Seeing yourself as you wish to become forges a mental roadmap which helps you begin closing the behavioral gap between your present self and that Higher Identity. Spark your *evolution* by spending time daily projecting into the mind and skin of your Ultimate Self!

## The Science of Dream Architecture

*A Quick Review*

Congratulations! You've now got your vision "Master List"—a detailed, written blueprint for the future you will come to enjoy.

Remember, your mental and physical powers generally rise in proportion to the challenges you place upon yourself, and *reality* begins to conform to the designs of the vision you keep locked inside your head on a regular basis.

So, let your imagination truly run wild, dream bigger than you ever have before, and return to your Master List as you become inspired to reach and stretch to even greater heights. Also, take no thought in where you will acquire the resources to make your dreams real. The ways and means will be made available to you, as long as you remain committed to what you're destined to achieve.

Select your destinations. Decide where you want to go. And when you do, your road and your chariot will *appear!*

*"The past is history and only the future*
*can give you happiness.*
*So, everybody must prepare for their future*
*and create their future."*
-Bruce Lee

Putting your dreams to paper was a great, first step in the process of transforming them from mind to matter. You've come a long way, but your journey into the realms of mind science and peak performance has only just begun.

If you're ready to take your visionary powers to the next level, it's time to discover the *"Vision Maximization System"*...

# 14

# Mastering the Art of Vision

*The "Vision Maximization System"*

*"The bravest among us are those who possess the clearest vision of what is before them—glory and danger alike—and yet, notwithstanding, go out and meet it."*
-Thucydides

**What's the "Vision Maximization System?"** The *V-Max System* is a set of advanced mind control applications designed to help you increase your visionary powers, as well as your skill in using them.

Whether you're in pursuit of a destiny of biblical proportions, dream of becoming a legend in your field or simply want to master your golf swing or become more persuasive with the opposite sex, the V-Max System can help.

The V-Max System is designed to help you see your future through a much sharper mental lens. This is important since your ability to transform dreams into reality increases in direct proportion to your skill in exercising your visionary powers. By putting the V-Max System to work for you, your ability to *foresee* what you plan to do, have, and become will begin to rival that of the world's top achievers.

Simply put, nothing is beyond the reach of the visionary who takes a systematic approach to dream acquisition by way of the Vision Maximization System...

# The V-Max System

*7 Ways to Maximize Your Visionary Powers*

## #1) Master the Art of "Mental Movie-making"

In your Mental Theater, you play the roles of owner, manager, producer, director, screenwriter, sceneshifter, sound editor, audience, and star of the show…all in one.

Want to become a master visionary? Begin to think of yourself as a Hollywood producer, and your vision for your future as a "Mental Movie" over which you have total creative control.

As owner and manager of your Mental Theater, your first order of business is to take your vision Master List and begin transforming it, in your mind, into a streaming motion picture of how you want the most important aspects of your future to *play out.*

### How to Produce a Mental Movie

Below, are some tips for producing the visionary blockbuster that will become your future.

- **Select a Sequence of Key Events**: Decide how you want your future to "play out." View your anticipated successes, triumphs, and peak performances as a series of *scenes.* Then begin assembling these scenes—in a logical sequence—into a cohesive, full-length Mental Movie.

- **Foresee Your Starring Roles:** Determine what "starring roles" you will play in life and business. Then practice projecting yourself into these roles, through the eyes and skin of the Ultimate You, in your Mental Movie. Remember, the roles you play in your Mental Theater set the stage for the roles you will play in real life!

• **Assemble Your Cast:** Every award-winning motion picture (and every great life) includes a cast of important people. Who will play "supporting roles" in *your* life in the future? An ideal mate you've yet to meet? A perfect assistant you've yet to hire? The happy family you plan to build? A financier with whom you've yet to cross paths? Begin *casting* these characters into your Mental Movie in the context by which you plan to interact with them in real life.

• **Pre-script Key Dialogue**: Hollywood actors memorize clever scripts to deliver Academy Award-winning performances and you can, to a degree, do the same thing in real life. Imagine in advance what "pitch" you will give when asking for a raise, business loan or date with someone special. The world is a stage. Anticipate choice encounters and rehearse the clever, funny or romantic things you'll say, as well as how you expect others to respond. You'll be surprised at how often your cast of characters goes with the flow of the script *you've* got in mind!

• **Add *Dimension* to Your Mental Movie:** Add dimension to your Mental Movie by building great detail into every scene. For instance, don't just visualize your dream car in your garage, *pre-experience* the thrill of ownership. What was the purchase process like? Did you finance or negotiate with cash? What does it *feel* like to accelerate down the road in your dream car? How does the engine *sound?* How do your neighbors react when you pull into your driveway? Generally, the more dimension your Mental Movie has the more "transformational power" it contains.

• **Connect with Your Audience**: Master filmmakers connect with their audience by making them feel happy, excited, sad, and even angry. In your Mental Theater, however, *you* are your audience. To get truly motivated about your future, don't just see yourself winning, commanding the spotlight, and giving memorable performances; immerse yourself in the *energy* and *emotion* of your self-selected starring roles!

• **Produce Your Film in Color**: There's a reason Hollywood films have switched from black-and-white to color. Movies made in color are more realistic and more stimulating to the audience's senses. Likewise, projecting a full color Mental Movie onto the viewing screen in your Mental Theater makes for a more realistic and stimulating visionary film. Dream in color!

**GURU'S TIP**: The world is a stage and life is a performance. To prepare for the starring roles and award-winning performances of your choosing, practice producing a *Mental Movie*—based on your vision for your future—onto the viewing screen in your Mental Theater. And remember, what goes on inside your head today represents the "coming attractions" for the movie that will become your life tomorrow.

Aim to produce and direct the epic, mental blockbuster of a lifetime!

## #2) Reinforce Your Vision with the Power of Reasons

Years ago, I had an eye-opening experience related to the power of *reasons.*

When my daughter was very young (perhaps six or seven years old) I received a report from her mother which made me cringe. Our daughter's teacher had informed my wife that Haley had joined in with some other children who were teasing a boy with "large ears." The boy was so humiliated he was brought to tears. I was heartbroken for the boy and immediately sat Haley down to explain what she'd done wrong.

"Haley," I began. "Mommy told me what you did today and I'm very disappointed. Haley, you are very fortunate to have been born with your looks and brains, and functional body parts which are properly proportioned. Some children are not so fortunate. This is a tough cross to bear and being made fun of only makes it worse."

Behind my girl's big blue eyes was a brain processing the lesson.

"Haley, you never pick on the disadvantaged. You stick up for them. You protect them. Don't ever again follow kids who are mistreating others. You're smarter than that. And because you're so smart, you've got to think for yourself, as well as for those around you. Do you understand?"

"Uh, huh," she nodded. And I knew she got it.

Not only did Haley apologize to the boy, she soon brought an "out-casted" girl into her circle of friends and over to the house to play. Haley's days as a follower also ended subsequent to our talk. She has since maintained a 4.0 grade point average and was invited to an Ivy League university to enjoy an advanced placement program at the age of 15!

What can we learn from this story? Knowing *why* we're doing something reinforces our commitment to doing it.

Ask yourself: *Why* must I fulfill my dreams? What will I gain personally, professionally, physically, emotionally, spiritually, financially, and socially by succeeding? How will my family, friends or community reap the benefits of *my* success?

Make a list of reasons why your vision is important, and read it often. The more reasons you have for succeeding, the less inclined you will be to abandon your mission in the months, weeks—or even fateful days—before your wildest dreams come true!

## #3) Gather Evidence that Supports the "*Feasible Attainment*" of Your Dreams

Kids are masters of the philosophy, "If he or she can do it, so can I!" However, this sassy declaration of personal power is just as applicable to the adult aspiring to new heights in life or business. After all, it's much easier to be sure you can achieve something when you know someone else has already done it.

*Mind Contrology* ® was designed with this fact in mind. Throughout this series, you'll discover inspiring stories about hundreds of ordinary people who've made their dreams come true in the face of every obstacle under the sun. Study the stories that support the *feasible attainment* of the goals you may be pursuing. Copy your favorite stories and hang them by your bedside, on your refrigerator, or at your cubicle for inspiration. Let these real-world triumphs infuse you with the confidence and excitement necessary to achieve your *own* important objectives.

Remember the rule: If they can do it, so can I!

## #4) Spend a Day in the Life of the Ultimate You!

Becoming visionary and transforming your dreams into reality is not an overnight event; it's a process. With that said, one of the most effective methods for taking your visionary prowess to the next level and *accelerating* the dream transformation process is to man your Mental Theater and work on your Mental Movie by spending a day in the life of the Ultimate You. Here's how…

### How to Spend a Day in the Life of the Ultimate You

Let's say you envision yourself becoming the wealthy CEO of your own top-flight management consultancy, a nationally-acclaimed best-selling author and speaker, and a devoted family man or woman.

Spend a day in the life of your Ultimate Self by going to a place of limited distraction (perhaps your bedroom at bedtime or your office at break time.) Then close your eyes and visit your Mental Theater.

Next, you might visualize your day unfolding as you drive to the airport at 5 am in your $130,000 Maserati. You watch the sunrise through the clouds as your Falcon LX 900 jet whisks you away to a coastal destination where you hold a seminar on the topic of your renowned expertise. The seminar ends with a standing ovation. Since you've written a book, you stick around to sign dozens of copies and mingle with your fans.

Then, on your return flight, you perhaps hold a video conference with your CFO and advisors regarding your diverse investment portfolio and your firm's latest global initiative.

Once home, you enjoy a meal prepared by your personal chef and spend some time with your kids in the game room. You then take a dip in the Jacuzzi with your spouse before climbing a marble staircase to your master bedroom suite.

Finally, standing on the balcony overlooking your estate, you consider the wonderful little world you've worked hard to create for your family. You think about the countless lives you've touched through your life, work, and charity. You draw in a deep, satisfied breath, thank your Creator with a grateful heart, and then retire for the evening. It's good to be the *Ultimate You!*

*"Nothing happens unless first a dream."*
-Carl Sandberg

Every time you man your Mental Theater and spend time fine-tuning your grand vision (or *Mental Movie*) you move your dreams one step closer to reality. Spending time in the life of your Ultimate Self triggers the following important processes:

- It teaches you how to begin to "live life" through the eyes and skin of the Ultimate You.
- It lets Life know what you want, often leading to personal miracles and favorable occurrences.
- It emboldens you to take decisive action!

## #5) **Create a Destiny Environment Filled with "Vision Enhancers"**

What are "vision enhancers?" *Vision enhancers* are travel brochures, architectural plans, photos, magazine spreads, drawings, floor designs, inspirational quotes, and anything else that represents your vision objectives and gets you excited about your future.

### Creating a Destiny Environment

Over the next few weeks, make an adventure of hunting down vision enhancers which represent the grand objectives you're pursuing. Find a photo or plan of the type of home you will live in. Download an image of your dream car or ideal physique. Stop by a travel agency and get brochures for the places you plan on traveling to. Or scour a trade or business magazine for a photo of your future office.

Next, create a "Destiny Environment"—a room or area filled with vision enhancers which represent everything you plan to do, have, and become. Visit your Destiny Environment often so you can avoid negative influences and draw inspiration from your surroundings.

**GURU'S TIP**: Creating a Destiny Environment is a fun and effective way to stay focused and motivated along your journey to your chosen destinations.

## #6) Open Your Spiritual Eyes—Expect Miracles!

Many people are convinced that miracles don't take place in today's world. To the contrary, miracles take place *every day*—in our *own* lives—often while we're too busy or distracted to recognize them taking place. As your visionary eyesight becomes sharper, you will become super-attuned to how your thoughts and prayers influence your life, career, relationships, and finances. And as your experiences with the Mind/Reality Relationship become more frequent, you will become increasingly aware of the small, and sometimes large, miracles that take place in your life on a regular basis.

Sometimes the smallest miracles teach the greatest lessons.

For instance, I used to jog with a friend whom I mentored professionally. One day, while jogging in the city, our conversation shifted from Shane's career to the simple wonders of Nature. I mentioned that I'd always been fascinated with the praying mantis.

I told Shane that I'd love to come across one again. I realized, of course, that the odds of crossing paths with a mantis in the middle of a busy city would be somewhere in the area of winning the lottery.

48 hours later, I met Shane for another run. Perched on his finger was a large, green praying mantis! Spotting this magnificent insect in the city, hours after wishing for it, in the very place where my friend and I met, at the precise time we met, and after not having seen a Mantis in this area for decades, was nothing short of a miracle.

Only adding more mystery to the experience, the mantis had landed directly on Shane—as if staging its own dramatic entrance—just as I arrived!

That mini-miracle reminded me of three important things:

(1) We're issued great power over our surroundings.

(2) God loves to reward us for helping others.

(3) Our Creator—God of the Universe and Architect of the Mind/Reality Relationship—begins where we end!

*"The Kingdom of God is within you."*
-Jesus Christ

**GURU'S TIP**: Want to see more miracles take place in your life? Start by opening your *spiritual eyes*. Miracles tend to take place in the lives of those who believe in miracles, and in a God who enjoys delivering them.

In the meantime, *become* a miracle. Strive to develop your visionary powers and use them to build a future which benefits you, your family, and your fellows. In doing so, you will become the *physical hands* of your Creator.

As for your reward? Let's just say that the person who becomes a good steward of his or her powers invariably reaps the benefits of God's limitless favor.

## #7) **Create a Destiny Statement**

What's a "Destiny Statement?" A *Destiny Statement* is a brief, personalized declaration that summarizes your vision for your future.

Your Destiny Statement should answer the questions: *Where* am I headed? *What* are my ultimate goals? *Who* am I aspiring to become?

An excellent Destiny Statement might resemble, "I will become a first-class operating executive who earns $175,000 per year. I will write a business book based on my expertise in managing franchise operations. I will use my wealth and influence to the benefit of my family. I will mentor multiple protégés in order to give back to others in my field. I will stay fit by eating healthy and exercising regularly. And I will hit my knees every night in a prayer of gratitude."

### **Drafting Your Destiny Statement**

Use the space below to draft your own personalized statement of destiny.

________________________________________________________

________________________________________________________

________________________________________________________

________________________________________________________

Okay, now that you've got your Destiny Statement, here are three simple ways to *supercharge* it!

(1) Recite your Destiny Statement aloud, until you *believe* it.

(2) Retool at will. As your confidence grows, you may feel the urge to raise the stakes. Welcome these promptings and *reach higher!*

(3) Thoroughly *enjoy* your journey toward the life of your dreams.

*"We need not be afraid of the future,*
*for the future is in our hands."*
-Thomas E. Dewey

As you continue to master the secrets and sciences of visionary mastery, you'll begin to find yourself in much greater control of your life, career, relationships, and finances. Next, let's delve into the 3rd Element of the *Dream Acquisition Formula (DAF)* found exclusively in *Mind Contrology* ®. Get ready to awaken within you a surge of internal motivation unlike anything you've ever known.

It's time to *ignite your passions…*

# Ignite Your Passions!

*The 3rd Element of the Dream Acquisition Formula (DAF)*

# 15

# Passion

*The Fuel that Drives Dreams and Makes Life Worth Living*

*"We all have reservoirs of energy and genius within us of which we do not dream."*
-Dr. William James

Have you ever been so *excited* about something that you couldn't even sleep? Your mind races and your heart pounds as you lie awake in bed, staring at the ceiling, unable to think about anything but that which you desire? Orville Wright had that very feeling during the nights proceeding December 17, 1903, and he would go on make history because of it…

Wright's story begins in 1896 when, after studying birds in flight through the window of his two-story brick storefront bicycle shop in Dayton, Ohio, the 25 year-old business owner imagined achieving the impossible. Orville and his brother, Wilbur, 21, would build a "flying machine" capable of carrying them into the sky like a giant, mechanical bird. Of course, two major obstacles stood between Orville and his desired outcome:

- Orville had no engineering credentials or piloting experience whatsoever.
- There were no aviation experts or aerodynamic principles from which to draw critical data because air-travel itself did not yet exist!

A miracle would be required to transition Orville's dream into reality. Wright's vision, however, blinded him to deterrents such as ridiculous odds…and gravity. The shop owner saw only his desired outcome—flight. And that purpose awakened within him a level of *passion* so powerful, so inspiring, that he simply *had* to take action.

*"Feeling and desire are the motive forces behind all human endeavor."*
-Albert Einstein

Committed to discovering the fundamental principles by which man could take to the sky, Wright turned to the most logical of teachers—birds.

Throughout 1896, Orville became increasingly obsessed with learning how birds fly. Poised for hours by the window of his shop, Orville observed the habits of sparrows as they swooped down to snatch the bread he'd supplied before flying off to nearby trees. All the while, Wright scribbled notes, engaged his imagination, drew diagrams, and, perhaps most importantly, welled up with energy and emotion.

Driven by the prospect of flying, the Wrights converted their bicycle shop into an engineering lab where the first rudimentary sketches of Orville and Wilbur's "flying machine"—a giant leap in the process of giving their dream physical properties—were strewn across countertops. The aroma of coffee and the bustle of progress filled the air as the Wrights worked their crude drawings into detailed schematics, a production schedule, and a list of materials by which to build their mechanical bird.

Between 1896 and 1900, while selling bicycles to finance the building of their machine, Orville and Wilbur began chatting up their project to every customer that walked through the door. "Never in a million years!" was the typical objection. "If man were meant to fly, he'd have wings!" But the Wrights were convinced they would get their wooded bird off the ground, and the time was quickly approaching when they would prove their gravity-defying destiny of choice to the world…

*"Passion is contagious.*
*And whatever makes us either think or feel strongly adds to our power and enlarges our field of action."*
-Ralph Waldo Emerson

From 1900 to 1903, the Wrights transported a series of rickety, wooden aircrafts to their makeshift runway in on Huffman Prairie in Kitty Hawk, North Carolina. During each attempted take-off, amused spectators pointed and laughed as the Wright's machines did everything but fly.

Committed to their dream, however, the Wrights refused to allow their failures to define them. Following each unsuccessful take-off, the brothers returned to their makeshift lab where they brainstormed improvements, fine-tuned their inventions, and then tried again. The vision of rising above the Earth kept the Wrights loyal to their project long after lesser motivated men would've thrown in the towel. It was during the twilight hours of a night in mid-December when Orville Wright found himself lying in bed, staring at the ceiling, unable to think about anything but how to get his flying machine into the air. History's clock ticked and Wilbur's place in its books grew ever more certain as the self-taught aviation engineer burned the midnight oil imagining his next test flight. He beckoned his brain to provide the solution which would allow him to make his dream real.

At last, the answers arrived: a more powerful engine, tighter controls and an *angled* wing!

On the morning of December 17, 1903, after having made the final, fateful improvements to their flying machine, the Wrights hurriedly moved their latest aircraft to Huffman Prairie. Onlookers on horseback and on foot lined the Wright's compressed-dirt runway. Adrenaline surged through Orville's veins as he climbed aboard and manned the controls. Brother Wilbur started the engine. Flight conditions were superb as Orville rumbled down the runway, pulled back on the controls, and then soared into the sky like a giant, mechanical eagle!

The skies would never be the same again.

*"The passions should be held in reverence."*
-Edgar Allen Poe

In 1903, Orville and Wilbur Wright achieved the impossible by daring to dream and then transforming their dream into reality on the wings of passion. Want to start producing the kind of passion by which you may usher your grandest dreams—even an "impossible" dream such as flying—from mind to matter?

You may begin by learning about your "Internal Motivation Mechanism (IMM)"...

## Your "Internal Motivation Mechanism"

*Source of the Passion-driven Lifestyle*

Powering dreams from mind to matter and living a life brimming with prizes like endless energy, joy, and excitement is largely a function of what I refer to as your "Internal Motivation Mechanism," or IMM. Scientifically speaking, your IMM is the working relationship between your brain's limbic system, your central nervous system and a dozen neurotransmitters which deliver the varying degrees of "electrochemical euphoria" you interpret as excitement, desire, and so on.

Simply put, your Internal Motivation Mechanism is the power-source behind what we refer to as *passion.*

### How to Trigger Your IMM into Action

As it relates to everyday life, there are a few specific ways you can stimulate your IMM into producing more of the passion that makes life worth living.

- You can incite your passions by developing a purpose for your life and vision for your future.
- You can discover what you enjoy most about yourself, others, and your world.

- You can earn a living doing what you love, or learn to love what you already do.
- You can pursue a great and noble cause. Those who pursue such morally-charged missions, you will find in later material, often discover the power to change the world in the process.

You can also use any combination of the above approaches to further increase your access to, and daily operating levels of, passion.

*"In Passion's Strife, no Medium can you have;*
*You rule a Master, or submit a slave."*
-Ben Franklin

Over the next four chapters, we'll cover each of the above-mentioned strategies for maximizing passion. Let's begin by learning more about how your vision and purposes in life activate your IMM and make life much more worthwhile.

## The Pursuit of an Energizing Purpose

*The Key to a Life Worth Living*

*"Great minds have purposes, others have wishes."*
-Washington Irving

Few things get the IMM revving like an energizing purpose. Your vision Master List and the Mental Movies you play out in your head based on your Master List represent an unparalleled source of direction and energy for your life both over the long run and on a daily basis.

Take Iowa's John Simplot, for instance…

Simplot was just 14 when he dropped out of the eight grade and went to work for a local potato farmer in 1923. At some point during the months he spent in the blazing sun sorting potatoes, tending the fields, and taking care of his employer's hogs, the young farmhand dared to dream of owning his *own* potato business.

From that moment forward, Simplot no longer showed up for work with intentions of trading labor for pay. Instead, John began to use his employer's farm as his own personal "Potato University." As if studying to earn a degree, Simplot learned everything he could about the potato business.

While scratching out a meager living, Simplot gained an understanding about what weather conditions, soil quality, and length of harvest cycles were needed to grow the biggest and tastiest potatoes. Simplot also learned strategies for packaging and pricing the product, and for acquiring customers. It wasn't long before Simplot decided he'd learned everything he needed to know in order to go into business for himself. At age 19, after saving every penny he earned for seven years, Simplot purchased a $250 potato sorter and then founded the J.R. Simplot Company in 1929.

*"The great and glorious masterpiece of man*
*is to learn to live with purpose."*
-Michel de Montaigne

Over the next 30 years, Simplot's energies shifted from simply growing potatoes to growing his business and serving the community.

In his quest to introduce his high-quality potatoes to a national market, Simplot purchased nutrient rich land by the hundreds—and then thousands—of acres. As sales increased, Simplot invested in a lab where the merging of technology and agriculture led to a process that made his (as well as other company's) potatoes bigger and tastier, and less prone to bruising and decomposition. Before he knew it, Simplot was providing jobs to 3,500 people, operating 10,000 acres of land, and known for pioneering the process by which French fries are frozen.

Although his wealth enabled him to buy a mansion on a hill, Simplot never allowed his wealth go to his head. Upon his nightstand could be found two items: Forbes Magazine and the Bible. And Simplot didn't just read the Bible; he practiced its teachings by donating millions of dollars to universities across Idaho.

It was in 1967 that John Simplot worked into existence one of those miracles of personal triumph that can be performed only by those who possess a worthy purpose and pursue their goal with a degree of physical vigor scarcely found in a *dozen* average beings. As a direct result of his consuming purpose of producing the nation's biggest and tastiest potatoes, Simplot attracted the attention of McDonald's founder Ray Kroc. Based on a handshake and a promise, Simplot was awarded a contract as the fast-food chain's primary supplier of top-quality potatoes worldwide. Almost overnight, Simplot had become the largest producer of spuds on the planet.

In 2008, some 50 years after launching his little company, John "King of Spuds" Simplot earned a place on Forbes's list of the world's richest people with a net worth in excess of $3.6 billion!

*"Without a purpose,*
*nothing at all shall be done."*
-Marcus Aurelius

## Driving Purpose: The Zest for Life Itself

The spectacular turnaround of a group of ailing seniors at a Wisconsin retirement home opened the eyes of the center's administration to the power of *purpose*.

It was a startling dilemma. A widespread wave of depression and illness swept through the senior living center like nothing the staff had ever seen. Administrators began to panic as they watched the center's residents begin withering away as if being overtaken by some otherworldly and unstoppable epidemic.

Once doctors confirmed that disease was *not* the culprit, the administration held an emergency meeting in order to brainstorm possible solutions. Medications were adjusted. Diets were changed. Heck, the staff even began throwing parties and serving cake in an attempt to lift the elders' broken spirits. Nothing had any effect.

Then something truly magical happened…

*"Passion is the wellspring of life."*
-Ralph Waldo Emerson

In a fortuitous unfolding of events, the facility's clinical director received a call from the owner of a nearby day-care center. The caller wanted to know if any of the center's seniors would be interested in volunteering to read to groups of preschoolers.

Many seniors immediately signed on; in coming days, many more. Before long, nearly every senior in the facility was among the volunteers. Within days, residents began to laugh again. Appetites returned. And seniors throughout the facility began to dress, move about, and carry themselves as if every new day was the single, greatest day of their lives.

By what miracle did the seniors manage such a spectacular turnaround? The residents discovered invigorating purpose as educators of the youth. The job of reading stories to groups of beautiful, happy children rekindled within the seniors the zest for life itself!

Whether you're looking to fulfill an impossible dream, dominate the workplace or change the world in some legendary way, an ignition of passion will provide the fuel necessary for you to complete your mission.

*"Within all of us, there are wells of thought and dynamos of energy."*
-Thomas Watson, IBM

Perhaps you're beginning to feel the fires of passion kindling within you at this very moment. Maybe you feel as though you're ready and able to accomplish anything you choose to set your mind to.

Well, imagine the power you'd wield by increasing your current level of passion by 100%—or even 1000%.

Consider, if you will, the euphoria you would experience on a daily basis if you could learn to derive mood-altering levels of energy and excitement from a boundless banquet of motivators amidst the world around you.

Now see yourself turning the page and doing just that…

# 16

# Igniting Your Passion!

*Discovering your "Magic Recipe" for Living Life to the Fullest on a Daily Basis*

*"We should live for the future, and yet should find our life in the fidelities of the present."*
-Henry Ward Beecher

You're very fortunate…

As a visionary with a detailed blueprint for your future, you get to enjoy the wonder and excitement of transforming your dreams from mind to matter in a series of calculated steps. The dream acquisition process indeed has a way of igniting one's inner fire like nothing else on Earth. Of course, it's also important to learn to derive joy, inspiration, and satisfaction from the people, places, and things that surround us on a daily basis. If you're like most people, however, you've probably devoted far too little time to discovering what you truly enjoy about yourself, others, and your world.

In this chapter, we're going to change that.

A terrific method for building a life driven by joy, inspiration, and wonder is to shift your Internal Motivation Mechanism (IMM) into overdrive by filling your days with the people, places, and things that give meaning to your life.

To acquire this skill, you must first discover what truly *makes you tick* at the deepest levels…

## Discovering What Truly Makes *YOU* Tick!

*The Secret to "Turning On" Your Internal Motivation Mechanism*

*"To know what you prefer, instead of humbly saying amen to what the rest of the world says you ought to prefer, is to have kept your soul alive."*
-Robert Louis Stevenson

When my daughter was small we often played a game we called "favorites." Before putting my girl to bed, I would ask her to select her *favorites* from among a wide variety of topics—her favorite animal, book, color or season, for instance. Smiling widely, my daughter would go on, sometimes for hours, listing the people, places, and things she liked best.

This "game," however, is as educational and empowering as it is fun.

You see, discovering what truly makes us tick at the deepest levels—by getting to know what we enjoy most about ourselves, others, and our world—builds self-knowledge, which leads to self-confidence. This, in turn, enables us to handle life more skillfully and to enjoy each day more fully because we understand "who we are" and know how to go about filling our lives with what really makes us happy.

Everyone has their own unique tastes and preferences, including *you.* In order to get your IMM to begin delivering a steady dose of electrochemical euphoria into your life, you've got to understand what your own, personal favorites in life are.

Below, you'll find lists of questions designed to help you discover more about *who you are* and *what you like.*

(1) **What are *your* "favorites?"** What's your favorite color? Hot food? Cold food? Dessert? Restaurant? Place to have fun?

Who is your favorite comedian? Actor or actress? Musician? Neighbor? Relative(s)? Which president, author, and athlete stand out as your all-time favorite?

Who's your hero, and *why?* And who's your best friend ever?

What's your favorite movie? Broadway play? Season of the year? Holiday? Bible passage? Band? Song? Childhood memory?

What's the funniest joke you've ever heard? Best book you've ever read? Greatest favor you've ever done, and how do you intend to top it?

When was the last time you experienced your *favorite* things in life, and when will be the next?

(2) **Who are the most important *people* in your life?** Who are the most important people in your current sphere of influence? Your spouse? Children? Friends? A particular friend? Your boss or business associates? Coworkers or employees? Your customers? Has a mentor, teacher or doctor had a major impact on your life? Do you value your priest or pastor? Your hairstylist or mechanic? Your IT guy?

*What* about each of your special people makes them so special? And what small act of kindness could you initiate to show your appreciation for the terrific individuals who make your priceless relationships…priceless?

(3) **What "leisure activities" bring you the most pleasure?** Do you prefer *outdoor* recreation like jogging, biking, and camping? *Water sports* like swimming, surfing, and jet skiing? Or *indoor* activities like watching movies and curling up with a good book?

Do you favor a night out with friends or a long walk with the dog? Do board games with the kids equal fun to you? Or is spending hours at the computer, building your social network or downloading songs more your thing? Would you rather attend a sports event, comedy club, an opera or a concert played by your favorite band? Do you prefer a sunny day on the beach, a wintry night on the slope, or something in between?

What "leisure activities" bring *you* the most pleasure? And what new ones will you consider trying?

(4) **What do you love most about the endless bounty of Nature?** What about *Nature* stimulates your being? Do you love the sight of fresh, winter snowfall? The colorful mountainsides of autumn? Do you enjoy the scent of a rose in spring? The smell in the air after a

cleansing, summer rainfall? Are you more energized by day or at night?

Are you an animal lover? Could you sit and watch lions on Animal Planet, or squirrels in your local park, for hours? Are you fascinated by space, the stars, and the planets? Or do the endless wonders of sea life pique *your* interests?

When was the last time you took a long walk in the park, visited the zoo with your kids or watched a sunrise with the person you love? What are you waiting for?

(5) **What motivates you most about your plans for the future?** Is it the *power* that comes with being rich? The *joy* of eating well, exercising often, and living longer? Or the *thrill* of launching your own business or dominating your field?

Is it the *recognition* of gaining national fame or becoming a role model to your kids that drives you forward? Does the *adventure* of traveling the world, or the *rush* of taking calculated risks, light your fire? Or does the *satisfaction* of early retirement and philanthropic gift-giving top your hierarchy of motivators?

What about your vision really gets your IMM revving, and *why?*

*"As far as we can discern*
*the sole purpose of human existence*
*is to kindle a light in the darkness of mere being."*
-Carl Jung

If you've put some thought into the questions above, you've probably got a pretty good idea about what makes you tick. The next step to shifting your IMM into high gear is to begin filling your days with the people, places and things that make life worth living for you personally.

Below, you'll find seven passion-igniting tips for getting the most joy, inspiration, and wonder out of life on a daily basis.

## Shifting Your IMM into Overdrive!

*7 Passion-igniting Tips for Getting More Out of Life*

### Passion Igniter #1) **Try New Things**

Denise, the love of my life, is a great mother, but she's always had a problem trying new things and having fun.

Considering it my job to infuse fun into Denise's life, I once proposed that we spend the day at the shore riding jet skis. She was adamantly *against* the idea. Didn't like the water. Didn't like speed. Didn't like...anything *new*.

For her own good, I pushed and pushed until she caved. I'll never forget skidding across the bay, glancing beside me, and seeing the ecstatic smile plastered across Denise's face. The glare from her pearly whites could've blinded the captains of merchant ships sailing 20 miles off shore!

*"The joy of life is variety."*
-Dr. Samuel Johnson

Boring routines deprive us of excitement and creativity. Experiencing new things, on the other hand, sparks "neural connectivity," stimulates the senses, and arouses the passions. Make a point of trying new things—new hobbies and interests, new styles and viewpoints, new restaurants and foods, new routes and travel spots. Go to a game or concert instead of watching television or listening to your iPod. Play a *real* sport instead of a video game. Be spontaneous—take in a comedy show or go to dinner for no other reason but to celebrate Monday.

**GURU'S TIP:** Make self-discovery a priority, and have the time of your life in the process!

## Passion Igniter #2) **Manage a Home Improvement Project**

Management is an exhilarating field.

As a young construction project manager, I worked for a GC whose clients included Exxon/Mobil and Ruby Tuesday Restaurants. Managing projects in the range of $5 to $10 million was exciting and laid the foundation for my roles as a corporate turnaround manager and, more recently, as the president of my own consulting firm. I've learned through my experiences that managing people, capital, and other valuable assets provides great mental exercise, offers rewarding compensation, and is one of the most exciting jobs a person can undertake.

Want to experience the *thrill* of management? Launching a small home improvement project like a snap-block walkway or vegetable garden is a great place to start.

**GURU'S TIP:** Launching a small project is an excellent way to sharpen your project management skills, kick your IMM into overdrive, and exercise positive dominion over your own private, little world.

## Passion Igniter #3) **Adopt a Faithful Companion**

One of the most rewarding ways to breathe newfound joy into your life is to give a puppy, kitten or some other needy animal a loving home. Pet ownership teaches responsibility and promotes kinship among members of your family. Pets make for loyal, lifelong friends. Pets also have been known to alert their owners to dangers like fires and intruders, to improve their owner's quality of life, and to considerably reduce the stress levels of their owners.

Of course, pet adoption and ownership are major decisions which require careful consideration. However, if your living arrangements and finances support the idea—and you're looking to inject a whole new level of joy and love into your days—then adding a new member to your family may be just what the doctor ordered.

*"To affect the quality of the day, that is the highest of arts!"*
-Henry David Thoreau

**GURU'S TIP:** Every day in the U.S., nearly 7,400 lovable animals fail to become matched to a prospective owner and, sadly, are euthanized as a result. To adopt a pet, visit your local ASPCA or animal shelter online or in person. It just may save a worthy animal's life and change yours for the better for years to come.

## Passion Igniter #4) **Create Some Adventure!**

I'm a mild adrenaline junkie. If you're like me, the craving for thrills and adventure is in your DNA. Of course, you don't need to race superbikes or film gorillas in the wild to get your adrenaline fix.

Instead, create some *adventure* in your life by taking your kids horseback riding. Go sight-seeing with your spouse in a nearby city, or become a "tourist" in your own hometown. Book a paintball war with friends. Go indoor skydiving. Or take your family camping. Explore Nature, do some fishing, and roast marshmallows by the campfire. Nothing rejuvenates the spirit like the great outdoors.

*"Life is either a daring adventure, or nothing."*
-Helen Keller

If your finances permit, plan an exciting day trip. Hit an amusement or water park. If you enjoy coming within arm's reach of the world's most exotic animals, give Six Flags Safari Park a try.

Thrive on mystery and suspense? Book a "murder mystery" weekend at a famous bed and breakfast. Crave heights? Charter a helicopter ride at your town's harbor or airport. One of my secretaries once booked me a hot-air balloon ride for my birthday. Perhaps floating above the pastel clouds at dusk would lift *your* sleeping spirit.

**GURU'S TIP:** Rekindle your zest for life by scheduling some exhilarating fun with your family or friends. Rediscover the thrill of *adventure!*

## Passion Igniter #5) **Work Up a Good Sweat!**

A lack of physical exercise doesn't just dull the mind and deplete the spirit, it *corrodes* the body. Failing to get enough exercise can accelerate the build-up of plaque in your arteries, of fat deposits around your heart and other organs, and of toxins in your blood and glands.

Being physically active, on the other hand, helps keep you mentally sharp, speeds your metabolism (which facilitates the mobilization of fat,) helps *prevent* heart disease, minimizes cortisol levels, and causes your brain to release endorphins which make you feel good naturally. In other words, when you're physically active, you *feel* more alive—because you *are* more alive!

### Some Fun Approaches to Physical Exercise

Does the thought of a health club membership or triathlon make you ill? Well, relax. There are tons of fun ways to become more physically active. Following are a few tips…

Take up a new hobby like tennis or golf. Join a softball team or Pilates class. Try hiking or rock-climbing. Interested in martial arts? Take a Tae Kwon Do class or give kickboxing a try. Target your cardiovascular system by jogging around the neighborhood or by keeping along with a physical conditioning DVD. Or strengthen your muscles with a pair of good old-fashioned dumbbells.

Want some *more convenient* approaches to physical exercise? Try these: Take the stairs instead of the elevator. Opt for the "scenic route" when walking the dog. *Walk* to the store instead of driving. Park your car at the far end of the shopping mall or parking lot. Or mow your lawn yourself instead of hiring help.

*"Labor to keep alive that little spark of celestial power!"*
-George Washington

**GURU'S TIP**: Want to feel more alive, *become* more alive? Get your heart pumping and endorphins flowing by working up a good, healthy sweat!

## Passion Igniter #6) **Rekindle Your Relationships—without Breaking the Bank**

If you look back on your happiest memories thus far, chances are your family and friends are a large part of the picture. Taking family vacations and enjoying memorable dinners with friends are fantastic ways to nurture your inner circle. Of course, you don't have to fly to Tahiti or spring for lobster to strengthen bonds with loved ones and create wonderful memories you'll treasure for the rest of your life.

*"The purpose of life, after all, is to live it, to taste experience to the utmost, to reach out eagerly and without fear for newer and richer experiences."*
-Eleanor Roosevelt

### Some *Inexpensive* Ways to Rekindle Your Relationships

Want to spend more time with the ones you love, without breaking the bank? Following are a few ideas.

Dust off that old Yahtzee or Scrabble game and declare tonight "family board game night." Put together a card game with friends instead of dining out. Baking cupcakes with the kids costs only a few dollars and can be just as fun Chuck E. Cheese. And choosing a matinee instead of a twilight show can save you 30% or more on the price of movie tickets. Forget greeting cards (and save the cost of postage) by emailing greetings, inspiring quotes, and jokes to friends and relatives.

Got a project you're looking to start? Rely on the help of family and friends instead of hiring a contractor. And do more favors just for the personal bond it creates. Take more moonlight walks with the one you love. Also, a public park can be an affordable alternative to an amusement park. Long ago, Denise and I discovered a beautiful public park where we enjoyed such activities as hiking and biking the trails, feeding geese with our daughter, encountering wild turkeys, and sitting peacefully by a waterfall. Over the years, this park became our private retreat. "Our park" offered picturesque scenery and plenty of exercise. What's more, it never seemed to get old.

Find a public park you and your family can call your own. It may breathe new joy into your life and set the stage for memories you'll never forget. And like so many of the best things this world has to offer, it won't cost you a dime!

## Passion Igniter #7) **Consider that the Clock is Ticking!**

Time is a precious resource afforded to each man and woman in finite measure. Each moment that passes, the hourglass of life continues to drain; yet, statistics have shown that the average person wastes 15 hours per week watching television. Before you squander away another moment of your most valuable resource, *time,* consider the following.

There are 168 hours in a week. Each week, the average person spends 42.5 hours working. 56 hours are lost to sleep. 12 hours are passed on the road or stuck in traffic. 10 hours are devoted to preparing and eating meals. 3.5 hours disappear while showering and grooming. Errands (like grocery shopping) and chores (like doing dishes) demand 3 hours of time. 5 hours are spent surfing the web, talking on the phone or texting. And .05 hours are blown simply staring off into space! Factor in the 15 hours most people waste watching television each week, and you're left with just over 20.5 hours per week—or an alarming 82 hours each *month*—to enjoy your loved ones and live life to the fullest!

*"Seize from each moment its unique novelty."*
-Andre Gide

**GURU'S TIP:** "Dost thou love life?" posed the venerable Ben Franklin. "Then do not squander time; for time is the stuff life is made of." Time is precious, and your dreams won't fulfill themselves.

So, turn off the television, get off the couch, and make life happen!

## Passion Maximization Methodology

*Your "Magic Recipe" for Living Life to the Fullest... on a Daily Basis*

*"He who reigns over himself,*
*and rules over his passions,*
*is more than a king."*
-John Milton

Below, you'll find a list of the three main *ingredients* for getting more joy, inspiration, and wonder out of life every day. Mix into the formula your own tastes and preferences and you will discover your own, highly-personalized "recipe" for passion.

Ingredient #1) **Stay Future-focused:** Foreseeing what grand successes your future holds adds rich energy and emotion to the present.

Ingredient #2) **"Turn On" Your IMM by Filling Your Days with What Makes *You* Tick:** Know what your favorite people, places, and things are in life.

Then make a valiant effort to surround yourself with these treasures on a daily basis.

Ingredient #3) **Shift Your IMM into *Overdrive* by Exploiting the 7 Tips for Igniting Passion:** Try new things. Manage a home improvement project. Adopt a faithful companion. Create some adventure. Work up a good sweat! Spend more time with those you love. And never forget that the clock is ticking!

*"Live not in your yesterdays, not just for tomorrow,*
*but in the here and now."*
-Carl Sandberg

Okay, you've learned how to turn on your IMM, and you've got seven strategies for generating more joy, inspiration, and wonder on a daily basis. You've even discovered your very own, highly-personalized *magic recipe* for passion. Next, you're going to discover how to use the "professional passions"—enthusiasm and ambition—to dominate the workplace (or marketplace)...

# 17

# The "Professional Passions"

*How to Use Enthusiasm and Ambition to Dominate the Workplace (or Marketplace)*

*"While the mind is the greatest money-maker, the passions are the greatest motivators."*
-Michael LeBoeuf, PhD

In this chapter, you'll discover the difference between *enthusiasm* and *ambition* and learn how to use these "professional passions" to utterly dominate the workplace (or marketplace.) Let's begin with an example of how proper application of the professional passions can mean the difference between working a job that pays the bills and landing the career of one's dreams.

Raised in Albuquerque, New Mexico, Mike Judge was a smart, young kid who happened to be crazy about cartooning. When Mike began scouting colleges in the 1980s, however, the brainy teenager placed his artistic passions on the back burner and focused instead on pursuing a more "logical career" in science.

Judge eventually enrolled at the University of California where he earned a degree in physics in 1986. Ironically, after college, Mike's *logical career* failed to materialize. Instead, the physics scholar drifted into a series of underpaying, dead-end jobs, including a stint as a computer programmer and a gig as a bass player in Texas.

Fortunately for Judge, his enthusiasm for cartooning eventually resurfaced. It was after stumbling across an animation display at a local movie theater that the aspiring cartoonist within Mike began to take hold of him, gently directing his actions. So, Judge invested in his own animation equipment and began producing animated "shorts" in a flurry of pure, creative genius. And before long, this powerful combination of raw enthusiasm and natural ambition would launch him into the national spotlight.

In 1989, Judge wandered into an animated film festival in Dallas, Texas where he thought he might showcase his work. What happened next is representative of the timely miracles that are reserved only for passionate visionaries who dare to forge a living doing what they love. Judge's work was immediately acquired by Comedy Central. Shortly thereafter, Judge's second series of short films—an edgy animated series starring two zany cartoon teenagers named Beavis and Butthead—was picked up MTV.

Seemingly overnight, Judge's controversial creation took the world by storm. "Beavis and Butthead" would run for more than 200 episodes straight before going on to become one of the longest running animated series of all time!

*"Every production of genius*
*must be a production of enthusiasm."*
-Benjamin Disraeli

**POINT TO PONDER:** It was only after rediscovering his enthusiasm for animation that Judge found the ambition to take the actions that earned him riches and fame doing what he loved.

## Enthusiasm and Ambition

*The Professional Passions*

Big business has undergone a massive evolution over the past 120 years: the Industrial Revolution, the organized labor movement, globalization, digitization, and, most recently, the Age of Information.

For all that has changed in the world of commerce, however, one timeless principle has remained the same—passionate professionals inevitably rise to the top positions in every industry and company.

So, just what does it take to become a "*passionate* professional?" This author's research of 500 peak performers and 250 Fortune-level firms has identified two specific qualities which top experts in every field invariably possess:

- **Enthusiasm:** *Enthusiasm* relates to the excitement you feel toward some particular career goal, field, company or industry.

- **Ambition:** Your level of *ambition* determines what actions you will take in response to your enthusiasm. Ambition is the prism through which your passion is converted into results such as raises, promotions, perks, authority, etc.

Enthusiasm and ambition, which we'll refer to as the "*professional* passions," are the greatest weapons for anyone looking to utterly dominate the workplace (or marketplace.) So, how can you become more *enthusiastic?* And how can you begin generating the kind of *ambition* that translates into a raise, perks, promotions, authority, and more—regardless of what your career goals may be, and even if you can't stand your current, dead-end job?

I'm glad you asked…

## Becoming a Passionate Professional

*7 Steps for Building Enthusiasm, Becoming More Ambitious… and Dominating the Workplace (or Marketplace)*

### Step #1) **Discover Your "Niche"**

What's a "niche?" Webster defines a *niche* as "a position or activity for which one is particularly suited."

Discovering the position or business for which you are best suited can truly revolutionize your life. Research has shown that working one's ideal career generally leads to increased earning potential and a level of happiness that spills over into one's personal life.

I'll never forget one particular night in the late 1990s when I learned just how life-changing finding one's niche in life can actually be. My friend, Mike, and I, both in our 20's, were cruising along I-95 in Mike's brand new BMW after a night out on the town. Overhead lamps flashed by in a blur as Mike sprung the news on me.

"Johnny, I did it," said Mike. "I'm a millionaire."

People often use their net worth, including real estate and other assets, to describe themselves as millionaires. Not so with Mike. Mike had managed to generate $1 million in positive cash flow, a goal he'd set for himself after launching a business he truly enjoyed just a couple, short years before.

After congratulating Mike, I naturally asked his secret for success. Wise ahead of his years, the Irishman winked, advising, "Just find your niche, something you're good at and enjoy. Do that, brother, and the money will take care of itself."

Of course, landing your ideal position isn't solely about making money; it's simply about earning a living doing what you love.

Take Tabitha the comptroller, for instance. Tabitha's coworkers called her "Crabby Tabby" because she hated her job and never smiled. As comptroller for a tourist town in Virginia, Tabby plotted out the county's multimillion dollar budget.

During her seven years in charge of the town's finances, Tabby spent most of her days confined to her office, pouring over forecasting software, reworking spreadsheets, and slamming cup after cup of coffee to stay awake. Her only escape was the view through her window which overlooked the beautiful, nearby beach.

Tabby possessed a degree in finance, and she commanded an impressive salary—$137,000 a year to be exact.

However, as she watched the police patrolling the sun-drenched sands, Tabby secretly dreamed of trading her computer, calculator, and pants suit for a uniform and an *exciting* career in law enforcement.

In 2010, Crabby Tabby broke free from her shackles and climbed out of her shell. After resigning from her job as comptroller, Tabitha signed on as a corrections officer for the Pennsylvania Department of Corrections.

Tabby's starting salary was $35,000—roughly 25% of her former salary—yet she hasn't stopped *smiling* since her first day behind bars!

*"The high prize,*
*the crowning fortune of a man,*
*is to be born with a bias*
*to some pursuit which finds him*
*in employment and happiness."*
-Ralph Waldo Emerson

The peak performers in any company or industry around the world invariably are those who are most enthusiastic about their work. When we inhabit a position we truly enjoy, ideas flow freely, hours pass happily, and we're much more likely to exert the extra effort that places us head-and-shoulders above our less motivated workplace peers or marketplace competitors.

Want to know one of the greatest secrets to happiness and freedom, to unleashing your creative genius, and to maximizing your earning potential? *Either find a job doing what you love, or learn to love what you already do.*

**GURU'S TIP:** The average person spends 40-60% of his or her adult life earning a living. That's why it's imperative to either start enjoying what you do or make the career leap to your ideal position.

There's no substitute for doing what you love!

## Step #2) "Spin" Your Current Position to *Your* Advantage

So, let's say you're an hourly employee who dreams of starting your own business, a department manager who yearns for a plush position in the ivory tower, or a breast cancer surgeon who envisions becoming a movie star (a recalibration of vision that a friend of mine recently underwent.) Let's also say you're thinking to yourself, "How can I generate and maintain enthusiasm for my niche position when I have to spend the next several weeks, months or years in my lousy, current position?"

That, my friend, is where mastering your perspective comes into play. A conscious shift in the way you interpret your current situation can shed a whole new light on your present job.

### How to "Spin" Your Current Position to *Your* Advantage

Below are a few tips for "spinning" your current position to your advantage:

- View your current position as a "stepping stone" to the Ultimate Destination you've got in mind.

- Focus on what you *do* love (or at least like) about your job. Do you enjoy hanging out with your coworkers or helping your employer's customers? Do you enjoy the perks or freebies? The flexible hours or health benefits? Is your job close to home? Is your job paying your bills?

- View your position as a "valuable experience." All of your experiences are in some way beneficial to you, including your current job. Through your job, are you gaining knowledge, skills, experience, and/or relationships that could benefit you down the road? Are you exposed to industry experts or trade secrets? To problem-solving or decision-making? Are you developing transferable skills by managing people, property, activities, systems, equipment or money?

If you search hard enough, you will find the *value* in what you know.

- Interpret your position as an *opportunity.* Every job provides an opportunity to learn and grow, to teach and share, and to build important bridges and alliances.

Keep in mind: your current boss, superiors, suppliers, clients, and coworkers can provide critical references, contacts or advice related to the career transition that may exist in your future.

*"Enthusiasm is a great leavening force in the mental world, for it brings power to your purpose. It inspires you to initiative in both thought and action. It is very hard for one to do one's best if one does not feel or display enthusiasm."*
-Andrew Carnegie

**GURU'S TIP**: Enthusiasm in the workplace comes from loving what you do. And although you may never *love* your current position, you can grow to "like it" a whole lot more (and build motivation in the present) by understanding the benefits and advantages that your current job has to offer.

Use your powers of perception to identify all the ways in which your current professional situation is either serving you well now or may prove beneficial to you in the near or distant future.

## Step #3) **Make a "Strategic Shift" in Your Work Routine**

Being confined to a cubicle or office all week, clocking in and out at the same times every day, and breaking to the sound of a whistle (or not at all) can turn any work week into an occupational prison sentence. If this sounds familiar, gain a newfound sense of freedom and continue to build enthusiasm in the workplace by *shaking up* your mundane routine with a small "strategic shift" from the ordinary.

I once had a finance manager named Gia. Gia did her job well and was very likable. However, Gia's chronic tardiness began to set a bad precedent around the office. When warnings didn't work, it became time for a talk. I approached Gia in her office, shut the door behind me and she started to cry.

"What's wrong?" I asked.

"It's happening again, isn't it?" she replied.

I squinted curiously. "*What's* happening again?"

"I'm being fired…for being late all the time."

Gia went on to tell me that she'd been chronically late for every job she'd ever had. It had gotten her axed twice and kept her in a constant state of fear that she'd lose her job again. After all, you can only show up late so many times before the boss walks into your office and shuts the door behind him.

"You're not being fired. We can *solve* this problem," I coached. "Got any suggestions?"

Gia shrugged, assuring me that she'd tried everything.

I glanced at the clock. "How about starting an hour later, leaving an hour later?"

Gia's face lit up. She *loved* the idea. This small adjustment to her schedule ended her worries about being 20 minutes late because her new hours gave her a 40-minute head start.

Suddenly, Gia was reenergized about her career!

## Making a "Strategic Shift" in Your Routine

It's hard to maintain sharp insights, creative genius, and unceasing energy when you're trapped in a cubicle or office all day. Following are a few tips for shaking up your workday and putting some pizzazz back into the hours you spend on the clock.

- Try someplace new for lunch 2 or 3 times each week.
- Sign on for a new, challenging project. Or volunteer to handle a problem your busy boss is currently working on. Both *shifts* will provide valuable experience and prove to the boss that you're a real go-getter.

- Stop ravishing the vending machines and avoid energy-zapping junk food crashes by packing healthy snacks like fresh fruits or vegetables, skinless chicken breast, yogurt, and fitness bars.
- Do "stress-relieving" exercises (like deep breathing, visualization, and stretching) at least once per day for 5 minutes while at your desk or post.
- Break to your *body clock*, instead of to the clock on the wall.
- Don't break at your desk. Get up and get your blood flowing. Step outside for some fresh air. Or try a short power-walk around the corporate complex for a clearer head, renewed energy, and livelier spirit.
- Talk your boss into letting you choose your own hours, dress code, office design, brand of coffee, etc.

*"A man can become successful at anything for which he has infinite enthusiasm."*
-Charles M. Schwab

**GURU'S TIP**: A small, "strategic shift" saved Gia's $90k-a-year job and gave her a new lease on life. What simple change could you put into place (or ask your boss for) in order to revamp *your* routine, and perhaps, your life?

## Step #4) **Infuse the Element of *Fun* into Your Office Culture!**

As part of my firm's Cultural Revitalization Training, we teach CEOs how to make the workplace challenging and fun for managers and employees by implementing strategies such as company-wide quarterly award ceremonies, monthly competitions between branches, off-site team-building exercises, and dress-down Fridays.

Following are several strategies you can employ to make your own place of work more challenging and exciting…

*"Nothing great was ever achieved without enthusiasm."*
-Ralph Waldo Emerson

## How to *Liven Up* Your Office Culture

- **Conjure Up Some Competition**: Ask your boss to sponsor an off-site "Office Olympics" or a branch versus branch bowling night. Or create an office pool (company policy permitting) based on who can decode the current operational quagmire first or who can close the week's biggest sale. The winner takes the pot and the losers spring for sandwiches at the next after work get-together.

- **Become a "Social Ringleader:"** Organize off-site get-togethers with coworkers. Order up some sandwiches and drinks. Aim to forge friendships as well as strategic alliances.

- **Stage a Tasteful Prank**: Tasteful pranks promote kinship and lighten up the atmosphere. During my days as project manager, it was customary to initiate the new guy by ordering him to "go get the pipe stretcher." There is, of course, no such tool. It was only after watching the poor sap scour the site in vain that we would let him in on the gag. Even the new guy couldn't help but laugh. Liven up your workplace with a clever prank pulled in good taste.

- **Turn Your Office or Cubicle into a Home Away From Home**: Decorate your personal space at work with memorabilia, posters, props, photos, and furniture that bring a smile to your face and make you feel at home.

  Try a tiny fish bowl or miniature basketball game. Or simply turn your workplace into a "Destiny Environment" filled with vision enhancers, so you can remember where you're headed while you earn your current paycheck!

- **Pump Up the Volume!** Soft background music makes work more fun and has been shown to contribute to a more productive workplace environment. If you don't currently benefit from music in the workplace, pitch the idea to your boss. Include the catchphrase,

"Music has been shown to *boost productivity* in the workplace." Most bosses will do anything to boost productivity.

**GURU'S TIP:** A fun workplace benefits employees, bosses, and customers alike. Happy, motivated employees generally are more productive and treat customers better. This forms the basis for a more satisfied client base and repeat sales, which are the overriding goals of any sensible boss. Collaborate with your boss and coworkers on ways to infuse the element of fun into your office culture!

## Step #5) Channel Your Enthusiasm into Outright Ambition!

By following steps 1 through 4, it's likely that you'll discover enough enthusiasm to better enjoy your current job as you move boldly in the direction of your dreams. Your next order of business is to learn how to begin channeling your enthusiasm into *outright ambition.*

To learn how to accomplish this, let's turn to Jinny…

While working with a company that was in the process of expanding into a new geographic region, I assisted ownership by heading-up the search for a talented executive who could run the new branch.

Jinny, a passionate MBA with a background in marketing, was among the first candidates to interview. Although Jinny demonstrated about as much enthusiasm for the position as every other candidate, it was this candidate's *ambition* that caused her to stand out from the herd. Following her interview, Jinny emailed me a report that included detailed market analysis and some keen personal insights related to leveraging social media. Jinny's report was so professional and thoroughly researched that it could've come off the desk of a top marketing consultant.

Sadly, Jinny's skillset was not aligned with the company's need for an executive with a strong financial background. So, it appeared that we would be recruiting a different branch manager. However, I was so impressed with Jinny's report that I delivered it to the company CEO and recommended that he read the document in its entirety.

As we wrapped up the interview process, I called Jinny to inform her that someone else had been selected to head up the new branch. "However," I continued, "Another terrific position has opened up which ownership and I believe may be right your alley."

It was only after Jinny accepted the position that I revealed to her that this top management position had been designed specifically for her!

*"The meaning of life is not simply to exist,*
*to survive; but to move ahead, to go up,*
*to achieve, to conquer."*
-Arnold Schwarzenegger

**GURU'S TIP:** Experience has taught me that only about 1 out of every 500 "professionals" is a true go-getter. Dominating your workplace (or marketplace) requires doing the things that your peers or colleagues either haven't thought of, or are simply too lazy or too scared to do. Got a professional dream you wish to make real? Begin by channeling your enthusiasm into *outright ambition!*

## Step #6) **Act Like *You* Own the Place**

Want to impress the brass with your newfound ambition? Start acting like *you* own the company for which you work.

Obliviously, I'm not suggesting that you barge into your boss's office and demand access to guarded financial statements. What I *am* suggesting is that you start laying the foundation for organizational advancement or for future business ownership by beginning to think and act like a business owner. *(If you're a business owner, pay attention. You may discover some strategies below by which to take your operation to the next level of performance.)*

## 3 Ways to Think and Act Like a Boss

(1) **Brainstorm Ways to *Drive Revenue:*** Do you know of a product or service that would spark explosive revenues if acted upon? Could you develop a YouTube commercial, Facebook/Twitter marketing strategy or promotional "sweepstakes" capable of increasing in-store or online traffic?

Could your company increase recurring sales by using existing customer lists to email "10% off $100 or more" offers? Even the smartest bosses often fail to capitalize on this low-cost avenue of electronic advertising.

Where do *you* see the prospect for driving revenues?

(2) **Create Ways to *Cut Costs***: Could you locate a more reliable supply source for the company resources you're in charge of? Renegotiate a supply contract for better rates? Or help reduce "shrink"—a big problem in many companies—by devising measures to curtail the amount of merchandise stolen, lost or damaged?

Does your organization suffer high G&A costs? You might suggest reducing employee turnover, leveraging outsourcing, renting out unused or excess capacity, reducing energy costs, or creating a "paperless office" by automating business activities and shifting to cloud-based services. A combination of the preceding strategies can lead to reductions in G&A of 25% or more.

Practically every business spends more than it has to on labor, materials, supplies, equipment, processes, fuel, energy, etc. Where would *you* cut costs as the boss?

(3) **Devise Ways to *Increase Efficiency***: Efficiency is about moving from A to B by way of the most direct route. Is there some outdated methodology still being used by your company that slows the sales process, creates "operational bottlenecks," delays fulfillment or delivery, or that rubs customers or clients the wrong way?

Think hard. As an employee, you likely know more than you realize about running the place efficiently.

*"Great ambition is the anchor of a great character."*
-Napoleon Bonaparte

**GURU'S TIP**: Thinking and acting like a boss is an effective strategy for laying the foundation for internal advancement or setting the stage for actual business ownership. So, just one question remains: What should you do with your new, brilliant list of money-making, cost-cutting, and time-saving ideas?

That's easy; create a "performance contract"...

## Step #7) **Create a "Performance Contract"**

Now that you've got some ideas for improving the organization you currently work for, it's time to transform your *intellectual property* into the money, perks or expanded authority you deserve.

First, put together a "special report" listing all of your ingenious strategies. Then bring your report to your company's owner, president or CEO. In order to protect your intellectual property, bypass immediate supervisors and middle managers (who may claim *your* ideas as their own) and go straight to the chief decision-maker.

Do whatever's necessary to get some face time with top brass and then follow the script below.

### How to Pitch Your "Performance Contract"

(1) **Win 'em Over**: Set the tone by communicating to your boss why you're there and what your intentions are. Impress the brass with your *enthusiasm* for the company and its bottom line.

(2) **Present your report**: Confidently present your "special report." But don't allow your bright ideas to be tarnished by handing your boss notes scribbled on a bunch of loose papers. Let him or her know you mean business by delivering your report in an attractive presentation folder.

(3) **Appear Consultative**: Be prepared to explain the benefits of each of your ideas. Include projected dollar amounts to be generated or saved, productivity increases to be gained, and /or anticipated improvements in customer service.

(4) **Pitch your "Performance Contract:"** Assure the boss that there's more where that came from. Then negotiate your demands (a raise, expanded authority, setting your own hours, etc.) in exchange for your continued superior performance for a specific time-frame, ideally 3-6 months.

(5) **Close the Deal!** Persuade your boss to agree to a *definite date* upon which the conditions of your "contract" will be satisfied.

**GURU'S TIP:** If you pitch a "performance contract" to any sensible boss, you can be sure that your ingenuity and interest in the company's bottom line will be welcome surprise.

If, on the other hand, you are a boss on the other end of such a pitch, you can be certain that you are dealing with a professional who possesses the highest calibers of enthusiasm and ambition!

*"I know Dear Son, Ambition fills your Mind, and in Life's Voyage, is thy impelling Wind, but at the Helm let Sober Reason stand, to steer the Bark with Heav'n directed Hand; so shall you safe Ambition's Gales receive, and sail securely through the billows heave; so shall you shun the giddy Heroes Fate, and by Her Influence be both Good and Great."*

-Ben Franklin

Okay, now you know that passion is the "fuel" that enables you to move your dreams and goals from mind to matter. You've learned ways to maximize your passion and get the most out of every day. You've also discovered how to use enthusiasm and ambition to begin dominating your workplace (or marketplace.)

Are you ready to step up your game in life and business? If so, it's time to awaken your spirit of greatness and learn how to change the world with a lesson based on the fascinating rags-to-riches story of arguably the most accomplished *Mind Contrologist* of all time.

You're about to uncover a full-chapter *Guide to Greatness* as demonstrated by Ben Franklin…

# 18

# Guide to Greatness

*As Demonstrated by Ben Franklin*

*"Man is only truly great when he acts from his passions."*
-Benjamin Disraeli

What does it take to become great...to change the world? There is perhaps no better man in history to answer these questions than legendary *Mind Contrologist*, Benjamin Franklin.

Dissecting Franklin's life is like discovering a step-by-step guide to greatness. Ben is arguably the most accomplished, brilliant, and charitable man who ever lived. He is also the most underappreciated figure in American history.

Although Franklin never enjoyed the presidency, and his face doesn't grace the facade of Mount Rushmore, his list of achievements as a businessman, civil servant, statesman, engineer, scientist, mathematician, inventor, doctor, military strategist, and philanthropist is staggering. What's more, Ben's role in acquiring the capital and assets that sustained the American Revolution is one of unparalleled importance.

It's important to understand that Benjamin Franklin wasn't *born* great.

Franklin was born in 1706 in a small borough in Boston. When Ben was 12, his father—a man who once insisted that his son was "best suited" for menial work such as grinding metal and sharpening knives—sent Ben to work for Ben's older brother and print shop owner, James Franklin. At James' print shop, Ben the apprentice earned his keep by running errands and operating machines.

Like many younger brothers, Ben longed for the day when he could be just like his hero, James. After considering the prospect of one day running his own business, Ben began borrowing business books from a neighbor and then stayed awake well into the nights ahead while reading by candlelight. It was during these long hours of self-study that Ben strengthened his vocabulary, learned about world economics, and imagined what roles he would play in life and business in the years to come.

Franklin also suffered his share of stupid, adolescent mistakes. Proving himself a typical teenager at the age of 16, Ben used his burgeoning intelligence to get himself into trouble. After writing a well-versed article defaming the local British authorities, Ben snuck behind James' back and used the family's printing press to publish the article. The local authorities became furious. James' reputation was ruined. And young Ben was run out of Boston on a rail!

And *that's* when Ben Franklin's rise to greatness began…

## Ben Franklin's Secrets of Greatness

*7 Steps for Becoming Great and Changing the World*

Think you've got what it takes to follow in the footsteps of the mighty Ben Franklin? Now is your chance to start. The following seven steps represent a guide to greatness based on Franklin's fascinating rise to prominence and power.

This list will help you summon forth your own spirit of greatness and expand your sphere of influence from your immediate environment to your company, community, school, town, country, and beyond.

### Timeless Tip #1) **Awaken Your Spirit of Greatness; Aspire to Great Heights!**

Franklin was a 17 year-old runaway when he arrived by barge at a harbor in Philadelphia in 1723. Ben had no money, no contacts, and no specific plans. He didn't even have a place to live. But as he wandered down Market Street, with its bustling street-side commerce and endless opportunities for prosperity, the entrepreneur inside of the homeless teenager began to…awaken.

Franklin quickly developed a vision for his future. He saw himself becoming a wealthy man of industry.

Over the several next weeks, while sleeping some nights outdoors and staring into the moonlit sky, Ben figured out a way to get on his feet and realize his dream. Ben gathered some wood, borrowed a few tools, and built a cart from which he began selling homemade maps and print services. In coming months, Ben networked with local merchants, befriended key players of Philly's budding business community, and even convinced an aging politician to lend him the cash to open a legitimate print shop.

Within two years of his arrival in town, Ben Franklin, 19, was operating a full-scale print shop of his own.

*"If we are to be really great people, we must strive in good faith to play a great part in the world."*
-Theodore Roosevelt

**GURU'S TIP**: Great aspirations are the lanterns that light the way to the highest levels of performance in life and business.

### Timeless Tip #2) **Believe in the God of the Universe—and Yourself**

In 1727, Ben Franklin's focus shifted from entrepreneurship to faith in God.

Just 21 years old, Ben founded the "Junto"—a philosophical society devoted to unraveling the mysteries of God, truth, and creation.

Throughout his life, Franklin would nurture his relationship with God by doing good deeds for his fellows and regularly praying for the good grace of a Creator which Ben viewed as the loving Grand Architect of the Universe. Franklin believed that, "If a creature is made of God, it must depend on God, and receive all its power from God."

Do you believe in God, a loving Father in Heaven? Do you believe that your Father in Heaven loves you and wants you to succeed? That He filled you with fathomless depths of potential, and that your primary mission on Earth is to discover this potential and exhaust yourself in the glorious pursuit of a worthwhile purpose?

You certainly should.

At a time in America when religious freedom is under assault, it's a good idea to remember that those upon whose backs this country was founded were largely unabashed believers in a loving God, avid readers of the Bible, and men who strived to live as good stewards of the bountiful blessings and far-reaching powers bestowed upon mankind from above.

Topping the list of these God-fearing men is Ben Franklin.

*"You must retain the faith*
*that you can prevail to greatness in the end,*
*while retaining the discipline to confront*
*the brutal facts of your current reality."*
-Jim Collins

**GURU'S TIP**: This author's studies of 500 of history's greatest figures have shown that great accomplishments are often the byproducts of great faith. Ben Franklin's Heaven-inspired, historic achievements provide no exception to this rule.

If you've got important dreams, follow the lead of Franklin. Practice uncommon faith in the God of the Universe, and in yourself.

## Timeless Tip #3) **Pay Attention to the Signs!**

As you begin pursuing your dreams, you can expect direction and assistance from a Higher Source. This help often takes the form of "signs." These *signs* tend to appear in direct proportion to our faith in God and our attentiveness to the workings of the Mind/Reality Relationship.

Ben Franklin benefited often from signs.

For instance, Franklin was 26 when a member of his Junto Society—impressed by Ben's keen insights into so many unrelated subject matters—suggested that the public might enjoy a book based on his knowledge and expertise. Considering his friend's suggestion a *sign* from above, Franklin set his mind to writing and subsequently authored a series of almanacs under his alter ego, Poor Richard.

Between 1733 and 1755, *"Poor Richard's Almanac"* became the most popular literary series of its time with readership rates of 1 out of every 100 colonists!

*"Some are born great, some achieve greatness, and others have greatness thrust upon them."*
-William Shakespeare

Does the God of the Universe really care enough about us to send us *signs* designed to show us how to proceed, to make our path straighter, and even to make our life more enjoyable and exciting? My personal experience assures me that the answer to this question is: Yes, God does care that much.

Allow me to provide you with an example…

Back in my 20's, I began entertaining the prospect of a better career but wasn't sure where to start. Then it happened. I was laid-off from the decent paying, yet highly unchallenging, union job I'd landed through that avenue of advantageousness known as nepotism. This "misfortune" might've devastated me, but for the fact that something inside of me assured me that the layoff was a blessing in disguise.

I drove from the workplace to a nearby service station, got out of the car, and was overcome by a sense of peace. Something assured me that a better opportunity awaited me ahead. The experience was so unusual that I told my father about it. However, the old man, a pragmatic police official, quite frankly wrote me off as crazy. Still, I held fast to my faith that a *better reality* was in the making.

Later that night, I drove by a church. On its billboard was the passage, "Humble yourself, so that in God's time, He may exalt you." I was certain that this message was meant for me to see and called my father to tell him about the *sign*. He politely told me that I was nuts and hung up the phone.

Days later, I was offered a very low-paying, temporary job. And although I considered the position "beneath me," I recalled the sign, *Humble yourself, so that in God's time He may exalt you.* Since the flexible hours allowed me to continue an active job search, I accepted the position. I had been working this crummy job for two weeks when I received a call to interview for a job as project manager for a large developer. I wondered why I was being asked to interview for a job for which I possessed no previous experience. Nevertheless, I eagerly complied. Later, during the interview, when I naively admitted being seriously underqualified for the position, my interviewer informed me that no specific construction management experience was required. As it turns out, the company president had a falling-out with one of his senior project managers. Upon firing the manager, the president assured the man that he intended to hire an "inexperienced kid" who would do a better job than the know-it-all who'd just lost his job. I was to become the boss's experiment.

Suddenly thrust into a role as manager of multimillion dollar construction projects (at a starting salary 1.5 times that of my former salary,) I was overjoyed. What's more, within six months, I was placed in charge of multiple, simultaneous projects, and was also asked to supervise *other* project managers who had been with the company for years! As for my father? After carefully considering all my talk about faith in God and of the *signs* I was being given, the old man reluctantly admitted, "Okay, okay, maybe you *are* onto something here."

## Paving Your Path with *Signs*

The subtle "signs" we receive from above let us know if we're on the right path and show us how best to proceed. These signs are best observed through the eyes of faith.

Want to benefit from a road-to-success that is paved by "signs" which make it seem as if God's grace and guidance are reserved for you and you alone? Simply place your faith in your Creator, tune into the connection between your thoughts and your world, and then pay attention to the *signs* the Universe is attempting to send you.

Below are some examples of the signs you might expect to find along your journey to greatness.

- A *knowing* you receive while in prayer or in the midst of some crisis
- A *highly-personalized, positive message* hidden in the lyrics of a song, on a billboard advertisement, on a bumper sticker, etc.
- The *timely advice* of a trusted friend, family member, coworker or even a stranger
- A sudden, energizing flash of images, a bright idea or an unexpected revelation (these are often signs which, if acted upon, lead to important insights or leaps of progress)
- A *blessing* or *opportunity* disguised as a difficulty
- A *Bible passage* or *inspirational quote* which motivates you to revolutionary action
- You may even discover a "physical sign," such as a *book* containing explicit instructions for attaining greatness and changing the world

*"I will go before you,*
*and make the crooked paths straight."*
-Isaiah 45:2

**GURU'S TIP:** You can find *signs* just about anywhere and through any number of everyday mediums, once you become open to receiving them. Heed the "signs" that direct *your* path to greatness!

## Timeless Tip #4) **Practice Changing the World—by Influencing Your Immediate Sphere of Influence**

By 1737, having conquered Philly's budding circles of commerce and haven proven himself a best-selling author, Franklin, 31, sold his business (at least temporarily) to a friend, and then undertook a career in civil service as postmaster of Philadelphia.

Although Franklin was a millionaire by age 30, he never let riches spoil him or corrupt him. In fact, Ben would go on to exhaust his 30's and 40's revolutionizing society for his fellow citizens.

Among Ben's contributions were the organization of Philadelphia's first police department, fire department, and public library. Recasting himself as a civil engineer, Franklin led the installation of the town's first paved roads and street lamps. Ben then founded a local hospital, as well as the academy that has since become the University of Pennsylvania. Some of Ben's other contributions include inventions such as: typeface, a crude hot water system, the urinary catheter, bifocal spectacles, a reusable battery, a primitive copy machine, and the common household stove.

By age 40, Franklin had already done more to improve his world than 100 average men combined!

*"For many centuries,*
*man has been using his powers*
*to change the world around him."*
-Hendrik van Loon

### Practice Changing Your World
*Impacting Your Sphere of Influence*

Like Ben, you have the power to change the world. And what better way is there to practice changing the world than by making life just a little bit better for those within your immediate *sphere of influence*; that is, those folks you live with, work or do business with, and come in contact with on a daily basis.

Below are a few small acts of kindness you can initiate to make an immediate impact on the world in which you operate.

- Buy your spouse or special someone a small, unexpected gift. Attempt to "personalize" the gift based on this person's uniqueness.
- Proactively encourage your kids about something they're into, excited about or working towards. Gain extra points for *participating* in it with them!
- Give a deserving boss, co-worker, employee, friend or neighbor a heartfelt thank you or compliment.
- Do a favor for a stranger and expect nothing in return.

**GURU'S TIP:** Start changing the world by changing your "immediate world" first!

## Timeless Tip #5) **Strive for Continuous Improvement**

Ben Franklin's mind was habitually focused on learning, growing, inventing, evolving, improving, succeeding, and giving. Ben's spirit was one of irreproachable greatness and unceasing progress.

In 1743, having exhausted himself in the mastery of more than a *dozen* different professions, Franklin expanded his mental horizons to include harnessing the forces of Nature itself. Reinventing himself as a scientist, Ben set out to confirm his suspicions that lightning was, in fact, electricity.

The year 1752 would prove to be a historical time for Franklin. Wagering his salvation against the prevailing superstition that lightning was a product of God's wrath, Ben ventured out into a thunderstorm with son, William, and raised a kite into the sky. By drawing a lightning strike to a key attached to the string of his kite, Franklin proved his theory that lightning was electricity and concocted his next revolutionary invention, "lightning rods."

Ben's lightning rods (metal spikes installed on building tops to control rogue lightning strikes) have become commonplace in modern commercial construction codes and have saved countless lives over the past 250 years.

*"All rising to greatness is by a winding stair."*
-Francis Bacon

Franklin's obsession with progress did not tarnish with age. At age 50, he played a largely undocumented role as a military commander in the French and Indian War. Then, after retiring from his military post, Ben took on a diplomatic role, and then exhausted his 60's building an elaborate network of high-level political contacts around the world.

Franklin's work as a diplomat seemed to flow forth from an almost supernaturally acute premonition of events to come. Following the outbreak of the American Revolution, Ben's political contacts would become indispensable to him in his quest to acquire the capital and assets that enabled the newly formed United States to sustain eight long years of battle against King George's army.

It was the designing of America's first known national map, however, that would become Franklin's most mysterious of feats. Using nothing more to guide his efforts than a combination of his own travels, mathematics, imagination, and the experiences of others, Ben designed a map of North America which, 200 years later, proved nearly identical to the satellite images featured on NASA's website!

**GURU'S TIP:** Ben Franklin didn't become a legend overnight. He did it incrementally, in his own time, on his own terms, and with total disregard for what the "ordinary men" who surrounded him considered *impossible*. Like Ben, you don't need a PhD to make a scientific discovery or an MBA to build a profitable business. There's no rule that says you can't change careers at 40…or even 60. And there's nothing stopping you from mastering a dozen different industries, instruments or languages, if that's what you aspire to do.

The only obstacles standing between you and greatness are your *own* aspirations and your *next* big move.

## Timeless Tip #6) **Achieve "Mastermindification"**

What's "mastermindification" you ask? In the pursuit of every dream or noble cause, there comes a point at which you wouldn't think of turning back, a moment at which your outcome as you foresee it graduates from a high probability to an inevitable reality suspended momentarily in time. To pass this "point of no return" in any pursuit or endeavor is to achieve *mastermindification.*

It can be said that Ben Franklin's role as one of America's most important Founding Fathers was scorched into the canvas of history during one particular moment of swift decision-making in the years *preceding* the revolution.

In 1770, Franklin was a 64 year-old grandfather and had already lived a remarkable life. Ben could've been content to retire, secure in the knowledge that he'd served his Creator and fellows as well as anyone who'd ever lived. Later that year, however, Samuel Adams, Ben's young friend from Boston, instigated an uprising of colonists against King George's abusive taxation practices. Before long, a bloody clash ensued between Boston colonists and the British soldiers who were currently policing the colonies. Sensing that the time was right to organize a full-scale revolt against the occupier, Adams beseeched the aging Franklin to put his brains, capital, and connections behind the cause of American independence.

After deliberating for weeks over a commitment to treason (a crime punishable by death,) Franklin became certain in his conviction that a revolution would serve the greater good of his fellow colonists. It was then that Franklin tossed away his walking stick and started planning not just for war, but for certain victory.

Between 1770 and 1775, Ben Franklin became committed to championing the cause of a free America. While operating behind the scenes and in total secrecy, Franklin went to work forming secret alliances with his political contacts at home and abroad, co-engineering a federal infrastructure, designing new money, acquiring capital to finance a lengthy battle, and convincing British agents to turn spy. The Boston Tea Party was staged and the Continental Congress was formed. By the time colonists across the east coast began joining the uprising, there would be nothing that King George's army would be able to do to stop it.

The American Revolution had evolved from an unlikely possibility, to a high probability…to an inevitable reality suspended momentarily in time.

In short, *mastermindification* had occurred.

*"We are very near to greatness, one step and we are safe. Can we not take the leap?"*
-Ralph Waldo Emerson

**GURU'S TIP:** Obsessively pursue your own glorious causes until you pass the point of no return, and wouldn't think of turning back. Achieve mastermindification!

## Timeless Tip #7) **Trust the Rule of Suspended Returns**

Ben Franklin made a large philanthropic investment before he passed. After earning interest over many years, Ben's investment grew to $7 million before being dispersed according to his will among the needy of his hometowns of Philadelphia and Boston.

As Franklin's rise to prominence has shown, attaining greatness and changing the world requires an "up-front investment" in the form of effort.

Fortunately, there's a universal law of success that enables us to cash-in tomorrow on stored-up benefits that accrue from an investment in focused efforts made today.

It's called the *Rule of Suspended Returns*.

Let me explain how it works…

*"Great events oft take their rise of small affairs."*
-Ben Franklin

In a company I once worked for, it became widely known that I enjoy helping people. One night, while working late, I heard a knock at the door to my office. It was Minnie, our janitor.

"What's up, Minnie?" I asked from behind my desk.

Mop in hand, Minnie stated bluntly, "Mr. John, I need more money to care for my family."

"Are you looking for a raise?"

"No, no, Mr. John. I want another job. A *better* job."

"What do you want to do?" I queried.

"Minnie shrugged. "Yo no se (I don't know)."

"Well, let's say you win the lottery, and no longer have to work," I posed. "What would you do simply because you *enjoy* doing it?"

Minnie smiled proudly. "I would write my stories. My children love when I read them the bedtime stories I write. I also love to draw."

Logically, I asked, "Ever consider writing a children's book?"

"Si, Mr. John. Many times. But—I need more money, *now.*"

"By starting a book, you *will* be making more money, *now.*"

Minnie was puzzled. "Mr. John, how is that possible?"

"The Rule of Suspended Returns," I explained. "Think of your dreams and goals as purchases made on an installment plan. The efforts you exert today in pursuit of your desired outcomes are like 'payments' which carry an actual cash value. And every payment brings you one step closer to owning your desired outcomes."

"So, starting a book…is like making money?"

"Every brainstorming session. Every word you put to paper. And every chapter you complete. It's like paying off an ideal reality suspended momentarily in time. And when the time is right and your work is complete, you'll be compensated for your effort, all in one bulk sum."

Minnie's eyes widened with excitement.

Over the next nine months, Minnie worked nights as our janitor while devoting a couple of hours each day to writing a children's book. Minnie's efforts netted her a multi-book deal for $30,000 (about equal to her annual salary) and a lucrative offer to continue creating illustrations at her leisure!

*"Great things are done not at once,*
*but by a series of small things brought together."*
-Vincent van Gogh

**GURU'S TIP:** The Rule of Suspended Returns assures that your dreams and goals are realities suspended momentarily in time.

Every small effort you make today in the direction of your dreams and goals is like making "payments" on the ultimate cost of the ideal realities of your choosing.

*Purchase* your destiny as you choose to define it at the manageable cost of small, daily efforts!

## Guide to Greatness

*The Final Word*

You now have a step-by-step Guide to Greatness as demonstrated by the mighty Ben Franklin.

Perhaps you're beginning to sense your spirit of greatness awakening within you as Franklin's did shortly after his arrival in Philadelphia as a teenage runaway. And maybe, just maybe, you are arriving at an understanding of the explosive energies that have been lying dormant inside you, waiting to be unleashed on the world in which you operate.

Well, know this: You can fulfill your dreams. You can become as great as you want to be. You can even change the world.

But first, you've got to *believe*...

# Harness the Force of Belief

*The 4$^{th}$ Element of the Dream Acquisition Formula (DAF)*

John Echols

# 19

# The Force of Belief

*Governing Force of Human Experience*

*"Verily, I say unto you,*
*that if you believe and do not doubt...*
*you will be able to say to this mountain,*
*'Get up, and throw yourself into the sea,'*
*and it shall come to pass."*
-Jesus Christ
(Matthew 21:21)

The *force of belief* governs virtually every facet of the broad spectrum of human experience. To harness this potent force of mental and physical energy is to gain greater control over every area of your life, career, relationships, and finances.

You are about to begin this process…

In this chapter, we'll expose the origins of belief. We'll examine some of your own beliefs, and show you how to begin operating strictly according to those beliefs that benefit and empower you. You'll learn about perspective, the "mental filter" which shapes your world. You'll discover how to use the *science of expectations* to your advantage. Then you'll find out how to begin using your belief system to your benefit going forward.

Let's start with the basics.

# The 7 Origins of Belief

Your "beliefs" can be defined as tenets you ascribe to, highly guarded views or messages you tell yourself, personal or religious doctrines, or governing principles you hold to be true and meaningful.

Your beliefs regulate just about everything you do on a daily basis. Sadly, while our beliefs regulate nearly every area our lives, for better or worse, few of us stop to consider how our beliefs are formed.

So, where do your beliefs come from? Your beliefs originate from just seven, primary sources:

(1) **Childhood:** A child's brain is like a new computer that's been programmed to download new environmental data from morning to night. The easily influenced, highly programmable mind of a child is the result of a combination of low-frequency (or delta, theta and alpha) brain waves and the trust kids place in their "programmers;" that is, their caregivers.

As a result of your *own* eager mind and trusting heart as a child, you, too, "downloaded" many of the beliefs of your parents or caregivers, for better or worse.

(2) **Family and Friends**: Throughout your life, family and friends continue to play a major role in the shaping of your beliefs and personality, due largely to the trust you place in these people and the considerable time you spend with them.

Einstein once asserted that most people are incapable of forming opinions that differ from those of family and friends.

We'll make sure that *you* are among the few who *can.*

(3) **Academic and Professional Origins:** Teachers, professors, instructors, and classmates help form your views and perceptions; as do your bosses, mentors, business partners, and coworkers. Academic curriculums and company cultures also play a significant role in the beliefs you choose to adopt.

There's a good chance that you are a detectable byproduct of the schools you've attended and the places you've worked.

(4) **Entertainment:** A portion of your perception is conditioned by the movies and television shows you watch, the music and radio programs you listen to, the books and magazines you read, and the events you attend.

Multi-sensory engaging sources of entertainment can be especially suggestive. For instance, an uplifting movie or tear-jerking opera can have a huge impact on your views about life, love or loss.

(5) **Marketers:** The top consumer product companies spend $25 billion every year in a frenzied attempt to win your loyalties and dollars.

Something as harmless as a box of cereal is actually a clever tool comprised of funny characters, "loaded messages," and emotion-evoking colors designed to influence your perception and convince you, and your kids, to choose their product.

Ever catch yourself recommending a product by insisting, "This or that is supposed to be really good," just because a company's television or radio commercial said so? If so, you now realize how easily your devotions can be manipulated and bought.

Just a friendly tip: For marketers, swaying your interest is a full-time job!

(6) **Church and Media:** Don't make the mistake of believing that religious and news organizations are *unbiased* and cater strictly to *your* best interests. Remember, if churchgoers stopped going to church and forking over donations, and news buffs quit watching the news and buying newspapers, these organizations would fold.

The primary concern of churches (aside from doing God's work) and media outlets is organizational survival. And guess whose dollars and loyalties these entities need to continue thriving?

(7) **Yourself!** Astonishingly enough, most of us spend our entire lives never discovering our own uniquely human ability to intelligently choose our *own* beliefs.

What, you missed the memo, too? Well, here's a news-flash with substance. You can, and should, exercise your God-given ability to ascribe strictly to those beliefs that benefit and empower you. Become your own "source of origin" by making everything from your views to your values a conscious, intelligent choice based on your unique dreams, goals, priorities, and responsibilities.

When should you begin this process? There's no time like the present!

## Becoming Your Own "Source of Origin"

My studies of the early lives of hundreds of the world's peak performers has shown that many super-achievers did not start out with the empowering beliefs that propelled them to the top of their respective fields. It was often only after coming to the realization that their long-held disempowering beliefs were holding them back—and making a *conscious* decision to adopt new, empowering beliefs, instead—that these masters of circumstance found the power to realize their true potential and achieve greatness.

If you want to begin operating according to a consciously constructed belief system which consistently acts in *your* best interests, three things must take place:

(1) What you choose to believe in must become a *conscious* decision.

(2) You must become acutely aware of the individuals and companies that are vying for your loyalties and dollars on a daily basis.

(3) You must ascribe only to those beliefs that benefit and empower you.

*"In order to be successful,*
*we must have a sound set of beliefs*
*on which to premise all of our policies and actions."*
-Frank Purdue

## Perspective

*The "Mental Filter" That Shapes Your Existence*

Your perspective acts as the "mental filter" between you and your world. This *mental filter* regulates the quality, or lack thereof, of virtually every aspect of your life, career, relationships, and finances.

*"Beauty exists in the mind which contemplates it."*
-David Hume

To better understand how our perspective shapes the quality of our existence, consider the starkly different life experiences of four individuals, each of whom were born with the genetic abnormality known as "dwarfism."

Matt, a "little person" in his 30's, long-considered his condition a curse and despised the attention it brought him. Matt's perception fostered anti-social behavior, feelings of inadequacy, and abusive drinking. Regularly drunk, often angry, and sometimes violent, Matt never failed to attract negative attention whenever he dared to leave his unkempt apartment. Matt passed away prematurely of complications related to heart disease and organ failure.

Salvatore and Marcy are a married couple who own a successful bakery. Sal and Marcy stay far too busy nurturing their relationship and running their business to fret about challenges of height. In fact, Sal and Marcy have together spent several years positioning their business as a leading producer of customized, gourmet chocolate sculptures. As a result, theirs is an existence defined by love and happiness, by sales and profits, and by the countless satisfied customers they serve.

Then there's Lisa, a smart, ambitious mother who as a child suffered grave medical complications as a result of her dwarfism. However, refusing to allow her condition or multiple surgeries to stifle her potential, Lisa has channeled her intellect and passions into becoming a physician. Lisa now spends her days doing what she loves—raising her family and helping *others* overcome illness!

So, how is it that four individuals who suffer from the same "genetic disadvantage" could encounter such vastly different life experiences?

It boils down to beliefs and perceptions.

*Disempowering* beliefs lead to a distorted mental filter which can transform a life of unlimited opportunities into one of "insurmountable challenges." On the other hand, *empowering* beliefs enable us to generate the rose-colored mental filter that enables us to convert a life of difficult challenges into one of ever-blossoming opportunities. Have you been allowing false or limiting beliefs like, *my earning potential stops at this point, I'll never lose that much weight, that's one habit I'll never overcome,* or *I'm not good enough for such and such,* to fog up your mental lens?

If so, change those counterproductive philosophies and start seeing life through a rose-colored perspective!

*"It is by believing in roses that one brings them to bloom."*
-French Proverb

**GURU'S TIP:** It sometimes takes an awareness of the struggles of others, and their superior point of view in spite of their challenges, to put our own "problems" and distorted views into perspective.

## Expectations

*A Force as Potent as Drugs*

Like our perception, our hopes and expectations are expressions of the core beliefs that underline them.

Your expectations can be viewed as a form of faith in an anticipated result. Just how reliable are our expectations in regard to facilitating a correlating outcome? A study conducted by Dr. Irving Kirsch, professor of psychology at the University of Hull, suggests that what we *expect* to happen can be about as reliable as the effects of prescription drugs.

In 2008, Dr. Kirsch, conducted an eye-opening study on the effects of antidepressant drugs. During a study that included 38 clinical trials involving 3,000 "clinically depressed" persons, Kirsch measured the effects of six commonly used antidepressant compounds, as compared to the *perceived effects* of harmless placebos.

Kirsch discovered that 75% of the patients could not tell the difference between the actual effects of the antidepressant drugs and the faux effects of sugar pills!

In spite of Kirsch's study, 30 million Americans (roughly 10% of the population) continue to swear by these drugs. According to a report by *Scientific American* in 2014, antidepressants remain the third most frequently taken medication in the United States.

So, what accounts for the disconnect between the "magical effects" that antidepressant consumers *claim* these pills produce, and what independent research *shows* they produce? This disconnect can be largely attributed to the *hopes* and *expectations* of those that label themselves "depressed" and desperately want these pills to work.

*"Believe that your life is worth living,*
*and your belief will help create that fact."*
-Dr. William James

Your expectations about a drug you may be using, an exercise program you may be undertaking, or a goal you may be pursuing, represent a neurophysiological operation that can influence—or outright control—your outcomes, for better or worse.

Your expectations about a result can even activate or inhibit your biological processes under entirely *false* pretenses, as is evidenced by numerous clinical studies in which participants who are told that they are being given drugs experience the anticipated symptoms associated with those drugs, although he or she is actually ingesting a harmless sugar pill!

Simply put, we are programmed at the molecular level to bring about the results we expect to receive.

*"Because of your faith, you shall be healed."*
-Jesus Christ

**GURU'S TIP:** Your perspective and expectations are potent forces of natural energy by which you can work wonders in your life, if you will but manage them intelligently and give them the reverence they are due.

You can waste your life away waiting for a "magic pill" that will solve all of your problems and motivate you to peak performance. Or, you can leverage the mental operations of perspective and expectations by interpreting your world in the best possible light, and anticipating spectacular results in all that you set your mind to.

But don't take too long deciding, for the quality of your tomorrows hangs in the balance.

## What You Believe Determines What You'll Receive

In 1894, the U S. treasury held just under $100 million in its vaults, more than enough to run the government and back its bonds. However, when a rumor began sweeping through Washington, D.C., and then across the eastern seaboard, that the Treasury needed a *minimum* of $100 million just to ensure liquidity for its bonds, alarmed investors across the country began a headlong stampede to cash in their bond drafts. By January of 1895, government coffers held only $45 million. Just four weeks later, only $10 million was left.

The Treasury was suddenly facing a full-fledged economic meltdown, sparked not by an inability to satisfy its bonds, but by investors' *mistaken beliefs* about a supposed financial crisis! But wait—it gets deeper.

In an attempt to sway public perception and avert an economic collapse, the treasury secretary negotiated the unconditional financial backing of banking mogul, J. P. Morgan. As soon as measures were taken to inform the public of Morgan's voucher in the "magic amount" of, you guessed it, $100 million, investor confidence returned, and the crisis ended.

*"The thing always happens that you really believe in."*
-Frank Lloyd Wright

The lesson? The U.S. banking crisis of 1895 was created and brought to an end by the same underlying force—the force of belief.

It didn't matter whether those beliefs were right or wrong.

Similarly, what we believe in our mind and heart, whether those beliefs are disempowering or empowering, will determine, to a large degree, what results we will receive in our own life, career, relationships, and finances. This is why it is so important to make what we believe in a conscious and intelligent choice.

Okay, you're now in a better position than ever before to manage the relationship between your belief system and your outcomes.

Next, let's move on to a unique, interactive chapter designed to test and strengthen your "moral fiber"…

# 20

# The Test of Moral Fiber

*Do You Have What it Takes to Pass the Test?*

*"If you will but arouse in yourself this fierce, ardent, insatiable desire, you will set into operation one of Nature's most potent mental forces."*
-Robert Collier

What's "moral fiber?" We can discover our answer in a story about the struggles and triumphs of boxing great, Jack Johnson…

Born in Galveston, Texas in 1878, Jack Johnson was the son of two former slaves. Jack's parents—a dishwasher and a janitor—encouraged their son to get an education. In spite of his parent's well-intentioned admonition, however, Jack, a headstrong youngster, decided to quit school after the fifth grade to go to work instead. It was during his teens that Johnson developed bold dreams of a career in boxing. At the time, there were a couple of major obstacles that stood between Johnson and his ideal career:

- Johnson was a black teenager during a time of racial segregation.
- The boxing establishment of the late 19th century didn't exactly lay out the welcome mat for black athletes.

Largely because Johnson's mother reinforced in him that he was loved and able to achieve anything he set his mind to, Jack never considered either the slim chances of going pro, or the enormous odds against going pro *black.*

Johnson would go on to exhaust his teens training under any coach who would have him. Convinced that he had what it took to be a top contender, Johnson tuned out his so-called disadvantages in education, finances, and color, focused on becoming the champ, and trained with intensity. After taking his first pro fight in 1898 at the age of 20, Jack began fighting his way into the limelight while being booed by crowds and denied prize purses by unscrupulous promoters who were eager to see Johnson quit. Instead of quitting, however, Jack fought harder…and kept on winning.

On December 4, 1908, in front of a packed arena, Johnson received his just dues when he made history by becoming boxing's first black, heavyweight world-champion!

Jack Johnson's victory of fame and fortune against unimaginable odds provides us with a perfect example of what I refer to as "moral fiber." *Moral fiber* can be defined as the combined force of your intellect, character, values, and spirit.

A few things you can do to develop this multi-faceted attribute include:

**(1)Flex your Intellectual Muscle**

- Learn to decipher *useful information* from disposable opinion.
- Be able to separate those who have your best interests at heart from those who may be harboring ulterior motives.

**(2)Build Character**

- Do your *own* thinking, researching, questioning, comparing, and deciding to arrive at your *own* conclusions.
- Exercise the audacity to choose your *own* beliefs.
- Have the sense to abandon those tenets you discover to be based on false logic or limited thinking.

**(3) Clarify Your Values**

- Determine what is, and is not, important to you.

**(4) Exercise Your Spirit**

- Summon the courage to demand the best life has to offer.
- Be willing to fight for what you believe in should the occasion arise.
- Pursue individuality. Express yourself as you see fit, and favor your unique preferences, regardless of what others might think.

Think you've got what it takes to command your thoughts and beliefs, to be your own man or woman, and to remain unscathed by the host of external forces that seek to pull you this way and that?

Then it's time to take the test of moral fiber.

## The Test of Moral Fiber

The following interactive assessment is designed to help expose your current level of *moral fiber* and get you on the road to strengthening it. Answer each question honestly. And keep in mind that this assessment is not about passing or failing; it's simply an exercise in self-awareness, and a tool for self-improvement.

Taken seriously, the following questions and suggestions will likely lead you to some new insights and help you to unlock those stubborn areas of your mind which have yet to be set free.

• Do you develop your views and decisions about earning and investing based on the earning potential and investment strategies of family and friends?

If so, are these people wealthy enough to model in these areas? If not, where might you find *better* models?

• Did you set exciting, new financial goals as part of your vision Master List? Have you already begun to figure out ways by which to make these goals real?

If so, you are well on your way to financial freedom. If not, take a moment to consider a few of the strategies by which you will reach your financial objectives.

• Do you consider yourself a "smart shopper?" Do you often purchase items that are 50% of the quality of premium products—in order to save 25% on price? Do you buy things you don't need (and will likely never use) simply because they're "on sale?" Do you regularly pay list-price, or do you negotiate down an item's asking price? Do you conduct your own market research by comparing prices, quality, features, warranty options, and service ratings before buying?

If you enjoy shopping, what are three ways in which you can become a much *smarter* shopper?

• Do you vote the same political party, use the same doctor, visit the same vacation spots, practice the same religion, drive the same car or live in the same school district as your parents?

Three or more *yeses* may indicate a stifled character. If you fall into this category, devise three ways in which you can exercise your *originality!*

• Would you "vehemently defend" the wrongdoings of a total stranger? Have you ever defended the publicly-exposed wrongdoings of a favorite celebrity, politician, athlete or some other *total stranger*?

• When watching your favorite sitcom, does the integrated laugh-track cue you to laughter the way canines once salivated to the sound of Pavlov's bell?

If you're not aware of the laugh-track, you should probably visit your vet—I mean, your optometrist. Your *mind* likely needs glasses!

• List the order in which you would consider doing a favor for the following: Spouse/lover. Needy animal. Boss. Friend. Child. Senior. Homeless person. Stranger. Coworker. Neighbor. Sibling. Celebrity. What does your list reveal to you about your hierarchy of values, or your relationships?

• Do you regularly read the newspaper and/or watch the news? If so, when was the last time you were truly enlightened by a columnist, or benefited from a real-time traffic or Doppler radar report?

Media sources are driven by doom and gloom, offer little useless information, and depend on ratings based on viewers with nothing better to do.

Try substituting your "news time" with an extra hour of sleep, a walk outdoors or a book cerebrally stimulating enough to replace the IQ points you likely lost…while watching the news!

• Can you name a dozen people for whom you would do anything? How about a dozen principles you'd fight for? What makes these people or principles so important to you?

• Are you locked into a single, narrow genre of favorite songs and bands? Or does your intellectual prowess and bold taste require an expansive playlist of songs and bands in multiple genres?

• Do you continue to operate according to the childish nicknames or defeating labels you were "assigned" in grade school or high school?

If so, isn't it time for a change?

• Would you rather donate money to an animal shelter or a homeless shelter? What underlying beliefs influence this decision?

• When was the last time you *disagreed* with someone? If you feel comfortable disagreeing with others (excluding your spouse,) and can articulate logical, informed reasons *why* you disagree, you exhibit strong moral fiber!

• In the past, have you settled for second-rate jobs, friends, lovers, merchandise, service, etc., because you believed you didn't deserve—or couldn't attain—"first-class?" If so, how might you upgrade to a *first-class* life experience?

• Do you have trouble voicing your thoughts, views or opinions in group settings? If so, try the following exercise during your next business meeting or social gathering.

Play the role of "expert" by starting a conversation on an issue about which you are well-informed. Articulate your views by using convincing facts, figures, analogies, and stories which support your position.

Make an effort to exercise your spirit and gain more say-so in a group dynamic.

• If you found a wallet or pocketbook (including the owner's ID) on the sidewalk, and inside of it was an envelope filled with $5,000, which would you do? Keep the cash and return everything else to its owner? Return the entire item to its rightful owner and hope for a reward? Or, return the entire item to its rightful owner and hope that someone would do the same for you?

• If someone "invades your personal space"—as people sometimes do while in conversation, in line at the store, and so on—do you typically (a) grin and bear it, (b) retreat to create an acceptable distance, or (c) politely insist that your *space invader* move to an appropriate distance?

If you picked (c,) I'm impressed. And you should be, too.

• Do you consider the *source* of the "facts" given to you in conversation? You should. Approximately 75% of what others tell you in conversation is either false, inaccurate or based on *their* opinion!

• Do you support racism? Are you in favor of "affirmative action" policies? These policies designate minimum hiring quotas for minorities, and offer minorities favoritism on academic entrance exams and in professional recruitment processes based on the applicant's race, instead of on qualifications and performance.

If you support affirmative action, you support racism.

• Do you adhere to the strict dogmas of a region just because you were born into it? If so, do you at least refrain from frowning upon those who practice other religions which they, too, were born into?

• Do you have trouble saying, "no?" If so, you are in danger of becoming a doormat to everyone you meet. Practice saying, *No…Nope…Not today…No thanks…Not a chance…Not in this lifetime!* Do it just for the moral exercise it provides.

• Do you believe that all criminals are inherently "bad people?" Are you aware that Ben Franklin, George Washington, and 54 other principled anarchists founded the United States through an epic act of *treason?*

What similar mistaken beliefs do you need to update or discard?

• If your boss asked you to do him or her a "favor" that involved signing a customer's signature to an undisclosed document, which of the following would most resemble your response? (1) Attempt to negotiate a benefit by complying. (2) Comply under the guise of "subordination." (3) Politely decline. (4) Decline with indignation. (5) Start the search for a more ethical employer.

Want an approximate estimate—on a scale from 1 to 10—of your current level of character? Simply multiply the *number* of your answer by 2.

Well, how'd you do? Have you identified some areas in which you display exceptional *moral fiber*? Have you also uncovered a few areas in which either your intellect, character, values or spirit could use some improvement?

Good news! You'll find plenty of strategies for strengthening your moral fiber, in one way or another, in coming chapters.

*"The belief that becomes truth for me…*
*is that which allows me the best use of my strength,*
*the best means of putting my virtues into action."*
-Andre Gide

Now, it's time to begin ascending the ladder of Self-power to a more confident you…

# 21

# Building Your Self-power

*Ascending the Ladder to a More Confident You!*

*"Faith in oneself is the best and safest course."*
-Michelangelo

Frank Sinatra was born on December 12, 1915, in Hoboken, New Jersey. Sinatra grew up in a gritty neighborhood comprised of low-rent tenements and bustling factories. By age 12, Frank had developed a reputation as a class clown. He also hung out on street corners and enjoyed a good street fight. In fact, the only thing Frank liked more than a good fist fight, oddly enough, was singing.

It was as a sophomore in high school in 1930, while most of his friends were battling acne and discovering the opposite sex, that Sinatra, 15, began envisioning what he would do with the rest of his life. For Frank, the decision was easy. He wanted to become a singer. So, emulating the same strategy that young Abe Lincoln used to learn the legal ropes, Sinatra looked to current entertainers to learn how to think, speak, and act like a star.

Frank particularly liked to study his hero, Bing Crosby.

Standing at the mirror in his bedroom, the aspiring heartthrob practiced Crosby's dance moves, vocal styles, song lyrics, and personal mannerisms. Frank even started dressing like Bing. And the more Sinatra practiced, the more certainty he developed that he had what it took to become an entertainer.

Sinatra was just 16 when he came home from school, proclaimed to his parents that he wanted to become an entertainer, and then convinced his parents to let him quit school so that he could pursue his chosen destiny.

While continuing to emulate the day's current heartthrobs, Sinatra took a part-time job delivering newspapers. Although the gig paid peanuts, it offered him something he valued more than money and education combined—the flexible hours he needed to perfect his song and dance routine.

*"Self-trust is the first secret to success."*
-Ralph Waldo Emerson

Throughout 1931 and 1932, Sinatra spent his days working for ridiculous wages, his nights crooning for his girlfriend, Nancy, and every moment in between auditioning for the big break he was sure his talents would one day land him.

Sinatra was unusually confident for a teenage dropout.

Frank's bold sense of self-worth could be seen in his piercing blue eyes, heard in his golden singing voice, and felt in the way he treated his peers not only as friends, but also as fans. In fact, Frank's smile, charm, and charisma became the magic combination that opened doors for him everywhere he went.

The first of those doors opened when Sinatra was just 17.

It was during a one-time audition for a popular radio talent show (an audition Frank landed by beating out 10,000 other applicants!) that Sinatra wooed the radio show host, as well as the audience, with his smooth vocals and magnetic personality. Following his performance, Frank propositioned the host for additional appearances. Although the host insisted that the deal was based on a one-time gig, Frank persisted. Using charm and the promise of packed venues as his bargaining chips, Sinatra finagled himself a 90-day contract to sing as part of a quartet at a series of venues around Jersey, and beyond.

The tour earned Frank local celebrity and further fortified his sense of certainty that he could do anything he set his mind to.

*"Self-confidence is the first requisite to great undertakings."*
-Dr. Samuel Johnson

On a fateful night in 1933, while attending one of Bing Crosby's final appearances as a lounge singer, Sinatra found just the incentive he needed to take his dream of becoming a professional entertainer to the next level.

As Bing Crosby commanded the stage, Sinatra, 17, sat on the edge of his front-row seat, studying his hero's every move with captivated attention. Nancy, who flanked Frank's side, couldn't help noticing the intensity with which Frank was studying Bing. It was then that something occurred to Nancy. Sinatra wasn't just enjoying Crosby's performance—he was *absorbing* Bing's *experience* as the star of the show. By the night's end, Sinatra's desire to take the stage could no longer be contained. "If Bing can do it," decided Crosby's gutsy admirer, "*so can I!*"

Over the next few years, as Bing Crosby made a transition to Hollywood films, Frank Sinatra joined a traveling band, cut a solo record, and then began taking his idol's place on the stages of amphitheaters in New York, Vegas, and Los Angeles.

By 1940, Sinatra, 25, found himself gazing out into the bright lights and excited faces of his own, loyal audiences. The charismatic kid from Hoboken was, at last, living his dream as the nation's newest singing sensation.

*"Nothing splendid has ever happened except by those who dared to believe that something inside themselves was superior to circumstances."*
-Bruce Barton

Frank Sinatra was a "gifted" entertainer. However, his *greatest gift* was neither his mesmerizing voice, nor his captivating dance moves. It was his ability to recognize his voice and moves as valuable and to leverage his talents in expediting his willful transition from high school dropout to mega-entertainer.

Sinatra's most important gift…was *Self-power!*

## The Skinny on Self-power

**What exactly is "Self-power?"** *Self-power* is the unshakable belief that you can do anything and everything you set your mind to.

Self-power was the source of Frank Sinatra's ability to transform himself from teenage dropout at age 16, to professional vocalist in his 20's, to Oscar winning actor (and co-star to his hero, Bing Crosby!) during his 30's and 40's, to mega entertainer of shows attended by 30,000-fan audiences during his 50's and 60's.

Self-power is the voice that screams out from inside, "Yes, I can! I *will* succeed. I'll learn the things I need to know, and do the things I need to do, to get to the places I want to go and make my dreams come true. And there isn't a person or obstacle on this Earth that can stop me!"

For the person who possesses Self-power, the world is a vast playground of unlimited opportunity.

> *"Immense power is acquired by assuring yourself in your secret reveries that you were born to control affairs."*
> -Andrew Carnegie

## Exposing the "Simple Secret" of Self-power

In 1952, a young doctor named Albert Mason was becoming quite a sensation around England's Queen Victoria Hospital due to his self-taught skill in curing wart infestations through hypnosis.

Dr. Mason's pioneering success in the realm of mind-medicine instilled the doctor with steadfast confidence that he could perform his medical magic on any patient who walked through the door. So, when a surgeon named Dr. Moore conferred with Mason about a 15 year-old boy whose torso was entirely covered with warts, Mason was up for the challenge.

Mason, however, had no idea what he was getting himself into…

*"To live without belief is a fate worse than dying."*
-Joan of Arc

Dr. Mason immediately began working with one of the boy's arms. After placing the boy under hypnosis, Mason employed the art of suggestion to convince his patient that the entire arm would return to health. As expected, the affected area scabbed up and gave way to new, healthy skin. Eager to boast of his success in curing the worst case of warts he'd ever seen, Dr. Mason returned the boy to the referring surgeon. That's when Dr. Mason received the shock of a lifetime.

"Mason, these aren't warts," explained the surgeon upon examination of the boy's cured arm. "This is congenital ichthyosis, [a rare and deadly skin disease from which there is no known cure.]"

Dr. Mason had used raw mental powers to facilitate a true-life, medical miracle!

How did Mason manage to *cure* an "incurable disease?" Simple. Information about the boy's true condition had somehow gone unspoken during Mason's initial encounter with Dr. Moore. As a result, Mason *believed* that he was treating warts and his faith in his ability to do so gave him the power to provide a cure.

But wait: That's only part of Mason's stunning story…

*"His supreme agony was the disappearance of certainty."*
-Victor Hugo

As word spread about Dr. Mason's "miracle cure," droves of other sufferers of ichthyosis were carted to the doctor's office for help. But strangely, Mason was no longer able to perform his medical magic with the same degree of precision.

So, why the sudden loss of power?

During an interview with the Discovery Health Channel in 2003, Mason attributed his inability to replicate, with other patients, the success he'd had with the boy to his lack of faith in himself. You see, when Mason was treating the boy, he *believed* that he was treating warts. However, once the doctor discovered that he was, in fact, treating a disease labeled "incurable," Mason's broken confidence thwarted his power to provide further cures!

The "simple secret" of Self-power is this: What you *believe* about your own powers and potential becomes *fact!*

## How Do *You* Measure Up on Self-power?

Are you a Self-powered Mind Contrologist? Do you believe you've got the ability to do anything and everything you set your mind to? Do you possess the heightened level of confidence with which miracles of personal performance are made?

Below, is a quick assessment designed to help you identify just how much *Self-power* you currently possess.

• Are you modest…to a fault? A little humility goes a long way, but too much may prevent you from going anywhere at all!

• Do you allow negative people at work or in social settings to take up too much of your time? Or do you quickly disassociate yourself from anyone who "brings you down?"

• Are you intimidated by your college-educated colleagues? Don't be. America's institutions of higher learning are a for-profit industry which hands out degrees to anyone who can pay tuition and keep from flunking out. As much as 90% of all college curricula are "filler material." About 49.9% of all students graduate closer to the *bottom* of the class than the top. And as much as 70% of college grads do not work in their field of study. What's more, some of the most unmotivated folks I've employed possessed college degrees.

Didn't go to college? Simply educate yourself and work hard. This leads to career progression about as often as paid-for diplomas.

• Do you automatically assume that everyone who is *older* than you is also *wiser* than you? Generally speaking, is a hard-working 25 year-old janitor not wiser than a 50 year-old wino?

• When reading or studying, and you come across a word you're not familiar with, do you usually (a) pretend you never saw it, (b) ask someone you trust for the definition, or (c) dart to the nearest dictionary?

If you've chosen (b) or (c,) your Self-power is alive and kicking.

• Do you readily abandon habits that serve you no purpose of good or make you feel bad? Or are you highly ritualistic, carrying out the same habits you've been carrying out for years, regardless of whether these habits hold you back or make you feel lousy?

If the latter sounds more like you, return to the *"7 Pillars of Mind Control!"* Revisit Pillar #2, "*Harness the Power of Redirection!*" and begin transforming habit energy into Self-power!

• When in a group, do you more often play the role of follower or leader?

• Are you intimidated by the opposite sex?

• Do you feel compassion for those who are mentally, physically or financially less fortunate than you? Self-powered legends of the past and present virtually all share the trait of *compassion* in common.

• Do you shy away from challenges or eagerly take them on? If you love a good challenge, you are brimming with Self-power.

• Would you rather pay a $10 tip than wait in an hour-long line? You should. Your time is worth more than $10 an hour, is it not?

• Has it been a while since you've learned something new? Or do you regularly "self-educate" by reading books, magazines or trade journals; referring to the internet; attending seminars or webinars; watching educational programs; questioning people in the know; and/or engaging in deep discussions with colleagues and friends?

If you're an aggressive *self-educator*, you are among an elite group of Self-powered leaders. This diverse group includes: Jesus Christ, Niccolo Machiavelli, Bill Gates, Walt Disney, and Donald Trump.

• Do you readily admit when you're wrong? Doing so builds Self-power.

• Finally, if you were on an overseas flight and both the pilot and copilot fell suddenly ill, would you possess enough confidence and courage to man the cockpit? If so, you've got Self-power of the highest altitude. From now on, I'm flying with *you!*

"Only those means of security are good,
are certain, are lasting,
which depend upon you and your own vigor."
-Niccolo Machiavelli

If you've answered the questions above, you should have a pretty good idea of where you stand in terms of *Self-power.*

Building more faith in who you are and what you can do will require doing things like practicing confidence (even if, at first, it seems like you're faking,) educating yourself and *applying* your newfound knowledge to real-life situations, heightening your awareness of all that is truly magnificent about you, becoming increasingly pro-social, growing in self-trust by making wise decisions that serve you well, and getting comfortable "chatting up" your strengths, accomplishments, and plans to others.

The rest of this chapter is devoted to increasing your Self-power...

## Victory Talk

*The Verbal Pathway to Unspeakable Power!*

*"You are who you declare yourself to be;*
*a matter wholly under your control."*
-Dr. Stanton Peele

Want to begin amplifying your Self-power, almost overnight? Become a "Victory Talker."

**What's "Victory Talk?"** *Victory Talk* is the habit of:

- Speaking comfortably about your abilities, qualities, and accomplishments
- Making declarations and predictions about your forthcoming achievements
- Labeling and branding yourself in the best possible terms

Victory Talk isn't about arrogance or putting others down. It's simply boldness in communicating to the world who you are, what you're made of, where you're headed, and what you intend to accomplish.

Ever watch a television show host interview a star who responds with confidence and excitement when asked about his or her life and career? The star speaks comfortably when discussing his or her current interests, latest good fortunes, and upcoming projects. This is the skill of Victory Talk in its most polished form.

It's also a brilliant display of Self-power.

## Victory Talk Provides the *Winning Edge*

*"I work harder than anyone who has ever lived."*
-Michelangelo

It was shortly after migrating to the U.S. during the 1960s that 6-time Mr. Olympia, Arnold Schwarzenegger, used Victory Talk to gain a winning edge over body-building adversary, Lou Ferrigno.

In an incident Schwarzenegger refers to as "psychological warfare," Arnold shared an *innocent* meal with Ferrigno and his father, shortly before Arnold and Lou were to face off against each other in the IFBB Olympia competition. While Ferrigno was trying to enjoy his meal, Schwarzenegger began confounding Lou with bold declarations and predictions about his inevitable, forthcoming Olympia victory. Arnold even referred to himself as a "7-time Mr. Olympia" although Schwarzenegger was, at the time, only a 6-time, Olympia winner.

Ferrigno was further befuddled after the contest when Schwarzenegger's Self-powered Victory Declarations proved true!

Reflecting back on his ascension to his tenure atop the throne of the IFBB, Arnold once revealed, "I knew I was a winner back in the late sixties. I knew I was destined for great things."

*"I'm tough, ambitious, and know exactly what I want."*
-Madonna

During her first television appearance, pop star Madonna was asked by interviewer Dick Clarke what her goal was going forward. Madonna painted a portrait of how she perceives herself when she answered without hesitation, "To rule the world."

Was this just the ridiculous fantasy of a young pop star who overestimated her abilities? Or another brilliant display of Self-power? Madonna's decades-long domination of the music industry, glamorous lifestyle, and recent $150 million annual income suggest the latter.

What we believe and confess about ourselves provides an accurate forecast of our attainable potential!

## The Staggering *Value* of Victory Talk

The world's foremost motivational coaches haul in upwards of $7,500,000 for a 50-hour, weekend seminar. Want to know how each of these motivational seminars ends?

It ends with the coach's admonition for you, the audience member, to continue finding ways to motivate *yourself.* You see, the best life coaches money can buy are of little use unless they instill in their students the understanding that motivating oneself is a full-time job. Once you exit a costly seminar (or put down this book,) it becomes your duty to keep your mind focused, your passions ablaze, and your body moving in the direction of your desired destinations. And one of the most valuable ways to stay motivated is by becoming a Victory Talker.

What exactly is Victory Talk *worth* to you?

If a 50-hour motivational seminar holds a market value of $7,500,000, it's fair to say that every *minute* you devote to motivating yourself (by tooting your own horn or predicting your next triumph) carries a staggering monetary value of $2,500!

Of course, Victory Talk is just one strategy of many that you can use to dramatically enhance your Self-power.

*"My final thought on the matter*
*is that I am destined for some great thing."*
-George S. Patton (early journal entry)

## Ascending the Ladder of Self-power

*7 Challenging Steps to a More Confident You!*

Taking on your world by believing that you can do anything you set your mind to comes naturally when you're driven by *Self-power.* Of course, generating the caliber of confidence by which you may perform miracles of progress in your daily life typically requires some effort on your part. You've got to want it, pursue it, develop it, and project it.

Below, you'll find seven progressively challenging, actionable steps for doing just that.

### Step 1) **Believe in Yourself!**

By now, you surely understand that your physical reality is a direct extension of your inner-self. Still, it's worth repeating that what you believe in and expect to happen, how you perceive and feel about yourself, and how you label and define yourself, most often, becomes *fact.*

*"If you believe you can, you will.*
*If you believe you cannot, you will not."*
-Chuck Norris

Believe that you've got what it takes to accomplish anything you set your mind to, and you *will* have what it takes!

Self-power is the underpinning of accomplishments small and large.

### Step 2) **Become a "Victory Talker"**

You're declarations and predictions tend to become self-fulfilling prophesies.

If you go around declaring, "I can't win for losing," or predicting, "Whatever can go wrong, will," you can be sure you'll suffer *additional* losses and find *another* monkey wrench stuck in the gears of progress. Instead, put your mouth to good use by becoming a Victory Talker.

Are you a masterpiece in-the-making? An up-and-coming expert in your field? Is winning in your DNA? Are you destined to land your dream job, to find true love, to attain greatness? Then *say* so! Heartfelt declarations and brave predictions are the acorns from which mighty trees of triumph grow.

*"I am seeking; I am striving;*
*I am in it with all my heart!"*
-Vincent van Gogh

**GURU'S TIP**: Practice *Victory Talk* in the mirror. Then, as you become more comfortable tooting your own horn and more confident about predicting your next personal or professional triumph, start integrating Victory Talk into your conversations with family and friends. Use Victory Talk against competitors in the workplace, during important interviews, or on any occasion in which you desire a winning edge.

If you're going to talk—*Victory Talk!*

## Step 3) **Readily Admit When You're Wrong**

The polar opposite of being pitifully modest is being hideously self-righteous.

Not being able to admit when you're wrong is one of the most unflattering traits a person can possess. It can also keep you from ascending the workplace ladder. Any smart boss knows that there's nothing you can't teach an "eager beaver." On the other hand, you can't teach a "know it all" anything at all.

Next time you're wrong, admit it squarely.

*"I think and think...ninety-nine times,*
*the conclusion is false.*
*The hundredth time, I am right."*
-Albert Einstein

**GURU'S TIP:** Remember, if Einstein can admit being wrong, so can *you!*

## Step 4) **Empower Others**

Ever notice how folks who are always encouraging others rarely get "down in the dumps?" There is a timeless principle of success hidden in this simple fact of life. The principle is this: It's virtually impossible to harbor negative thoughts, defeating feelings or resentments when you're regularly focused on motivating others.

Want to simultaneously build Self-power and improve your social standing? Attempt to bring out the best in others through compliments, advice, coaching, and good deeds.

**GURU'S TIP**: One of the great paradoxes of building Self-power is this: When you seek to empower others, you empower *yourself.*

## Step 5) **Control Your Daily Interactions**

Feeling sure of yourself? Here are a few "more challenging," pro-social strategies for building Self-power.

- Make "small talk" with a boss or supervisor you're usually subservient to.

- Strike up a conversation with a member of the opposite sex.

- Give more advice regarding fields, subfields, relationship issues, hobbies, and areas of interest in which you are knowledgeable.

- When dining out, demand preferential treatment (immediate seating, the best view, combinations of food which may not be on the menu but which you prefer, etc.) Then *tip* according to your service.

- Treat the less fortunate with compassion.

- Quickly disassociate yourself from anyone who brings you down.

- Pick the brains of those whom you consider to be older, smarter, and wiser than you. You may be pleasantly surprised at what you discover.

- Strike up friendly conversations with your doctor, your professor, local police, owners of businesses you frequent, or anyone else within the social structure that holds a position you once considered "unapproachable."

## Step 6) **Become an "Expert" in Your Field**

Research suggests that "experts" in any given field possess ready access to about 100,000 chunks of relevant information. These chunks can be a combination of easily accessible articles, statistical data, stories, case studies, diagrams, conversations with other experts, research findings, and personal experience.

Want to become an *expert* in your current or target field?

Gain "industry IQ" by reading relevant best-sellers, scouring trade journals, ingesting online articles, listening to audio programs, attending webinars and seminars, conducting case studies, modeling leaders, and, if you've got the guts, interviewing current experts. Then put all of your newfound knowledge into practice by starting a blog, authoring a book, conducting a speech, or by filming a video for YouTube that positions you as an expert in your field of choice.

Supercharge your career through targeted study, and by proactively positioning yourself as an expert.

## Step 7) **Master the Phenomenon of Self-power—and Take on the World!**

The vast realm of human experience is governed by the Mind/Reality Relationship. And just as sure as your thoughts stitch the fabric of your reality, the world will respond to you according to your own estimation of yourself.

*"Confidence is that feeling by which the mind embarks on great and noble courses."*
-Cicero

Portray yourself as weak, inferior or second-best and that's how *others* will perceive and treat you, too. Conversely, when you possess confidence in yourself and your abilities, you will project a commanding presence and people will perceive you as someone worth listening to, befriending, and doing business with.

Going forward, stand firm in the belief that you can do anything and everything you set your mind to. Become a *Victory Talker*—and speak confidently about yourself, your accomplishments, and your plans. Readily admit when you're wrong. Strive to empower others everywhere you go. And practice transforming self-study into expertise in order to maintain a competitive edge in your career.

Do this, and you will find yourself operating from the highest rung of the ladder of Self-power.

Next, let's work on honing your sense of *Self-destiny*…

# 22

# Honing Your Sense of Self-destiny

*Becoming a True Believer in Your Future*

*"Man has no other destiny than the one he forges for himself on this earth."*
-Jean-Paul Sartre

Take a moment to recall the most important aspects of your vision for the future. Project onto the viewing screen in your Mental Theater a brief Mental Movie based on these objectives. Then ask yourself: Am I *absolutely certain* that I will achieve all that I plan to do, have, and become in life?

This is important, because unless you possess total certainty in your destiny as you choose to define it, you are in danger of allowing your wonderful dreams and goals to lose steam and fade into oblivion long before you get the chance to bask in the glory of having fulfilled them.

So, what can you do to make sure that you don't fall victim to the forthcoming challenges of elapsed time, unforeseen setbacks or a gradual loss of passion?

That's easy; you've got to hone your sense of "Self-destiny."

## Decoding the Mystery of Self-destiny

The term "Self-destiny" may have a mysterious ring to it. But decoding this forward-looking, faith-centered concept is a fairly straightforward task.

A keen sense of *Self-destiny* will include the following:

- Total conviction in your ability to predict your own outcomes

- Confidence that you have what it takes to overcome any obstacle which may stand in your path

- Certainty that all that you plan to do, have, and become in life will *inevitably* come to pass

Simply put, *Self-destiny* is Self-power directed toward the future.

In this chapter, you will discover how Albert Einstein used the art of Self-destiny to overcome his troubled childhood, to transition himself from high school dropout to Princeton professor, and to revolutionize the world of science. You will discover strategies for honing your own sense of Self-destiny. And you'll also learn how to solve "destiny's equation."

Right now, let's find out what it means to develop and exploit one's powers of Self-destiny by studying the largely untold story of Albert Einstein's lifelong climb to greatness…

*"The destiny of a man is in his own soul."*
-Herodotus

## How to Master the Art of Self-destiny

*As Demonstrated by Legendary Physicist, Albert Einstein*

The Universe readily accommodates the dreams and goals of a man, woman or child who, by accident or design, develops a sense of control over his or her destiny.

Albert Einstein was no exception.

Einstein wasn't *born* great, nor did he become the world's foremost physicist by *chance.* To the contrary, Einstein achieved scientific stardom through a series of highly calculated steps taken in the direction of his increasingly challenging goals.

And he succeeded against enormous odds…

Albert Einstein was born in 1879 in Ulm, Germany. Albert possessed a grossly oversized head and failed to speak until the age of two. Around age three, Albert earned the nickname "dopey" after developing the strange habit of facing a lonely corner of his family's living room and mumbling to himself for hours on end. When the habit persisted, Albert's alarmed parents took him to a local physician who labeled him a "slow learner" and suggested that the Einsteins give their boy time to outgrow his impediments.

Albert showed his first interest in science at age five when his father bought him a compass in the hopes of cheering the boy up as he lay in bed with the flu. Young Einstein spent days studying the compass with sharp fascination. It was this singular incident that would spark Albert's fascination with the mysteries of the Universe. It wasn't long before his interest in science became stifled by his next struggle.

When Albert was eight the Einstein's made the mistake of enrolling their Jewish son into a Catholic School. The only Jew in school (except for his sister,) Albert was forced to endure daily ridicule from heartless classmates and to suffer occasional beatings on his walks home from school. The abuse left Einstein with no friends, and eventually drove him to introversion and temper tantrums at home.

And things only got worse for Albert.

Einstein's problems multiplied when his reluctance to participate in class—due largely to his fear of the jokes and jeers of his classmates—was misinterpreted as an unwillingness to cooperate with authority. After being confronted by a teacher about his behavior, Einstein lashed out. Following that confrontation, Einstein's father was summoned to a private meeting after school by the school headmaster. It was during that meeting that Mr. Einstein was rudely informed that his son would likely "never make a success of anything."

Albert finally received a break at age 10 when Max Talmud, a 21 year-old family friend, took young Einstein under his wing. Over the next few months, Talmud taught Albert the importance of self-confidence and helped him discover his dormant academic strengths and personal passions. Under the tutelage of Talmud, Albert began spending the hours after school locked in his bedroom where he listened to Mozart, scoured science books, worked on puzzles, built card houses, and solved mathematics problems.

With the help of Talmud's coaching, Einstein's psyche and mathematical prowess improved by leaps and bounds. Before long, Albert's mind for math far outshined that of his mentor—and even his teacher. By age 12, while the classmates who once tortured him struggled to learn the basics of algebra, Albert was easily interpreting the complex formulas of differential and integral calculus! Einstein's triumph over circumstance taught him a valuable lesson about his ability to do anything he set his mind to and won him the newfound respect of classmates who only vaguely understood the breadth of Albert's accomplishment.

Next, Einstein would learn to direct his Self-power toward the future. And he would begin to take charge of his destiny in progressive steps.

*"Men, at some time,*
*become masters of their fate."*
-Julius Caesar

In 1894, when Albert was 15, he began employing one of the great skills of a master visionary—thinking in *pictures.* "I very rarely think in words at all," Einstein would later reveal. Instead, the brainy teenager used his imagination to translate complex mathematical concepts into a language of images only he could understand. During one such Mental Movie, Albert visualized himself riding a beam of light. The revelations that occurred to him during this thought experiment led him to a key insight by which he would later unlock the mysteries of time and space.

Einstein was still a sophomore in high school when he shifted his newfound mental eyesight from science…to success. Imagining how he would earn a living in the years to come, Albert's future came suddenly into focus.

He saw himself becoming a teacher of physics.

Wasting no time in pursuing his dream, Albert contacted the dean of Zurich College with a brazen proposition. The ambitious German wished to skip high school and go straight to college. In his letter to the dean, he explained that he foresaw himself becoming a teacher in the mathematics and physics branches of the natural sciences. A new practitioner of Victory Talk, Einstein cited his "talent for abstract thinking" and his "desire to do that for which he had talent" as the basis for his request. Einstein also admitted in his written request, "I am attracted to the financial independence offered by the profession of science."

Albert's request for entrance was denied, but he refused to give up. Outsmarting the system, Albert finagled a doctor's note citing a sudden "nervous condition," and then quit school and spent the next year studying on his own for the college entrance exam. In 1896, Albert, 17, aced his exam and enrolled in Zurich Polytechnic College—bypassing a year and a half of high school in the process!

At Zurich, Einstein met his future wife, Mileva, before graduating in 1900 at age 21.

*"The future belongs to those who believe in the beauty of their dreams."*
-Eleanor Roosevelt

In 1900, after a short break from school, Einstein returned to college with plans on becoming a doctor.

While studying for his doctorate, Einstein began searching for work as a teacher. To his dismay, however, he was unable to land a position. Albert tried private tutoring but no one desired his services. Einstein could've become discouraged, but he believed in himself and his future. So, the aspiring scientist kept his dream alive by accepting the only job he could find, a humble position as a filing clerk for the

Swiss Patent Office. The job paid only $12.50 per week but enabled Einstein to work toward his two current goals: provide for his wife and newborn son, and work on his doctoral thesis.

It was in 1905 (later dubbed Einstein's "miracle year") that Albert, 26, produced three revolutionary papers while filing patent applications as an unknown clerk. The first paper purported the existence of photons; the second, the true size and nature of atoms; and the third was based on bold, new theories about space and time.

So confident was Einstein that his theories would prove true and earn him worldwide fame that he promised Mileva the prize purse for the Noble Prize he was sure to win in the years to come. Einstein's papers would simultaneously earn him his PhD and open the door to his toughest challenge yet—jealous colleagues. In 1909, Einstein, 30, fulfilled his childhood dream by securing, by a very slim vote, a professorship at Zurich College. The sweet joy of victory, however, was to be short-lived.

Problems mounted for Einstein when he began chatting up his still-unconfirmed, space-time theories among the older, more established faculty members who argued that Einstein's views didn't hold water. The more Einstein insisted that he was right, the more his colleagues held him in contempt. "Who are you to challenge us?" was the chant of the self-righteous professors to the cocky, young doctor. This culture clash resulted with Einstein being ostracized by the very faculty that had reluctantly taken him aboard. Einstein would devote much of the next 10 years to devising a method to prove true his theory that light "bends" around the sun on its way to Earth.

In 1915, Einstein concocted another theory—his General Theory of Relativity. Einstein would simplify "relativity" by explaining, "When a man sits with a pretty woman for an hour, it seems like a minute. But let him sit on a hot stove for a minute and it seems longer than an hour. That's *relativity*."

The buzz created by Doctor Einstein's Theory of Relativity won him a small triumph over his detractors, but his true victory came in 1919. It was through an experience during a total eclipse that year that the 40 year-old physicist's "light bending" claims were, at long last, confirmed by the global, scientific community. Einstein's reputation was restored and, seemingly overnight, the scientist was elevated to a level of acclaim surpassing that of his intellectual hero, Isaac Newton!

Remarkably, Albert Einstein's most impressive feats of Self-destiny had yet to unfold…

*"Our belief at the beginning of any doubtful undertaking is often the only thing that ensures the successful outcome of our venture.*
-Dr. William James

By the time of his 43rd birthday, Albert Einstein found himself hounded by the press for interviews, sought-after across Europe for lectures, and revered by leaders from nations near and far. Yet, as busy as Doctor Einstein had become enjoying the fruits of his labor, he still made time to keep his promises. In 1922, after winning the Noble Prize—*as predicted*—for his discovery of photons in 1905, Albert handed over the prize purse to Mileva as promised. The purse (225,000 German franks) equaled nearly 40 times Mileva's annual salary!

To Einstein, 225,000 German Franks could not compare to the riches, fame, and glory he would earn after moving to the United States and becoming a professor at Princeton. Now heralded as the most accomplished scientist of the 20th century, Albert Einstein would spend the rest of his life amassing a list of accomplishments which would include: developing a personal network of world leaders, serving as special advisor on atomic matters to President Roosevelt, performing humanitarian activities, lecturing around the globe, and championing his vision of a one-world government called "democracy."

Best known for his formula $E=MC^2$, Albert Einstein's true genius existed not in his mathematical prowess, but in his foresight in visualizing his ideal future, in his courage in taking the steps necessary to realize his objectives, and in his ability to navigate around obstacles and setbacks until all that he planned to do, have, and become in life inevitably came to pass.

Einstein's true genius was *Self-destiny*.

*"The brave man carves out his own fortune;*
*and every man is the sum of his own works."*
-Miquel de Cervantes

Reducing to its simplest terms his skill in orchestrating the events and affairs that led him to his chosen destiny, Einstein explains, "I have always done what lay in my modest powers." As for the headmaster who assured Mr. Einstein that his son would *never make a success of anything?* Well, the teacher certainly succeeded…in becoming a byline of irony in the Great Physicist's tale of grand-scale triumph!

## Honing *Your* Sense of Self-destiny

*3 Strategies for Keeping Your Dreams Alive*

Possessing a strong sense of Self-destiny is one sure way of keeping your visionary powers sharp and your dreams supercharged, until you *fulfill* them. Below, are three things you can do which are particularly useful in developing durable faith in your ability to control your future.

### (1) Put the *"Vision Maximization" System* into Daily Practice

Using the *V-Max System* is a great way to hone your sense of Self-destiny.

To refresh your memory, the V-Max System includes: producing Mental Movies based on your vision for your future, citing all the *reasons* why your goals are important, gathering evidence (stories, facts, and figures) that supports the feasible attainment of your important objectives, spending time visualizing what it will be like to experience life as the Ultimate You, creating a Destiny Environment filled with motivating vision enhancers, and reciting your Destiny Statement daily.

*"Man cannot discover new oceans*
*unless he has the courage to leave the shore."*
-Andre Gide

By practicing the V-Max System, you will feel more in control of your future and be more in control of your future, which is what Self-destiny is all about.

## (2) **Develop a Thick Skin to Criticism**

Along your road to success as you define it, you may encounter critics who try to knock you down, mislabel you, break your spirits or cast you aside. One's detractors can take the form of misguided family members, jealous opponents, envious friends, ex-bosses, disgruntled employees, estranged lovers, and the list goes on.

If, during your journey, you should come face to face with someone who's bent on stealing your thunder, remember this: Our sweetest victories often lie just over the shoulder of the critic who stands in our way.

For instance, Albert Einstein was labeled "slow" by his doctor before teaching himself calculus at age 12. Then, after being ostracized by his colleagues for his *ridiculous theories* about space and time, Einstein went on to win the Nobel Prize in Physics.

While serving as a Wall Street intern, J.P. Morgan was laughed out of a top-rated brokerage firm for demanding an expanded role in the company. Morgan answered the contempt by founding J.P. Morgan & Company. The 24 year-old CEO then went on to become his former employer's fiercest competitor!

Aspiring boxer Jack Johnson was treated like less of a man in the years before proving himself a world-class champion.

And during Harry Truman's entrance into the political field, his opposition discovered that he was a law school dropout. His detractors had a field day. After becoming the 33rd president in 1945, Harry lashed back at his critics by declaring, "The C students run the world."

*"A believer, a mind whose faith is consciousness, is never disturbed because others do not yet see the fact which he sees."*
-Ralph Waldo Emerson

**GURU'S TIP:** Developing a thick skin to criticism can mean the difference between faltering before the finish line and seizing the gold medal in your quest to realize your dreams.

## (3) Rid Yourself of Self-limiting Beliefs

Experience has taught me that a man's worst enemy is most often found in the mirror. More often than not, it is our own self-limiting beliefs (including self-doubts, irrational fears, and self-criticism) that deprive us of personal power and limit our true potential in life and business.

Our self-erected, mental barriers are reflected in "I can't" statements, such as:

- I'm too young/old to fulfill my dreams
- I don't have the finances to follow my dreams
- I lack the education necessary to get ahead
- I'm too deep in debt to ever become wealthy

*"There are those facts which cannot come unless a preliminary faith exists beforehand."*
-Dr. William James

Honing your sense of Self-destiny will require ridding yourself of any views or philosophies that present a threat to your future as you choose to define it. If you entertain any of the above-mentioned (or similar) restricting tenets, you're in luck. You'll find all the incentive you need to purge your belief system of "I can't" philosophies in the next, two chapters.

Right now, let's delve into "destiny's equation."

## Solving Destiny's Equation

*Self-power + Self-destiny = Mastery of Destiny*

*Self-power* (or the belief that you can do anything and everything you set your mind to) and *Self-destiny* (or the faith that *you* are in charge of your future) are two parts of the same equation—"destiny's equation."

During my first weeks on the job as a project manager during my 20's, I didn't have much confidence in myself because I didn't know much about my field and didn't have many successes upon which to build a foundation of self-trust. Of course, as I gained experience over the next few months, my level of Self-power increased. Managing mid-size construction projects created within me the confidence that I could handle even larger responsibilities. Yet, in spite of this newfound confidence, I still lacked an understanding of my God-given ability to dictate my own destiny.

After managing my first business turnaround at age 30, I caught an exciting glimpse into what it's like to influence events over an extended period. Leading a failing company from near-bankruptcy to the height of profitability over a period of more than a year afforded me a much better understanding of one's ability to orchestrate outcomes well into the future. Finally, after penning *Mind Contrology* ®; engineering the "Science of Dream Architecture" found in earlier material; and applying this science to my own life, career, relationships, and finances; I developed a firsthand appreciation of the precision with which one may chart one's own course in life and transform one's dreams into reality.

Similarly, you, too, cannot possibly understand the power you have at your disposal in the forms of Self-power and Self-destiny until you begin to cultivate these gifts and use them to carve out your desired place in the world. As you begin to apply these forces to your life, you will find that there is nothing you cannot do, and nothing within the expansive realm of human experience that will not surrender itself to your wishes.

It is only in putting what you've learned about Self-power and Self-destiny into practice that you will come to know what it means to solve *destiny's equation.*

*"Destiny is not a matter of chance, it's a matter of choice; it is not a thing to be waited for, it's a thing to be achieved."*
-William Jennings Bryant

Okay, over the last two chapters, you've begun to build Self-power and hone your sense of Self-destiny. Over the next two chapters, we're going to shatter all of your limitations and prove that *nothing* is impossible for you.

Take a deep breath and prepare to enter the next phase of your growing ability to harness the force of belief. You're about to be stripped of seven faulty beliefs that hold good people, like you, back…

# 23

# Shattering Your Limitations

## *Debunking the 7 Faulty Beliefs that Hold Good People—Like You—Back!*

*"The satisfaction and confidence that come from overstepping your supposed limits is enormous; but it never comes to those who fear to test their limits."*
-Arnold Schwarzenegger

Unless you are currently living your dreams, there's a good chance that you're harboring self-limiting beliefs. Maybe you think that you're too young (or old) to fulfill your dreams or fear you don't have enough money to set your plans in action. Perhaps you worry that so-called "bad luck" is keeping you from getting ahead or think that some physical limitation will keep you from making your way in the world. Or, maybe your current lack of education, experience or connections keeps you from reaching for the stars and fulfilling your true potential.

If any of these self-imposed barriers have caused you to construct a "performance ceiling" so low that you practically have to crawl through life to keep from bumping into it, this chapter will help you shatter your limits once and for all.

In this chapter, you'll discover:

- Seven common faulty beliefs that hold good people, like you, back
- The "real deal," or the stories, facts, and figures which expose these beliefs as fraudulent

As you read on, remember: you are a boundless being designed with a limitless mind, instilled with a spirit to energize you, and equipped with a body to carry out your wishes. No good purpose under the Heavens will be denied you if you will only foresee it, anticipate it, and pursue it.

There is just one obstacle on this Earth that can keep you from achieving all that dream of doing, having, and becoming in life. That "obstacle" is *you*...

*"No other passion so effectively robs the mind of all its powers of reasoning and acting as fear."*
-Edmund Burke

## Shattering Your Limitations

*Debunking the 7 Faulty Beliefs that Hold Good People—Like You—Back*

### Faulty Belief #1) I'm Too Young (or Old) to Pursue My Dream

Think you're too young or old to pursue your dreams? Think again...

**Too Young?** Douglas Barry was just 14 years old when he wrote his first business book, *"Wisdom for a Young CEO."* Virgin Group Ltd. CEO Richard Branson was only 16 when he launched his first venture, *"Student"* magazine. Branson now controls more than 200 businesses with annual revenues exceeding $5 billion! Spanish artist Pablo Picasso was 19 when he opened his first studio in Barcelona, where he devoted himself to the melancholy portraits that would be dubbed Picasso's "blue period."

Beautiful Alex Scott was just 4 years old when she launched "Alex's Lemonade Stand"—a national movement which has raised some $40 million for cancer research. Nascar's Ryan Newman started racing at age 5. By age 9, Newman had already seized 20 victory flags, a good indicator of his forthcoming Daytona 500, first-place finish in 2005.

And then there's Miley Cyrus. Cyrus' earliest accomplishments include roles as a singer, song-writer, television actor, and movie-star, all before the age of 18. From her triumph as the youngest artist to have multiple #1 albums within the same 12-month period at age 14, to her 2011 earnings of more than $50 million, Cyrus has proven that *youth* does not limit one's ability to make dreams real.

**Too Old?** Jack Miller was 82 when he sold his company to an office supplies superstore for $20 million. Then, deciding retirement was for the elderly, Miller launched another office supply business. Hulda Crooks made history by becoming the oldest person to ascend Mount Whitney (America's tallest peak) at age 91.

Fitness guru Jack LaLanne was 61 when he swam the length of the Golden Gate Bridge underwater. LaLanne was handcuffed and shackled…and had a 1000-pound boat in tow. LaLanne's motto? "Anything in life is possible!" And Rose Blumkin, owner of Nebraska Furniture Mart continued to run her $50 million retail empire until she was 103!

Want a few *more* examples of age-defying performance?

Sidney Sheldon, Claude Monet, and Albert Einstein each continued authoring mind-bending novels, painting million dollar portraits, and decoding the mysteries of the Universe, respectively, into their 70's. Pablo Picasso continued sculpting and painting into his 80's. And George Burns and Pablo Casals retained their comedic and musical genius, respectively, until beyond their 90th birthdays.

Others continue succeeding beyond age 100. Britain's Fauja Singh holds a record for the 10K marathon with 1 hour, 32 minutes…at age 102. And, in 2014, three sisters from Oklahoma fulfilled their long held dream of reuniting with each other at the same retirement community. The sisters were 101, 104, and 110 years young!

*"Nothing at all will ever be attempted*
*if all possible objections must be overcome before we start."*
-Dr. Samuel Johnson

**The Real Deal:** You're *never* too young or old to realize a dream or goal!

## Faulty Belief #2) I Don't Have Enough Money to Launch My Vision

If you are among those who've been bound by the false belief that "it takes money to make money," the following facts and figures may help you exchange your mental shackles for wealth-mindedness.

Walt Disney was 19 years old when his first business, Laugh-O-Gram, went bust. The bankruptcy left Walt with nothing but a used movie camera and a boat-load of debt. Refusing to surrender his dream of running his own animation studio, Walt went door to door to borrow spending cash from his neighbors. Then, after promising his lenders repayment, Walt packed up his camera and boarded a train from Kansas City to Hollywood. Disney studios would soon take the world by storm.

In 1862, J.D. Rockefeller shelled out $4,000 to start Standard Oil Company. As the business grew, Rockefeller used the profits to invest in real estate and build a portfolio of other businesses. By 1882, J.D. found himself sitting on a personal fortune of $70 million and was considered the richest man in all of New York.

Would you like to turn a modest, well-managed investment into $70 million over the next 20 years? $35 million over the next 10 years? How about $7 million over the next 2 years? Rockefeller has shown us that it *can be done!*

In the 1950s, Hugh Hefner launched "*Playboy*" magazine using $100 seed capital he'd borrowed from his mother. "*Playboy's*" 2009 circulation exceeded 1.5 million issues at a revenue value of about

$12.5 million. And in 1907, Jim Casey borrowed $100 to start a messenger service in Seattle, Washington. Operating faithfully to his mission of "best service, lowest rates," Jim earned enough business to purchase a truck…then a fleet of trucks…then a fleet of 747's.

Since its inception, Casey's one-man messenger service has evolved into the $4 billion parcel giant, UPS.

When it comes to transforming small cash investments into multimillion dollar businesses, my friend, Mike Girm, immediately comes to mind. One night back in the 1990s, Mike was flipping through the television channels when he came across an infomercial advertising a "real estate riches" video. Casting his doubts aside, Mike invested $40 and used the how-to video for instruction and inspiration. A couple of years later, Mike was a millionaire. Today, Mike controls a multi-industry business portfolio worth *many* millions!

*"Our doubts are traitors,*
*and make us lose the good we oft might win,*
*by fearing to attempt."*
-William Shakespeare

**The Real Deal:** You can launch your vision and build an empire with little more than the cash you've got in your pocket!

## Faulty Belief #3) My "Bad Luck" is Keeping Me from Getting Ahead!

Do you have a habit of telling yourself (or others) that a mysterious "black cloud of doom" follows you around, keeping you from getting ahead?

If you do, your morbid philosophy has likely transformed you into the very *doomsday magnet* you believe yourself to be. To break the spell of your own limited thinking, consider that Donna Williams transformed her grave misfortune into a unique opportunity, and, in the end, a best-selling book…

Donna Williams was diagnosed with autism at age two, and that was just the tip of Williams's iceberg of hardship.

After spending her early years in a school that provided inadequate care for her special needs, Donna returned home to an abusive family situation. Terrified and confused, Donna developed "multiple personality disorder"—a defense mechanism which helped the little girl cope with the conflicts in her mind and with the trauma caused by her confusing world. Surrounded by people and circumstances that suggested that she was *different* and *inferior,* Donna left home at age 13 and found a surrogate foster family where she was able to regroup and begin transforming her "bad luck" to good.

That's where Williams' story gets interesting...

*"You have to create your own luck."*
-Bruce Lee

Outsmarting autism itself, Donna employed the assistance of a psychiatrist and social worker to help her enroll in college. Temporarily freed from the grips of autism at age 18 by focusing on her future, Williams became an honor student and went on to earn degrees in sociology and education. After college, Williams, 24, moved to Europe, got a job and rented an apartment.

It was during a relapse into the throes of autism that Donna returned to treatment. Treatment, it turned out, was a godsend which awakened Williams to the realization that for the past seven years she had unwittingly conquered an "incurable disorder" by the power of her own unstoppable will. And this time, it would be for good. Newly empowered, Donna acquired a typewriter and composed the story of her life, a best-seller which took Donna just four short weeks to write!

**The Real Deal:** There is no such thing as bad luck, only self-limiting thinking. And this you have the power to change at any time you choose.

## Faulty Belief #4) **My "Physical Disadvantage" Is Preventing Me from Making My Way in the World**

Physical disabilities do not preclude one from achieving grand dreams. The world of success is chockfull of examples of human beings whose superior mentality enabled them to transcend such "limitations" as impaired senses, crippling diseases, lost limbs, and more. These folks are the warriors whose hard-won victories teach the rest of the world that a man's potential lies not in the strength of his body, but in the force of his will.

For example, Ray Charles and Stevie Wonder both saw fame and fortune as blind piano players. And Lou Ferrigno refused to let his hearing impairment stop him from becoming a world-class bodybuilder and television actor.

Beethoven composed some of his greatest symphonies while deaf. Nathanael Greene refused to allow his crooked leg, acute asthma or lack of education to prevent him from becoming George Washington's favorite general. Napoleon Bonaparte used a "giant ego" to compensate for his miniature stature. And Franklin Roosevelt fought through a crippling case of polio instead of resigning as governor of New York. After becoming so weak he couldn't even stand, Roosevelt used a combination of metal leg braces and sheer will power to overcome his illness and see through his term.

Helen Keller (a blind, deaf mute) used her inner-force to attend college, write a book, and become a famous lecturer. And after losing her arms in a horrible accident, one middle-aged housewife continued to care for her family by learning to cook, clean, and wash dishes…with her feet.

When cancer threatened to steal away the dreams of cyclist Lance Armstrong, Armstrong fought the disease into remission and won the Tour de France as his reward. And after suffering a severe leg injury, former Philadelphia 76er's owner, Pat Croche, stunned his doctors by pulling off a recovery in a timeframe that most medical professionals would've agreed was "impossible." How'd Croche do it? Pat attributes his miraculous recovery to *wanting* and *expecting* a speedy recovery!

*"Nature equips each man with some faculty which enables him to do easily some feat impossible to others."*
-Ralph Waldo Emerson

And then there's Ralph Braun. Braun was just six years old when he contracted spinal muscular atrophy, a crippling disease which would eventually confine Ralph's body to a wheelchair, but not his ambitious spirit.

Refusing to be slowed down in high school, Ralph built himself a motorized wheelchair to keep up with his peers. After graduation, Braun spent the next several years working at a local factory and engineering motor-chairs for other disabled persons in his spare time. Over time, Braun's custom-made wheelchairs became "professional grade." Word spread and demand increased. At age 23, Ralph realized that maybe he was selling himself short by working for somebody else. Braun opened his own business and began selling motorized scooters and equipping vehicles with electric lifts for wheel chair accessibility.

In 2009, Ralph's little company "BraunAbility" generated nearly $200 million in revenues!

**The Real Deal:** Physical "disadvantages" generally exist to the degree to which a person acknowledges them!

## Faulty Belief #5) **My Lack of Education Is in the Way of My Dreams**

Think you need a PhD or MBA to get ahead? Think again.

Billionaire John Simplot dropped out of grade school. Kirk Kerkorian also dropped out of grade school. Kerkorian later purchased a piece of land in Las Vegas on which he would build the MGM Grand. And Richard Branson dropped out of high school before becoming a billionaire 5 times over.

Paul Allen dropped out of Washington State University so he could tinker around with "electronic boxes" with his friend, Bill, in Bill's garage. Months later, Paul and Bill—Gates, that is—launched their fledgling company, Microsoft. Bill Gates? Also a college dropout. Computer giant Apple was the brainchild of two college dropouts, Steve Jobs and Steve Woznick.

Music mogul David Geffen dropped out of college, too. Geffen was working as a mail clerk before he reached for the stars and, as a result, made millions. Ralph Lauren never attended fashion school. And the only degree real estate guru Mike Girm possesses is a PhD in street smarts.

Harry Truman dropped out of law school, yet became a U.S. president. Actors Kevin Bacon and Christina Applegate both dropped out of high school. Comedians George Carlin and George Burns dropped out of high school and grade school, respectively. And novelist Agatha Christie never attended school at all!

Walt Disney dropped out of high school before launching Disney Studios and building Disney Land. Henry Ford's education stopped at sixth grade. And J.D. Rockefeller dropped out of high school before becoming America's first billionaire.

Abraham Lincoln attended only one full year of formal schooling. Thomas Edison spent just three months in the classroom. And remember "Mrs. B," the 103 year-old furniture magnate? "Mrs. B," who retired with a net worth of approximately $50 million, could neither read nor write!

*"The C students run the world."*
-President Harry S. Truman

**The Real Deal:** When you believe in the inevitability of your dreams (no matter how grand the dream,) your current level of education (no matter how limited) will be more than sufficient!

### Faulty Belief #6) I'm Too Deep in Debt to Become Wealthy

When you total the debt you owe to your mortgage company, bank, credit card company, auto dealer, etc., what's the total? $5,000? $50,000? $500,000 or more? Do you feel like you're so deep in debt that you'll never get out?

Well, what if I told you that it's entirely possible to transform debt (even debt totaling millions) into wealth? It's true. And the businessman in the following story is one of the all-time masters of this principle.

*"The only limit to our realization of tomorrow will be our doubts of today."*
-Franklin Delano Roosevelt

During the 1970s, Uichiro Niwa, a Japanese businessman who was working out of an Itochu Corp. sub-office in New York, lost $100 million dollars in a business deal gone awry. Stop for a moment and consider the magnitude of Niwa's loss. Imagine the panic. The pressure. Your mind races in a hundred different directions as it attempts to grasp the devastation of having lost…$100 *million* dollars!

Faced with this very dilemma, Niwa found himself with two options: resign in shame, or summon the Self-power and Self-destiny to engineer a turnaround and get back in the game. Against all odds, Niwa chose the latter. Citing his faith in God as a chief source of strength, Niwa unlocked his mind and brainstormed a solution. He harnessed his energies and summoned his resources. Then he achieved the impossible by recouping the entire $100 million!

Niwa was later appointed *president* of Itochu Corp.

*"According to your faith be it unto you."*
-Matthew 15:23

**The Real Deal:** Generally speaking, your philosophies and habits surrounding money dictate what you'll earn, own, and owe.

Want to earn more? Raise the cognitive "wealth-ceiling" that governs your current earning potential. Wish to increase your net worth? Start operating according to the wealth philosophy: *generate revenue/income and purchase undervalued assets.* Need to get out of debt? Ditch the strategies that landed you in debt in the first place, and then shift your focus, energies, and resources toward designing your financial comeback!

## Faulty Belief #7) **My Humble Beginnings Preclude Me from Grand-scale Success**

When you look in the mirror, do you see the forthcoming *Ultimate You?* Or do circumstances such as your current crummy job, low earnings, and unsavory living conditions prevent you from seeing the new and improved person you are destined to become? If you're having trouble "seeing" how you'll ever get from where you are to where you want to be, here's some facts that might help improve your vision…

Actor Sean Connery polished coffins before becoming 007. Sylvester Stallone cleaned lion cages at the Central Park Zoo before climbing into the ring as Rocky Balboa. And Colin Powell unloaded trucks on his way to the White House.

James Dean was a stunt dummy before becoming an American icon. And Marilyn Monroe was an orphan and a nude model before storming the gates of Hollywood. And this author held positions that included busboy, laborer, collections agent, and limo driver, before becoming a business expert, mind guru, author, and speaker.

In 1940, an Albanian teenager named Agnes foresaw her destiny of serving the poor and joined a Catholic convent. In 1946, Agnes challenged the pope to bless, and finance her self-ordained mission to provide assistance to the poor. She got her wish. By 1954, Agnes was living her dream of running an orphanage in Calcutta. Agnes later founded her own order of missionaries which has grown to more than 3,000 sisters serving the poor in 85 countries. Perhaps you know Agnes by her *other* name—Mother Teresa.

*"Every man takes the limits of his own field of vision as the limits of the world."*
-Arthur Schopenhauer

Want a few more inspiring, Cinderella stories? Harry Helmsley was a mailroom clerk before unleashing his inner hotel magnate. Al Pacino sold shoes before winning Oscars. And Mohandas Gandhi served some seven years behind bars before becoming the global figurehead for the cause of non-violent resistance.

Steven King wrote reports as a janitor before penning best-selling novels. Sharon Stone worked at McDonald's. Danny DeVito worked as a hairdresser. And singer Mariah Carey swept the floors of a beauty salon before becoming a singer.

Then there's Cornelius Vanderbilt...

Vanderbilt quit school at age 11 and went to work at his father's business. At age 16, Vanderbilt found work as a humble, ferry operator. Cornelius was busy shuttling people and goods between Manhattan and Staten Island, yearning for a more rewarding career, when something caught his eye in the distance beyond the river's edge. That *something* was the bustling city of New York. Vanderbilt wanted a piece of it, and vowed not to stop until he received his share. The year was 1810.

In 1811, Vanderbilt launched his *own* ferry service. He operated the business for six years, and then sold it in order to purchasing a large steam ship. Vanderbilt would spend the next decade amassing an entire fleet of merchant vessels.

After adopting the title "Commodore" during the 1840s, Vanderbilt purchased a fleet of luxury liners before making a lucrative living in the budding industry of "vacation travel." In 1857, Vanderbilt reinvented himself again after undertaking a new quest to build railroads across New York and its surrounding regions. In the end, Vanderbilt would gain control of much of New York's commercial waterways and railways, amass a $100 million fortune, and enjoy the life he'd once dreamed of living while working as a lowly, ferry operator!

*"Be concerned with the ends, not the means. Master your own manipulation of force."*
-Bruce Lee

**The Real Deal:** Virtually all grand-scale success takes its rise from the humblest of beginnings.

Okay, we've debunked the seven, most common, faulty beliefs.

The next chapter is devoted to proving that *anything* is possible for you, if only you will *believe*...

# 24

# Disproving the Myth of Impossibility

*Placing the 7 Timeless Rules of Belief on Your Side*

*"We have found that by reaching for what appears to be impossible, we often do the impossible."*
-Dr. Jack Welch

Through my decade-long study of 500 of the world's most fascinating figures and 250 Fortune-level firms (and their CEOs,) I have discovered this to be true: nothing within the expansive realm of human experience is "impossible" for the man or woman who believes in *unlimited possibilities.*

You are about to discover this truth for yourself.

The goals of this chapter are to:

- Introduce you to the 7 *Timeless Rules of Belief*
- Remove any last shred of doubt you may be harboring about your limitless nature
- Begin the process of aligning your belief system with your vision for your future

# The 7 Timeless Rules of Belief

## The 1st Rule of Belief) **If You Can Believe It, You Can Achieve It**

In 1999, Taylor Swift, a 10 year-old from Wyomissing, Pennsylvania, decided what she wanted to do with the rest of her life—become a country singer.

According to her interview on the *Tonight Show*, Swift believed that Nashville was the place where dreams come true for aspiring country singers. So, after pleading with her parents to take her to the famed music town, the Swifts found themselves on a family vacation in Tennessee's capital.

For Taylor, the trip wasn't about pleasure; it was business.

While being chauffeured by her mother, Taylor, determined to break into the music business, visited several, local record companies where she dropped off copies of her demo and introduced herself as an aspiring, country music star. It was a feat that required guts, and Taylor's efforts would be rewarded.

After the Swifts returned to Pennsylvania, Taylor sat by a metaphorical phone which never rang. Still, she refused to give up. Taylor continued attending school, writing songs, and singing at local clubs. She even landed a gig to sing the national anthem at the U.S. Open tennis tournament. Perhaps newly motivated by her first major appearance, Taylor convinced her family to *relocate* to Nashville in 2003. Soon afterward, Swift, at last, received Destiny's Call.

In 2005, 16 year-old Swift was picked up by a major record label and—after her debut album went "gold" in just 13 weeks—Taylor was soon whisked into a world of recording studios, music videos, and award shows.

In 2009, *"Rolling Stone"* magazine named Taylor Swift one of the top people changing America, and by 2011, Swift's earnings had skyrocketed to $45 million!

*"I never had any patience with the multitudes who theorized that my dreams were impossible."*
-Booker T. Washington

**GURU'S TIP**: Whatever you believe you can achieve, you *can* achieve!

The 2nd Rule of Belief) **If You Believe You're Destined for Greatness, You *Are* Destined for Greatness**

Greatness is attained far less by royal lineage than by regal aspirations. Take Alexander Hamilton, for instance…

Alexander Hamilton was born in 1755 on Nevis Island in the Caribbean. Ridiculed as the bastard son of two "sinful locals," Alex longed to escape the island and move to a place where his embarrassing stigma would no longer haunt him.

Alex's wish came true in 1768 when, at age 13, he found work as a clerk for an international dealer of fish, horses, and alcohol in St. Croix, the central trading hub of Britain, France, and Spain. Although Hamilton's position was a step up from his troubles in Nevis, it wouldn't be long before his ambitious spirit outgrew it. "I condemn the groveling conditions of a clerk," complained Hamilton. And the longer Alex watched the endless stream of money flow through the hands of his boss, the more intrigued the young clerk became with the economics of international commerce.

Using his employer's success as a measure of possibility, Alex began to envision *himself* becoming a man of wealth, stature, and intellect. And that was enough to get the materialization process in motion.

*"You must do the thing that you think you cannot do."*
-Eleanor Roosevelt

Fortune began setting the stage for the manifestation of Hamilton's bold dreams during a major hurricane that ravaged the islands in 1772.

It was after Alex managed to get his poetic, written account of the storm into a regional newspaper that a wealthy, local businessman happened across the story and fell in love with Alex's colorful journalism. Recognizing "academic potential" in the 20 year-old Hamilton, the businessman tracked down Alex, and then offered to foot the bill for him to travel to New York and attend the academy that would later become Columbia University. Over the next three years, Hamilton's studies of economics afforded him keen insights into the strategies by which King George was looting the commerce channels which connected the colonies of North America to neighboring countries. Before long, Alex would use his newfound understanding of economics to begin positioning himself into the career roles for which he'd been preparing.

In 1775, as a full-scale revolution took rise across America, Hamilton entered the fray on the side of the colonists by organizing a small militia in Manhattan comprised of fellow students who believed in the cause of American independence. After promoting himself to "captain" of his militia, Hamilton ran considerable interference in the rebels' quest to block Britain's access to commerce channels in the region. Word of Hamilton's growing reputation as a loyal rebel and economics expert spread through the region—at the perfect time. When General Washington swept through New York in the heat of battle, Washington was informed of Alex's heroics, and the general wasted no time in rewarding the captain.

Just 20 years old, Hamilton was initiated into Washington's guarded, inner circle. Although young, scrawny, and inexperienced in battle, Alex's bright mind, ambitious spirit, and expedient attendance to Washington's beckon call soon catapulted Hamilton to a coveted position as Washington's chief of staff!

*"There's absolutely no limit to what plain,*
*ordinary people can accomplish."*
-Sam Walton

Alex the clerk would go on to become a lawyer, member of Congress, board director at the First Bank of New York, and secretary of the U.S. Treasury! Hamilton revealed one of his secrets of success as, "I am an enthusiast in my notions."

What possibilities are *you* enthused about?

**GURU'S TIP:** Nothing is impossible for the man, woman or child who believes he or she is destined for greatness, and takes bold action when the opportunity for which he or she is waiting arises.

## The 3rd Rule of Belief) **Wealth Responds to Those Who Believe It Will**

The 3rd Rule of Belief can be seen in the remarkable career evolution of famous financier, J.P. Morgan.

In 1857, John Pierpont Morgan, 20, began an apprenticeship with a Wall Street brokerage firm. Morgan didn't like that he was treated as an errand boy, didn't appreciate being made to take notes and keep quiet, and wasn't happy about being locked out of meetings attended by senior executives. So, Morgan—intent on securing his share of the money and perks he felt entitled to—immediately took action to put an end to his being treated as the "office mascot."

Unusually headstrong and confident for a kid with zero experience in his field, Morgan took it upon himself to court special-interest clients which were supposed to be off-limits to him, to broker deals he had no authority to oversee, and to build forbidden alliances with competing brokers whom he flattered in order to finagle trade secrets it had taken them *years* to learn for themselves. Because he was making money for the firm and clients seemed to like him, ownership allowed Morgan to continue pressing his luck. The more latitude Morgan was given, however, the more the *apprentice* began to act like the chairman of the board.

In 1861, just three years after being hired, Morgan decided that he was either going to sit among the firm's partners, or compete with them. When bigwigs laughed off Morgan's "offer" to make him a partner, J.P. responded by opening the doors of J.P. Morgan & Company. By 1864, Morgan's tax statements revealed an income of $50,000, an incredible 50 times that of the average annual income in the U.S. for that year!

*"If more of us would strike out and attempt the "impossible," we would very soon find the truth of the old saying that nothing is impossible."*
-Dr. C.E. Welch

Through J.P. Morgan's evolution from cocky clerk to top-rated financier, we see the 3rd Rule of Belief at work: wealth responds to those who believe it will.

Morgan's belief that he was entitled to riches (largely a result of his belief in his ability to deliver results to his clients) enabled him to reach beyond his "assigned role" within the firm that had hired him. Morgan's harmless ego enabled him to acquire the actual investment experience and expert reputation it otherwise may have taken him years to gain had he acquiesced to the company culture and "waited his turn." Newly empowered as 24 year-old CEO of his own firm, Morgan expanded his mental horizons to include investments in the railroad and steel industries. A series of multimillion dollar deals only served to reinforce Morgan's growing reputation as Wall Street's brightest money manager.

To Morgan, money was an asset, a trusted friend, a faithful companion, and a necessary requisite of the glamorous lifestyle he believed himself put on this Earth to enjoy. And, as a result, Morgan's fortunes continued to increase. Continuing to prove himself the wise steward of a progressively larger fortune, Morgan would soon go on to purchase Carnegie Steel for $492 million before becoming chairman of the U.S. Steel Corporation—the world's first *billion dollar* company.

Morgan would also use his personal fortune to twice bail-out the U.S. Treasury in 1893, and again in 1907!

**GURU'S TIP:** Want wealth to respond to you? Believe it will.

## The 4th Rule of Belief) **Those Who Have Faith in a Comeback, Get It**

The 4th Rule of Belief states: *Those Who Have Faith in a Comeback, Get It!* Below, are a few examples of men and women whose outright refusal to buy into the concept of "failure" has enabled them to transform setbacks into milestones.

Home Improvement star Tim Allen served seven years in prison before reinventing himself as America's injury-prone dad, Tim "the Toolman" Taylor. Author Jack London suffered dozens of rejections before getting his first work published. Dick Cheney flunked out of Yale before returning to school and earning his degree. Oprah Winfrey got canned from her job as a television reporter before bouncing back as the "Queen of TV Talk Shows." And Soichiro Honda—yes, *that* Honda—was turned down by Toyota for a position as an engineer before deciding to open his *own* company.

Oscar-winning filmmaker, Oliver Stone, originally set out to become a novelist. So, when his manuscript was shot down by a series of publishers, Stone was devastated. Perhaps working up the courage to try again, Stone took on a teaching job, as well as a tour as a soldier. Finally, after summoning the audacity to pursue his dream, Stone applied his writing talents to the arts of screenwriting and film-making. This time, Stone found fame, fortune, and a living legacy as one of greatest motion picture producers of all time!

Writer Henry David Thoreau went jobless for *years* as an adult. Henry lived with his friend, Ralph Waldo Emerson, in Emerson's back room for two years before living off the land at Boston's Walden Pond for another year. It was during his years-long stretch of homelessness, however, that Thoreau quietly penned the manuscripts which have come to be considered among the most genius literary works of all time.

Before becoming president in 1861, Abe Lincoln tried his hand at running a grocery store, but failed miserably.

And after David Needleman was fired from his executive position at Southwest Airlines, Needleman proceeded to do what "comeback artists" do best—reinvent himself. Needleman rebounded as CEO of his *own*, brand new airline, JetBlue!

*"The well-built mind is aware of the world's infinite possibilities and reaches out in every direction."*
-Marilyn vos Savant

Novelist Kurt Vonnegut authored a particularly poetic comeback. After his professor at college assured him that his writing was "terrible," Vonnegut dropped out of school and devoted the time he might've spent under the professor's thumb to studying the dictionary, traveling to interesting places, and fine-tuning his self-taught profession of choice—story writing. Vonnegut, of course, would go on to gain a cult following as one of the most celebrated novelists of the 20th century.

Finally, turnaround artist Nelson Mandela says, "There is no passion in playing small, in settling for a life that is less than the one you are capable of living." After spending 27 years in prison for protesting against apartheid in Africa, Mandela became *president* of the very country that had once held him captive.

Mandela's motto? "It always seems impossible until it is done."

**GURU'S TIP:** Your life's defining milestones often lie just beyond your next, fearless attempt. Suffering a setback provides an opportunity to engineer a *comeback!*

## The 5th Rule of Belief) **Believing You Can Beat the Odds…Evens the Odds**

The 5th Rule of Belief involves one's ability to level the playing fields of life and business by believing that one has just as good a shot (or even a *better* shot) as anyone else does at becoming victorious.

For instance, in 1985, Jim Koch started a microbrewery called Boston Beer and delivered, in person, his first 25 cases of product to local bars around Boston. Many business experts agreed that Koch's attempt to break into a market that had long been dominated by giant breweries like Anheuser-Busch and Miller was a laughable endeavor. But Jim believed in his product, and in his company. And that's all it took to begin leveling the playing field against the big breweries.

In coming years, the mega breweries would become intoxicated with surprise at the rapid growth of Koch's microbrewery. By 2004, Boston Beer was bringing in $217 million in revenues. And in 2010, revenues topped $463 million!

When a group of teenage boys from Alabama decided to start a rock band, their high school gym teacher, Leonard Skinner, told them they didn't have a prayer. In fact, Skinner assured the boys they would "never amount to nothin'." Exercising faith in their chosen destinies, the boys went ahead and formed their band anyway.

They called it, Lynyrd Skynyrd—a name they selected in tribute to their harshest critic.

*"Nothing is impossible unless you believe it is."*
-Chuck Norris

The fast-paced world of technology provides another inspiring example of the unfailing precision of the 5th Rule of Belief.

When Michael Dell launched his little computer company, analysts predicted that Dell would fail for three, specific reasons. Michael had no previous experience running a company. Large technology firms already dominated the market. And Dell's access to capital was very limited. Dell might've been discouraged by his so-called "slim chances" of survival if he wasn't so busy *gaining* experience running his company, *stealing* market share away from his large competitors, and implementing his genius customer-direct distribution model to *compensate for* his lack of capital.

In the face of Wall Street's best analysts, Michael Dell, at age 27, became the youngest CEO of a Fortune 500 company. In recent years, Dell's little company was processing an average of $120 million per day in sales!

**GURU'S TIP:** Got a particularly tough personal or business venture you plan on undertaking? Begin evening the odds by *believing* that you can beat them!

## The 6th Rule of Belief) If You're Certain You Can Change the World…You *Can*

Joe Weider was born in 1920 in Montreal, Quebec.

Weider was still a jobless teenager when he informed his family that he was going to quit high school to launch a fitness magazine by which to introduce body-building and physical exercise to the mainstream public.

Oblivious to the magnitude of her son's forthcoming accomplishments, Joe's mother suggested he should take a job at a local factory instead. Fortunately, Joe, 18, stuck to his guns, followed his heart, and put together his first, crude fitness magazine, "*Your Physique*." Copies were initially sold primarily by word-of-mouth advertising within the restricted circles of the body-building community. Of course, Joe didn't stop there. Weider's next publication, "*Muscle and Fitness*," boasted a team of writers, improved content, and a reader-base that would grow steadily into the *millions* over coming decades.

The figurehead of the new-age fitness movement, Weider would organize the International Federation of Body Building (IFBB)—the world's first organized body-building circuit. It was through Weider's IFBB that body-builders such as Arnold Schwarzenegger and Lou Ferrigno were discovered. Schwarzenegger and Ferrigno were massive, human specimens who generated publicity for the sport of body-building and supplied momentum to Weider's dream of enlightening the global consciousness to the health benefits associated with the fitness lifestyle.

*"Always remember that your mind is infinite and your doubts are limiting."*
-Robert Kiyosaki

By the turn of the 21st century, Weider found himself presiding from the throne of a fitness empire which included 17 different magazines sold in 128 countries, multiple international fitness organizations, and a mile-long line of health and fitness products generating hundreds of millions in annual sales. In fact, if you read fitness magazines, use fitness equipment or take body-building supplements, chances are a *physical piece* of the Weider vision has muscled its way into your life.

Once asked if he foresaw his trend-setting success in the world of fitness, Joe responded, "You can't start something as big as a magazine without believing that it's going to change the world."

**GURU'S TIP:** The mark you will make on your world—in terms of dollars earned, relationships built, battles won, ground gained, goals accomplished, dreams fulfilled, and value added—will be based largely on what you *believe* your destiny holds.

If you're certain you can change the world, you *can!*

## The 7th Rule of Belief) **When You Believe That Anything Is Possible, Anything Becomes Possible!**

Imagine the level of mental mastery it would require to walk into a fast-food restaurant for the very first time and, while you're waiting in line to be served, figure out a way to run the place more efficiently and arrive at a decision to buy out the company. Now, imagine the level of faith it would require to become so confident that you could convince the owners to agree with your plans that you would leave your current life behind to pursue your vision?

Amazingly, that's exactly what Ray Kroc did just over 50 years ago, and it would make him fast-food legend…

In 1954, Ray Kroc, 52, walked into the McDonald Brothers' hamburger joint in San Bernardino, California. McDonald's was then just a small chain run by Dick and Maurice McDonald. As Kroc stood in line for a hamburger, he became captivated by the unlimited possibilities he envisioned for McDonald's. Kroc saw a national chain of fast-food restaurants with sparkling clean facilities, a friendly atmosphere, limited menus, and speedy service. Kroc also envisioned *himself* as CEO. And although the McDonald brothers had never heard of Ray Kroc and had no intentions of selling their business, Ray immediately went to work on a genius, take-over plan.

Later that year, on a quest to learn the nuts and bolts of the McDonald Brothers' business model, Kroc joined the company as a franchise manager. After a 12-month crash-course in McDonald's 101, Kroc purchased his own franchise in Illinois.

Then, in 1961, just seven years after waltzing into a McDonald's restaurant for the very first time, Ray Kroc negotiated a $2.7 million buyout from the McDonalds brothers, crowned himself the new king of fast-food—and then took the chain global.

Today, more than 35,000 McDonald's can be found in 120 countries!

*"All things are possible for him that believes."*
-Jesus Christ

**GURU'S TIP:** There is no such thing as "impossible" for you when you believe in the reality of unlimited possibilities!

So, what outrageous, new possibilities do *you* believe in?

Over the past two chapters, you've shattered your limitations and dispelled the myth of "impossibility."

Next, you're going to discover your subconscious *Master Thinking System (MTS)*—a powerful assembly of neurophysiological programs which, once understood and intelligently directed, can guide you effortlessly toward the realization of your dreams and goals, even as you sleep…

# 25

# The Master Thinking System (MTS)

*Unlocking the Mysteries of the Subconscious Mind*

*"Turn your eye inward and you will discover 1000 roads of your mind yet untraveled."*
-Henry David Thoreau

Let's begin unlocking the mysteries of your subconscious mind by answering an important question: What is the ***"Master Thinking System (MTS)?"***

Your *Master Thinking System* (or *MTS*) is a complex system of highly self-regulated interplay between: (1) your amazing brain, (2) the environmental data and stored information your brain processes as you move through life, and (3) your central nervous system. Much of this neurophysiological interplay is based on preprogrammed molecular directives which elicit *conditioned responses* so quickly that they seem automatic. This unceasing interplay of subconscious activity effectively controls the large majority of what you think, say, and do—often without any input required from the *conscious* you.

Simply put, your MTS is what's running your life when the *conscious* you isn't.

In order to get a better understanding of the Master Thinking System at work in your life, think back to your first days behind the wheel of a car.

Can you recall the mental and physical challenge of learning to drive? Do you remember how much concentration it took simply to steer the car, maintain proper speed, brake smoothly, and park within arm's length of a curb? Do you also recall how, just a short time later, you were not only operating your vehicle with ease, but navigating a complex course of highways and intersections, chatting comfortably with passengers, and enjoying a cup of coffee while behind the wheel, all seemingly without devoting a moment of *conscious* thought to the once demanding task of driving?

Who—or what—was operating the vehicle while your focus and attention were devoted to all of these *other* activities?

Ah, yes, your *Master Thinking System.*

*"The assumption that the mind is a real being... is the only one compatible with the facts of experience."*
-Dr. William James

As you go about your day, your Master Thinking System is busy processing a staggering 25 million bits of environmental data and stored information per second, compared to your conscious mind's roughly 50 bits of data and info per second.

This means that during any given *minute* you spend behind the wheel of your car (while you devote your conscious thoughts to say, chatting with a passenger,) your subconscious MTS is presiding over approximately 1.5 *billion* bits of environmental data and stored information. The broad range of stimuli and info your MTS might be managing include: visuals of the roads; judgments about steering, acceleration, and braking; memories about how to get to where you're going; essential bodily functions; your entire mental vault of life experiences; and much more.

Your MTS represents the operating system of "mental software" programs that effectively controls every move you make from sunrise to sunset, and remains highly active...even as you sleep.

## Your Master Thinking System

*A Brain unto Itself*

Just as your Master Thinking System assumes control over your vehicle when you're paying attention to other things, your *subconscious* thinking system often takes over other important aspects of your life without your conscious consent.

If you're not careful, this could spell real trouble for you over the long-run in your "conscious quest" to master your mind and world.

For instance, have you ever wondered how a pretty woman can *believe* she's overweight or unattractive despite many compliments about her looks? Or how a man remains *convinced* that quitting smoking is "impossible" when he knows many others who've quit successfully? Or how it is that a person who possesses the advantage of full, physical capabilities *maintains* that he or she "can't do" what is being done elsewhere by folks with missing limbs?

The source of this phenomenon of overriding belief can be found within the programming of a person's Master Thinking System.

Think of your MTS as an operating system for your beliefs. This operating system governs the large majority of your daily activities with the help of an assembly of "Master Thoughts" (or core beliefs) which may or may not serve your best interest. Just like your computer or smart phone's operating system, your MTS needs to be programmed correctly in order to provide you the best possible service.

So, let's learn a little more about Master Thoughts, and begin the process of reprogramming your MTS.

*"The controlling intelligence knows what it does,*
*and whereon it works.*
-Marcus Aurelius

## The "Master Thought" Assembly

*Invisible Guide to the Ultimate You*

So, how does your MTS…*think?* And, more importantly, how can the "conscious you" begin to *outthink* it? The answer to both of these questions can be found in your "Master Thought" assembly.

At the epicenter of your subconscious MTS is an assembly of mental directives which I refer to as *Master Thoughts.* Each Master Thought is a preprogrammed directive made up of:

- **A *mental picture* you show yourself**
- **A *message* you tell yourself**
- **A *feeling* you experience**

For instance, a non-smoker might *see* someone smoking, *tell herself,* "that's a disgusting habit," and *feel* repulsed. A smoker, on the other hand, may *see* the same person smoking, *tell himself,* "I could really use a smoke," and *feel* an urge to fire up.

Each of the above responses is an expression of the Master Thought that underlies it. Each Master Thought in your MTS represents an unquestioned mental program which elicits a conditioned response. Your Master Thought assembly is essentially an assortment of your most fundamental beliefs. And this self-governing, subconscious programming is currently running your life, steering you in the direction of who you are to become, for better or worse, even as you sleep!

So, just how are new, empowering Master Thoughts "installed?" You're about to find out.

## Reproramming Your Master Thinking System

Installing new, empowering Master Thoughts into your MTS is like rewriting the operating system that governs your belief system, and your life. This process begins by selecting your choice of new, empowering Master Thoughts. Let's begin this process…

Throughout the initial chapters of *Mind Contrology ®,* you have been exposed to stories, facts, and figures about ordinary people who have achieved extraordinary feats in the face of every obstacle under the sun. These stories, facts, and figures are designed to deprogram you of the self-imposed limitations and performance barriers that have long held you back from fulfilling your true potential in life and business.

These limitations and barriers represent Master Thoughts which were installed without your consent and to your detriment.

It's time to reprogram your Master Thought assembly, and get your Master Thinking System entirely on your side. The first step is to begin reprogramming your MTS through the power of conscious choice.

Below, list any new, empowering Master Thoughts you wish to adopt about your ability to control your mind and destiny; about your powers and potentialities; about your ability to get out of debt and generate wealth; about others, your world or your Creator; about your ability to achieve the impossible and fulfill your dreams; etc.

Don't forget to list *supporting evidence* (stories, facts, and figures that verify that your new belief is grounded in truth) and *anticipated benefits* related to each new Master Thought you wish to program into your MTS.

For instance, a new Master Thought, "I've got millionaire potential," may include *supporting evidence* such as, "There are 12 million millionaires living in the U.S. as of 2016." This Master Thought may include *anticipated benefits* such as, "As a millionaire, I will be able to travel the world and contribute to my family, friends, employees, and/or community in profound ways."

New Master Thought:
**Supporting Evidence-**
**Anticipated Benefits-**

New Master Thought:
**Supporting Evidence-**
**Anticipated Benefits-**

New Master Thought:
**Supporting Evidence-**
**Anticipated Benefits-**

New Master Thought:
**Supporting Evidence-**
**Anticipated Benefits-**

New Master Thought:
**Supporting Evidence-**
**Anticipated Benefits-**

*"The mind not only serves a final purpose, but brings a final purpose."*
-Dr. William James

All right, you've begun the process of "reprogramming" your MTS with new, superior Master Thoughts which will afford you the best use of your powers, and will support your vision for your life, career, relationships, and finances. You are well on your way to harnessing the full force of belief, and to crossing the threshold of the place where the old you ends and the Ultimate You begins.

Next, let's turn to an advanced Master Thought installation methodology designed to fortify your MTS reprogramming efforts.

## Ego Reformulation Methodology

*The Master Thought Installation Process*

**What is "Ego Reformulation Methodology?"** *Ego Reformulation Methodology* (or ERM) is an advanced, Master Thought installation technique which combines the powers of visualization, Victory Talk, and gamma-frequency-producing emotion.

**Who Uses ERM?** The U.S. military uses ERM as part of its basic and specialized training programs in order to deprogram and reprogram the psyche of new recruits so quickly and completely that militaries around the world have sought to replicate it.

If you've ever observed a soldier return home from boot camp a changed person (in just weeks,) you've witnessed the transformational effects of ERM!

Used properly, ERM is the single, most effective technology for driving new Master Thoughts through the barrier of consciousness and into your subconscious Master Thinking System.

## The Ego Reformulation Process

*How to Install "Ultimate You" Mental Software*

Installing empowering Master Thoughts (or overriding, neurophysiological software) into your subconscious Master Thinking System is a relatively straightforward, 3-step process.

Step 1) ***Visualize*** **a future scenario in which you see yourself acting in accordance with any new Master Thought(s) you wish to make permanent.**

For instance, let's say your professional vision includes becoming an expert in your field and making millions doing it. Maybe you're new, empowering belief is, "I'm a world-class leader and sought-after professional in-the-making." In this case, you might *visualize* yourself in the boardroom at your company's headquarters, skillfully calling the shots among your top executives in marketing, finance, and operations. On the wall, you might *foresee* a glass-encased *"Forbes"* magazine cover with your face on it. The magazine headline reads, "*Manager of the Decade!"*

Step 2) **Incorporate** ***Victory Talk*** **into the installation process.**

Victory Talk adds an additional, critical facet to the Master Thought installation process.

At the same time that you are foreseeing yourself act in accordance with the new Master Thought(s) you wish to make permanent, proclaim the Master Thought out loud. Referring to the example above, you would declare, "I'm a world-class leader and sought-after professional in-the-making!" while you are visualizing your company, your boardroom, your executives, and your awards on the wall.

Remember to *say* while you *see.*

Step 3) ***Supercharge* the installation process!**

The final step to successfully "installing" your choice of Master Thoughts into your MTS is to add positive energy to the installation process.

Get *excited* about the great progress your future staff will make because of your effective management skills. Feel the *satisfaction* of banking your first million as a result of your hard work and wise investment decisions. Anticipate the unspeakable *joy* of revolutionizing your field and of giving back in major ways to your supportive family, friends, associates, employees, and community.

Adding positive energy to your visualized statements of belief will cause you to generate gamma frequency (or peak performance) brain waves. This will also help you to maximize the benefits of the Mind/Reality Relationship.

**ERP** = + +

*"To believe your own thoughts...is genius."*
-Ralph Waldo Emerson

**GURU'S TIP:** When using Ego Reformulation Process, it's important to "time" the *seeing, saying,* and *feeling* precisely together. Performing these steps simultaneously creates the ideal Master Thought installation environment, enabling your desired Master Thoughts to penetrate the barrier between your conscious and subconscious minds.

Now that you understand the ERP, you're in a terrific position to begin accelerating your evolution into your Ultimate Self and expediting the transformation of your dreams from mind to matter.

However, we're not done with the Master Thought installation process just yet. Below, is a trick to make the ERP doubly effective.

*"You have a conscious mind,*
*and an unconscious mind—or subconscious mind."*
-Dr. Milton Erickson

## Add *Anchoring* to the Master Thought Installation Process

Add power to the Ego Reformulation Process by incorporating "anchoring" into your ERP efforts.

For instance, let's say your chosen Master Thought is, "I'm a millionaire, or multimillionaire, in the making!" Or perhaps it's, "I will lose 10 pounds of fat and build visible muscle over the next six months by joining a gym and eating right!"

Simply *place your hand over your heart* or *touch two fingers to your temple* as you visualize yourself acting in accordance with your chosen Master Thought and declare your new Master Thought to yourself, God, and the Universe.

The physical actions of *placing your hand over your heart* and *touching two fingers to your temple* provide the anchoring which helps your brain register the changes you wish to make as "important."

Use the ERP methodology (and add anchoring to the process) each day upon rising and before bed for 30 days. You can be sure that the Master Thought installation process is complete, and largely automatic, once you firmly believe the content on which your choice of new Master Thoughts is founded.

*"When you believe in a thing,*
*believe in it all the way,*
*implicitly and unquestionably."*
-Walt Disney

## Harnessing the Force of Belief

*A Quick Review*

Throughout the 4th Element of the Dream Acquisition Formula, you've learned a great deal about harnessing the force of belief.

For starters, you learned that the primary "origins of belief" include: your childhood, family and friends, schools and workplaces, marketing and advertising, church and media, and, most importantly, *yourself*.

You took the test of moral fiber, started ascending the ladder of Self-power, and began honing your sense of Self-destiny. And after shattering your limitations and dispelling the myth of impossibility, you're now more prepared than ever to reach new heights of personal and professional performance. You even discovered your Master Thinking System (MTS) and found out about a method for reprograming your MTS with new, empowering Master Thoughts designed to help you fulfill your dreams and realize your goals…even as you sleep.

At last, you've got what it takes to harness the *full* force of belief.

Are you beginning to feel as if there is nothing on this Earth that you cannot do? Is your mind reeling with an assortment of wonderful goals you wish to accomplish in the years, months, weeks, and days ahead? If so, now is the perfect time to introduce you to a pioneering system for making goals real, with mathematical accuracy.

You're about to become a Goal Scientist…

# Become a Goal Scientist

*The 5th Element of the Dream Acquisition Formula (DAF)*

# 26

# Goal Science 101

*An Introductory Course in Goal-setting*

*"Experts on the science of success know that the brain is a goal-seeking organism."*
-Jack Canfield

Welcome to the University of Goal Realization. Your highly-focused, time-compressed, three-chapter curriculum will enable you to:

(1) **Master Goal Science 101** by discovering the science of goal realization as demonstrated through the rags to riches story of retail king, Sam Walton.

(2) **Discover the "Goal Realization System"**—a 7-step discipline for getting everything you want out of life in the *specific time-frame* of your choosing.

(3) **Graduate with a PhD in Goal Science** by performing three, exciting goal science projects.

Let's begin your studies with a lesson about how a young, J.C. Penny management trainee named Sam Walton used the power of goal science to realize his objective of building a multi-billion dollar retail empire, and did so in less time than it takes most folks to pay off their mortgage…

When Sam Walton graduated from the University of Missouri in 1942, he had no real work experience and little savings. What he did have was an inspiring vision—he wanted to become a successful businessman.

Realizing that he didn't want to work for peanuts in the crowded aisles of someone *else's* enterprise, the ambitious southerner set a long-range goal to open his *own* retail shop. Intuitively grasping the need for short-term goals by which to light the path to his chosen destination, Sam focused on what he currently needed: real-world management experience and the capital necessary to finance his dream.

On a quest to learn the ropes of the retail industry and bank some coin, Walton signed on as a J.C. Penny management trainee for $75 per month. There, Sam learned three things. He despised being managed. He was terrible at accounting. And the road to riches definitely didn't run through J.C Penny.

So, after gaining the insights he felt he needed to manage his own store, Walton took what cash he'd saved, and then arranged to borrow the $20,000 he needed to open a shop in nearby, Newport.

*"Hitch your wagon to a star."*
-Ralph Waldo Emerson

By 1945, following a two-year tour in the Army, Walton was living his dream as the owner of a Ben Franklin 5&10 retail shop. The 27 year-old Walton barely had time to enjoy the rewards of his first write-offs before discovering that he was "being taken" by his franchise supplier. The astronomical costs that Walton was forced to pay for his merchandise made it impossible to turn a decent profit without beating his customers over the head with high prices at the register. So, Sam—an honest shopkeeper who believed that his customers deserved better—set out to find a cheaper supplier which could help him cut costs and pass the savings along to his patrons.

Over coming months, Walton scoured the area for a new supplier, but was thwarted by local business politics. Sam's primary supplier, Butler Brothers, managed to convince the area's smaller suppliers (most of whom purchased *their* supplies from Butler Brothers) not to deal with the young shop owner directly. Refusing to be beaten, however, Walton traveled outside the state to locate a willing wholesaler. At last, he struck gold when he found a cheap supplier which allowed him to undercut Butler Brothers. Sam's rock-bottom prices soon brought customers stampeding through his doors!

With his first major victory under his belt, Walton set a new goal for himself: to "become the best, most profitable retail shop in Arkansas within 5 years."

And the reliable operations of goal science immediately went to work on Sam's behalf.

*"The person who makes a success of living*
*is the one who sees his goal steadily*
*and aims for it unswervingly."*
-Cecil B. DeMille

By 1952, just five years from the time Walton had set his objective of becoming the best retailer in Arkansas, Sam's 5&10 had already become the franchise system's top performing store (at $250,000 in sales and $40,000 profit,) not only in Arkansas, but in the surrounding six-county region. Throughout the 1950's, Walton grew his shop into a profitable portfolio of a dozen similar stores. Business was booming. Customer loyalty was steadily improving. And Sam was living the life of his dreams.

It was around 1960, however, that Walton identified a curious, new trend in the retail industry. Mass retailers like Kmart and Woolworth's began cropping up across the country, threatening to put variety stores like Walton's out of business. Sam saw only two options: expand or die. Sam adamantly refused to throw up the white flag and surrender and become a casualty to big business. An unusually gutsy visionary, Walton returned to the drawing board with his next, enormous objective—to open his own one-stop market and grow his empire into the "nation's largest retail chain."

In response to his enormous new goal, Walton's mind supplied him with a crafty strategy by which to meet his target objective. Specifically, Walton began visiting Kmart and Woolworth's stores, where he studied their displays, compared prices, and interviewed customers about what he could do to earn their business. During each of his visits, Sam filled his trusty notepad with new ideas about how to outperform his new rivals. By 1962, Walton's purpose of becoming the nation's largest retailer was beginning to materialize. Pony rides and free watermelon marked the festive, grand opening of Sam's first, giant, retail outlet—Walmart.

Over nearly the next decade, Walton personally oversaw the opening of a series of Walmart box stores. At each grand opening, Walton could be found speaking up his vision for Walmart as the *nation's #1 retail chain*. In fact, Walton once admitted, "I love to get in front of a crowd and speak something up—an idea, a store, a product, the whole company—whatever I happened to be focused on right then." Sam's strategy of speaking goals into existence worked wonders.

By 1970, Walton was operating 32 stores and generating $31 million in sales. By 1980, Sam's Walmart was 275 stores strong with $1 billion in annual sales. Walton's dream of becoming the nation's largest retail chain was rapidly transitioning from mind to matter. However, Sam was just getting started…

*"Aim at the Heavens and you will get the Earth thrown in."*
-C.S. Lewis

During the 1980s, Walton became eager to raise the bar again. This time Sam's mind began reeling with visions of a *global* business empire.

One can imagine the fateful meeting at Walmart headquarters during which an aging Sam Walton, armed with his trusty notepad and a soul fueled by passion, paced the boardroom while discussing his newest plans for Walmart's future—the grand goal of becoming the world's biggest retailer. The deadline? 1990.

In order to make his impossible dream come true, Sam employed the same goal realization system he'd been using for most of his life—a system based on *prioritizing, writing, discussing, believing in,* and *setting deadlines* for *specific goals* which *excite* and *motivate* the goal-setter. The results would prove historic.

By 1990, Walmart revenues topped $26 billion worldwide. Then, in 2002, Walmart's global domination of the retail industry was made official when Forbes Magazine named Sam's company both the "world's largest retailer" and "world's largest company!"

Speaking about his remarkable discipline in converting vision into goals, and goals into billions, legendary CEO Sam Walton once revealed, "I've always held the bar pretty high for myself; I've always set extremely high personal goals."

Goal realization is a *science*, and Sam Walton was a master goal scientist.

*"Once a goal is set, it's just a matter of time before that goal becomes a reality."*
-Pat Croche

Whether you're looking to build a global business empire over the course of a lifetime, put your first million—or next million—in the bank by next year, or improve your marriage or love life over the next 90 days, your chances of success improve astronomically by filtering your ambitious goals through the *Goal Realization System (GRS)* found exclusively in *Mind Contrology* ®.

You will discover this amazing goal actualization system in the next chapter…

# 27

# The Goal Realization System (GRS)

*An Advanced Studies Course on Making Goals Real*

*"If we want to discover the unlimited possibilities within us, we must find a goal big enough to push us beyond our limits and discover our true potential."*
-Anthony Robbins

**About the "Goal Realization System:"** The *"Goal Realization System" (or GRS)* is the most effective Peak Performance Technology available today for moving goals, large and small, from mind to matter.

The most powerful goal attainment system ever designed, the GRS offers the combined power of seven, goal-mastery strategies which have been effectively employed by a diverse assortment of the world's top peak performers.

Just how powerful *is* the Goal Realization System?

Each of the GRS's seven components is, in and of itself, an effective tool for taking your goal actualization capabilities to the next level. By working all seven components as a system, however, you will be able to transform your vision for your future into a logical and actionable format by which to realize your objectives in every category of life, with *scientific* precision.

# The Goal Realization System

*7 Principles for Setting Goals—and Getting Results*

## Goal-mastery Principle #1) **Divide, Prioritize, and Conquer Your Plans for the Future**

*"You need to visualize your whole life in terms of the goals you are pursuing, and the steps necessary to get there."*
-Dr. Stanton Peele

The vision Master List you created earlier works hand-in-hand with the *Goal Realization System (GRS.)*

The first step in using the GRS to your advantage is to divide each life-category of your vision Master List into a hierarchy of highly manageable objectives. An effective hierarchy might include your ultimate, long-range, and short-term goals for each major life category.

For instance, you might divide and prioritize your professional objectives in the following way:

- **Ultimate Goal**: 5 years or more
- **Long-range**: 1 year or more
- **Short-term**: less than 1 year

Topping each life-category of your Master List should be your ultimate goal of the distant future, descending down to the daily, supporting goals that represent rungs of a ladder toward your ultimate destinations.

Want an example? During college, Sam Walton dreamed up the ultimate goal of becoming a successful businessman. Sam then set a specific, long-range goal to "open a local retail shop." Next, in order to work his way toward business ownership, Sam set three supporting, short-term goals: to get a job to gain real world management experience, to bank some "seed capital," and, later, to borrow $20,000 to finance his dream.

So, if Sam were to divide and prioritize the professional life-category of his vision Master List, it would look like this:

| **Professional Objectives** |
|---|
| Ultimate Goal: Become a successful businessman |
| Long-range Goal(s): Open a retail shop of my own |
| Short-term Goal(s):<br>• acquire a business loan<br>• save 30% of every paycheck<br>• land a job in management<br>• gain business expertise |

**GURU'S TIP:** Structuring each life-category of your vision Master List into a logical timeline of attainable goals should be your first order of business if you want to transform your vision for your future into a highly actionable plan for success.

*Divide, prioritize, and conquer* your plans for the future!

## Goal-mastery Principle #2) **Set Specific, Detailed Goals**

Vague goals confuse the brain and fail to arouse the whole of our resources. Knowing that you want to retire a "millionaire" is a terrific long-range financial objective. But it's not enough.

In order to generate the momentum it takes to increase the zeros on your bank statement from three or four to seven or more, you've got to get *specific.* A precise, ultimate financial goal such as "retiring at age 50 with a net worth of $2,500,000" gives your brain a clear understanding of what you're looking to achieve, and of what types of business and investment strategies it'll take to make it happen.

*"No wind serves him who addresses his voyage to no certain point."*
-Miguel de Cervantes

Just how important are *details* when it comes to realizing your goals? In a landmark Yale University study, researchers asked a graduating class who among the group had a detailed, written plan outlining their goals for their future. Only 3% of the class did. Twenty years later, that small group of competent goal scientists had a larger collective net worth than the other 97% of the study group combined!

**GURU'S TIP:** *Specific goals* beget *specific results*. Sweat the details.

Goal-mastery Principle #3) **Write Your Goals into Existence**

If I told you that each time you put your goals to paper it represents one small step (or even large step) toward making your plans real, would you believe me? Celebrated cartoonist Scott Adams admitted using this very tactic to transform his dream career of cartooning from mind to matter.

In 1988, Scott Adams, 31, was working as a manager for Pacific Bell when he began entertaining the thought of leaving his cushy job to become a cartoonist. Through a stroke of genius, Adams began putting his goal to paper multiple times each day. "I will become a cartoonist," was Scott's written declaration of destiny.

The act of writing his goal, and of seeing it on paper, emboldened the obscure telephone company manager, raised his levels of confidence, and strengthened his commitment to art. By cartooning during the early hours before work at the phone company, Adams was able to get the first of his cartoons published in 1989. The $389 monthly royalty check he received was enough to fan the flames of Adams' passion. Eventually, Adams' prediction grew into, "I will become the world's best cartoonist!"

In 1990, Adams' cartoon strip—Dilbert—was being printed in 100 newspapers. Three years later, Dilbert was in 400 papers, and Scott found himself edging closer to the exit door at Bell. Finally, by 1996, Adams was able to devote himself to cartooning full-time. Appearing in some 800 newspapers, Dilbert had become one of the most recognized cartoon strips outside of Peanuts, and Adams was just getting started.

By the year 2000, Dilbert could be found in 2,000 newspapers in 57 countries.

*"The discipline of writing [goals] down*
*is the first step to making them real."*
-Super-CEO Lee Iacocca

**GURU'S TIP:** The act of writing goals is a critical part of the goal realization process. Putting your goals to paper—a *dozen* times a day if you've got it in you—is an effective way to articulate your goals, and to begin to transition your plans from that which you intend to achieve to that which you have already accomplished.

Forge the destiny-defining habit of putting your thoughts, ideas, plans, and goals to paper.

## Goal-mastery Principle #4) **Speak Your Objectives into Reality!**

Herb Kelleher was the mastermind behind the remarkable success of Southwest Airlines. During his tenure as CEO, Kelleher set an enormous goal for his growing airline—to become the "best service provider" in the air travel industry.

Kelleher's primary vehicle for realizing his goal? His *voice.*

Using his mouth as a megaphone, Kelleher preached the message of superior service to everyone who had ears. He discussed his goal at corporate meetings, repeated it during luncheons, and reminded his employees in the hallways.

Why was Kelleher so relentless? The legendary CEO understood that the communication of one's goals to others holds a special magic in the process of making them real.

Kelleher continued proclaiming Southwest's future as the industry's best service provider until it permeated the entire organization, from the executive ranks to the clerk hired yesterday. Did Herb's verbal approach to goal actualization work? Southwest has won the airline industry's coveted "Triple Crown Award" for service no less than 30 times!

*"A secret goal cannot benefit*
*from the participation and force of others."*
-Dr. Charles Garfield

Those who've developed the discipline of confidently proclaiming their goals to the world, as if they've already achieved them, have stumbled upon one of the great secrets of the Mind/Reality Relationship; that is, specific objectives respond faithfully to the sound of their master's voice. This is what makes reciting your Destiny Statement so important in your quest to fulfill your dreams.

### The Advantages of *Speaking Up* Your Goals

By regularly talking with family, friends, and colleagues about your long-range and short-term goals, you can expect the following clear advantages:

- Your Self-power will soar!
- You will develop hardwired, neurological commitment to your objectives.
- You will become comfortable in articulating your plans.
- *Others* will become committed to your causes, too!

**GURU'S TIP:** Chatting up your goals to your spouse, boss, business partners, money manager, and/or potential lenders enables you to win the critical, interpersonal support by which to accelerate the goal realization process.

Practice *speaking* your goals into reality!

Goal-mastery Principle #5) **You Must "Buy Into" Your Goals**

While it's great to have the support of family and friends as you pursue your ultimate long-range and short-term goals, there's one person you absolutely must get on your side, and that person is *you*. Buying into your goals becomes much easier when your hierarchy of ultimate, long-range, and short-term goals is one that includes logical steps, like rungs of a ladder, by which to ascend your hierarchy of goals over the years, months, weeks, and days ahead.

For instance, let's say you're a department manager and your ultimate goal for your career is to "become president of the company" you currently work for. Below are the right and wrong ways to approach this ultimate objective.

| **WRONG** (Illogical gaps in goal hierarchy) | **RIGHT** (Hierarchy of logical, supporting goals) |
|---|---|
| Professional Objectives | Professional Objectives |
| Ultimate Goal: Become president of firm | Ultimate Goal: Become president of firm |
| | Long-range: Become vice president |
| Long-range: Become division manager | Become division manager |
| | Become branch manager |
| Short-term: Become branch manager | Short-term: Win company's "department manager of the year" award |
| | Weekly/Daily: Manage my department more effectively |

In the scenario above, the ultimate goal of "becoming president of firm" is supported by a series of logical long-range and short-term supporting goals. With these additional long-range and short-term goals added to the goal hierarchy, the pathway forward becomes quite clear. Furthermore, establishing a *weekly/daily* action step allows for immediate participation in the realization of one's future outcomes.

*"You must buy into your goals."*
-Dr. Stanton Peele

**GURU'S TIP:** When establishing a hierarchy of goals, your objectives should come across as logically progressive, completely attainable, and immediately pursuable. This is the key to being able to *buy into* your goals.

Goal-mastery Principle #6) **Set Goals That Challenge and Motivate You!**

One of my firm's most transformational services is our *"Ultimate Coaching & Consulting"* package. This high-end service includes: limousine service for our client, a helicopter flight to a luxury hotel and banquet hall, and a comprehensive strategic plan developed over a fine-dining luncheon.

The purpose of all these bells-and-whistles is to get the client—typically a CEO of a company that generates less than $225 million in annual revenues—to start thinking, leading, and managing like a Fortune-level CEO. After an exhilarating day of operating at a higher level of performance than these executives are used to, our clients find it easier to expand their mental horizons, and to set new, challenging goals for themselves and their organizations.

Fortunately, you don't have to charter a chopper or dish out $10,000 to establish goals that challenge and motivate you. All you've got to do is remember the 1st Rule of Mentality: *The mind rises to the challenges you place before it.*

Set uninspiring goals and your performance will be limited. Continuously raise the bar, however, and you'll subject yourself to an increasingly higher caliber of ideas, strategies, smarts, energy, skills, and resources by which to reach new heights of success.

*"It is for us to pray...for powers equal to our task, to go forward with great desire beating forever at the door of our heart, as we travel toward our distant goal."*
-Helen Keller

**GURU'S TIP:** Want to achieve spectacular results? Establish challenging goals that excite and motivate you!

Goal-mastery Principle #7) **Commit to Definite Deadlines**

You wouldn't consider booking a flight with an airline that wasn't sure what time its aircraft was arriving at your chosen destination, would you? Well, you also shouldn't establish a system of important goals unless it includes *specific deadlines* by which you will arrive at your chosen destinations in life and business.

Attaching deadlines to your goals (large and small) does three important things:

- It adds commitment and a sense of urgency to the goal actualization process.
- It provides a metric for measuring progress.
- It provides a date for celebrating, and a starting point for your next, major goal.

*"Arriving at one goal is the starting point to another."*
-Thomas Dewey

**GURU'S TIP:** Anytime you say, "I will achieve this specific goal by this particular date," you are exercising your ability to master time, marshal your resources, and trump circumstances.

Attach reasonable deadlines to your goals, and then do everything within your means to meet them!

## The Goal Realization System

*A Brief Overview*

Remember, realizing an objective is a *science*. And there's no better way to maximize your goal attainment capabilities than to set and pursue your objectives according to the seven, goal-mastery principles of the Goal Realization System.

Let's review the GRS…

**1. Divide, Prioritize, and Conquer Your Plans for the Future**

**2. Set Specific, Detailed Goals**

**3. Write Your Goals into Existence**

**4. Speak Your Goals into Reality**

**5. "Buy Into" a Hierarchy of Logical Goals**

**6. Challenge Yourself—the Motivation Will Follow!**

**7. Commit to "Definite Deadlines!"**

So far, you've examined a case study based on the extraordinary goal actualization capabilities of master goal scientist, Sam Walton. You've also discovered the Goal Realization System (GRS) found exclusively in *Mind Contrology* ®.

You're accelerating through the University of Goal Realization with the highest honors.

It's now time to become a certified *goal scientist…*

# 28

# Becoming a Goal Scientist

*Earning Your PhD in Goal Science*

*"He turns back not who is bound by a star."*
-Leonardo da Vinci

In the last chapter, you gained an intimate knowledge of the mechanics of the GRS—a 7-step system for making goals real. You know goal science in *theory*. However, making your dreams come true with scientific precision will require putting your new knowledge into *practice*.

If you're ready to earn your PhD in goal science, you'll need to manage three goal actualization projects:

(1) Transform your vision Master List into an actionable, personal agenda for success
(2) Add depth and deadlines to your Destiny Statement
(3) Initiate a "goal discussion"

The following projects are designed to help you hitch your wagon to a star by becoming more than a superior goal-setter, more like a *goal scientist*.

## Your 3 Goal Actualization Projects

### Goal Science Project #1) **Transform Your Vision Master List into a *Personal Agenda* of Actionable Goals**

Your first task as an aspiring goal scientist is to convert your vision Master List into a prioritized hierarchy of objectives in each of the seven life-categories.

**How It Works:** Let's say you're a salesperson with little experience and a grand professional goal of becoming the nation's hottest sales guru. This is a feasible goal which has been achieved by others. One example is Tom Hopkins, author of, "How to Master the Art of Selling."

Below, you'll find an example of an actionable personal agenda based on the ultimate professional goal of "becoming the nation's top sales guru."

**Professional Objectives**

| **Ultimate Goal:** Become the nation's top sales guru (within 10 years) |
|---|
| **Supporting Goals:** (long-range and short-term) |
| • Write a book on effective selling (ready to publish in 5 years) |
| • Become my company's top sales manager (within 5 years) |
| • Become a regional/district sales manager (within 2 years) |
| • Become top branch salesperson (w/in 1 year) |
| • Increase my close rates by 50% (over next 6 months) |
| **This Week's Goal?** Attend a sales seminar or webinar this weekend |
| **Today's Action?** Buy a book written by *today's* hottest sales guru and begin applying what I learn to my very next sale! |

**GURU'S TIP:** The trick is to establish your Ultimate Goal in each life-category of your vision Master List, and then work backward, setting supporting goals with deadlines, until you arrive at a daily goal you can act on immediately.

## Your Personal Agenda for Success

To begin drafting your actionable personal agenda, simply transfer the objectives from each life-category of your vision Master List to the framework provided below.

The goal is to create a logical timeline of specific goals which challenge you and that you can buy into.

### (1) *Professional* Goals

Ultimate Goal:

How will achieving this goal change my life?

Supporting Goals (long-range and short-term):

-
-
-
-
-

This Week's Goal:

Today's Action:

### (2) ***Home/Living*** **Goals**

Let's say your ultimate *home/living* goal is to buy land in a developing area, build a bed and breakfast, and live in it. Commit to a deadline for completing construction and for booking your first suite. Is it 10 years? 5 years? 24 months?

In this case, your logical supporting goals might include acquiring a business loan, acquiring a business license and insurance, locating a GC and architect, conducting site analysis, and incorporating.

Weekly goals and daily actions might include locating a potential lender to discuss your plans, looking into zoning laws, and researching property in developing areas.

Ultimate Goal:

How will achieving this goal change my life?

Supporting Goals (long-range and short-term):

- 
- 
- 
- 
- 

This Week's Goal:

Today's Action:

### (3) ***Relationships*** **Goals**

Maybe your ultimate relationship goals are a rewarding marriage, a large family, and a dozen grandkids. Perhaps your aspirations include attending black-tie affairs among the premiere players in the music industry, political arena, corporate world or Hollywood scene. Or maybe you want both.

Whatever your chief relationships goals may be, determine what new alliances or social habits *logically support* your vision. Then, once you decide when you must acquire these alliances or master these habits, attach definite deadlines to each step of your goal hierarchy.

Ultimate Goal:

How will achieving this goal change my life?

Supporting Goals (long-range and short-term):

- 
- 
- 
- 
- 

This Week's Goal:

Today's Action:

### (4) ***Financial* Goals**

If your ultimate *financial* goal is to retire with a net worth of $5 million, what is your absolute deadline for retiring and enjoying your $5 million in combined assets, real estate, investments, and available cash?

Commit to a date by which you will achieve your ultimate financial goal, and then work backward with logical supporting goals which you will use to climb the ladder to your ultimate financial destination.

Want some inspiration? Oprah Winfrey made a transition from an unknown news reporter to a nationally recognized television show host in less time than it takes most U.S. Treasury Bonds to mature!

Ultimate Goal:

How will achieving this goal change my life?

Supporting Goals (long-range and short-term):

- 
- 
- 
- 
- 

This Week's Goal:

Today's Action:

### (5) ***Travel/Adventure* Goals**

Let's say your ultimate travel/adventure goals are to spend three months in Australia, and to learn how to pilot a helicopter.

Supporting goals for an Australian vacation might include visiting a travel agent, acquiring a passport, Googling timeshare options in Sidney, and dropping $50 of each forthcoming paycheck into a special "vacation fund."

For chopper piloting, your supporting goals might include: acquire a license, pass FAA-mandated physical, enroll in a pilot's class, and start pricing out courses this very weekend.

Below, outline *your* travel/adventure goal hierarchy. Don't forget deadlines!

Ultimate Goal(s):

How will achieving this goal (these goals) change my life?

Supporting Goals (long-range and short-term):

- 
- 
- 
- 
- 

This Week's Goal:

Today's Action:

### (6) ***"Advance Payment"* Contract**

Take a moment to revise your "advance payment" contract.

If you've upped the ante on your goals, you may also have bigger ideas about what you'd like to *give back* in exchange for the success you seek. Make any adjustments you see fit, and then attach deadlines to your list of contributions.

Don't forget to make good on your contract once you're living your dream.

My Ultimate Contributions:

How will my contributions change the lives of others?

Contributions I will make along the way:

- 
- 
- 
- 
- 

This Week's Contribution:

Today's Contribution:

(7) **The *Ultimate You!***

Let's say you envision your Ultimate Self as the next Ben Franklin, Arnold Schwarzenegger, Oprah Winfrey or, dare I say it…your favorite Kardashian.

Some goals that would support an evolution into the roles above might include mastering multiple fields, hitting the gym five times per week and study politics, developing business savvy and media contacts, or…mastering the art of publicity.

When it comes to accelerating your evolution into your Ultimate Self, the key is to determine what supporting habits, alliances, traits, awards, memberships, licenses, self-studies, defining moments, and new endeavors will enable you to close the gap between the person you are now and that Highest Self you will, at last, unveil!

Define the *Ultimate You* in one sentence:

How will my evolution into this role change my life?

Supporting Goals (long-range and short-term):

- 
- 
- 
- 
- 

This Week's Goal:

Today's Action:

Okay, you've converted your vision Master List into a personal agenda of highly-attainable goals. This actionable agenda for success represents a living contract which will help guide you to your chosen destinations in life and business within the "specific timeframe" of your choosing.

Let's move on to your next goal science project.

## Goal Science Project #2) **Add Depth and Deadlines to Your Destiny Statement**

Adding depth and deadlines to your Destiny Statement will supercharge your goal attainment capabilities. Doing so is a simple, two-step process:

**Step 1)** Revise your Destiny Statement to reflect any increases in the scope of your vision for your future.

**Step 2)** Add deadlines to give your statement of destiny new meaning and power!

**Example:** Say your original Destiny Statement resembled, "I will own a specialty-foods store that generates $1,000,000 in annual revenues," and so on. If you've expanded the scope of your vision to include the ultimate goal, "I will become president of a chain of specialty-foods stores that generates $10,000,000 in annual revenues," then retool your Destiny Statement to reflect these changes.

Otherwise, simply insert deadlines into the details of your original Destiny Statement. When will your claims prove true? 10 years? 5 years? 2 years?

**Put your revised Destiny Statement to paper below:**

______________________________________________________________

______________________________________________________________

______________________________________________________________

______________________________________________________________

**GURU'S TIP:** A descriptive Destiny Statement driven by firm deadlines supercharges the goal actualization process. However, it only works if you use it. Proclaim your destiny predictions (including deadlines) daily, until you believe it!

### Goal Science Project #3) **Initiate a "Goal Discussion"**

**The "Goal Discussion" Project:** Learning to talk about your dreams, goals, and plans to others is a critical step in the process of realizing your goals. In fact, it can be said that each time you discuss your goals brings you one step closer to making them real.

Over the next 30 days, actively pursue opportunities to discuss your goals with family or friends, your boss or coworkers, your priest or pastor, or your accountant or money manager.

**GURU'S TIP:** When initiating a "goal discussion," be sure to discuss your objectives only with those you trust for encouragement and sound advice. Don't be discouraged by constructive criticism. And don't stop after just one *goal discussion*. Continue chatting up your plans on a regular basis.

*"There can be no happiness except in the realization that we've accomplished something worthwhile."*
-Theodore Roosevelt

## The University of Goal Realization

*Your Graduation Ceremony*

Congratulations—you've earned your PhD in goal science!

As a certified Goal Scientist, you know *who* you are, *what* you want, and *where* you're headed. You also have a very good idea of *when* you'll arrive. However, have you stopped to consider *how* you'll get there?

What strategies will you use to tackle, or sidestep, the obstacles you may find along the way to your chosen destinations? What tactics will you use to deal with, or influence, those who stand between you and your objectives? And what broad range of resources will you begin to mobilize in your quest to realize your goals and to approach each day with the effectiveness of legends past and present?

If you're ready to begin operating with a level of life-effectiveness on par with that of the world's most fascinating figures, you'll find everything you need in the 6th Element of the Dream Acquisition Formula (DAF) found exclusively in *Mind Contrology®*.

It's time to *master the art of strategic living…*

# Master the Art of Strategic Living

*The 6th Element of the Dream Acquisition Formula (DAF)*

# 29

# Strategy

## *Mobilization of Power and Resources*

*"Envision the future and plan a route to it."*
-Super-CEO Al Dunlap

What is "strategy?" And how can you begin exploiting it to gain unparalleled effectiveness in using what you've *got* to get what you *want?*

This chapter aims to answer these questions, and more.

Born in 356 BC, Macedonian prince Alexander used the unusual combination of military might and graciousness to form an unprecedented battle strategy which would come to prove legendary.

While King Philip II was busy ruling Macedon between the years of 356 and 336 B.C., Philip's wife, Olympias, catered with loving care to her newborn son Alexander's every whim. Olympias was a visionary who believed her son was destined for greatness. In her vision, Olympias foresaw Alex upon the throne of a kingdom that stretched far beyond the Macedonian kingdom that the boy's birthright entitled him to. Alex was just a baby when Olympias, whispering softly in the young prince's ear, began programming Alex's brain with the noble plans for his future.

When Alex was 10, Olympias arranged for her boy to study under the tutelage of a local philosopher named Aristotle—the perks of being a prince. To Aristotle's dismay, however, Alex showed little interest in academics. His mental programming assured him that military command was going to be *his* claim to fame.

So, with Olympias' prophesies of world domination guiding his focus, his decisions, and his footsteps, the young prince eagerly devoted the next decade to the captivated study of King Philip's every move. Throughout his teens, Alex absorbed the ways in which Philip mobilized his army, noted how Philip rewarded loyalty and punished crimes, and discovered the virtues of showing mercy, all the while preparing to assume his own Ultimate Role as king and conqueror.

*"Recollect the strength,*
*the resources,*
*and above all the spirit,*
*which when raised know no opposition."*
-John Dyke Acland

Alex's big day came in 336 BC when King Philip was killed by a Royal Guardsman. Following a swift act of retribution, Alex assumed the throne of Macedon. He was just 20 years old.

Operating according to his cognitive encoding, Alex wasted no time putting into place a plan to conquer neighboring Persia. After carrying out a broad "regime change" by executing conspirators, dismissing incompetent or disloyal officials, and replacing dubious soldiers with warriors which he deemed strong and loyal to himself, Alex began mobilizing the whole of his military resources. Driven by a brain focused on large, specific goals and a strategy which was about to make him "great," Alex, the boy king, mounted his horse, and then led his vast, inherited army into Persia.

Alex's army of 35,000 quickly conquered Egypt. However, to the surprise of both the Egyptians and his soldiers, Alex chose not to pillage villages or take prisoners. Instead, King Alexander made *friends*.

After ordering his soldiers to take camp among the Egyptians, Alex went out of his way to treat the locals with kindness. Alex ate with the locals and spoke to them as if they were his own people. Then, after building trust by subjecting himself to Egyptian customs, the young king promised the locals freedom from strict, Persian rule.

Of course, there was a method to Alexander's madness. You see, by portraying himself not as a ruthless invader, but as the Great Liberator of Persia, Alex was able to win the hearts, and loyalties, of the Egyptians. Top generals and foot soldiers alike marveled at Alex's undeniable genius and unexpected finesse after he managed to convince the Egyptian people to take up arms…on the side of the invading army! As the boy king continued his region-by-region charge toward the capital of Persia, he not only managed to keep his soldiers from harm and his army intact; he also amassed a growing army of new recruits willing to fight the "Persian oppressor" on behalf of their new, beloved king.

Alexander the Great's genius battle strategy enabled him to conquer Persia by harnessing the power of his greatest resource—Persia's *own* people!

*"Hope is not a strategy."*
-Donald Trump

Several years ago, I worked with a $10 million construction company that was in bad shape. Sales had declined for the third year straight to $8.7 million. The sales force's closing rates were below the industry average. The company was operating at a $300,000 deficit. And more than 100 contractors and employees thought *they* were running the show.

Because ownership was in such financial straits, and because I believed in my team, I promised this CEO that I would help him get the place turned around, or our services would cost him nothing. As you can imagine, this client was eager to get started.

First, my team and I developed a long-term strategic plan for the company. Then, after presenting our plan to ownership and getting the unconditional support of the CEO, we went to work. For starters, we recommended the dismissal of several marginal managers. Once those terminations were enacted, we conducted a companywide presentation to share with every employee the details of ownership's new vision for the future. Those that were on board with the company's new direction could stay. Anyone who was attached to the status quo would be looking for work elsewhere. Following one swift landmark termination of a marginal contractor that had been earning $150,000 per year for doing far too little (a termination carried out very publicly,) the company was suddenly working with a broad spectrum of cooperative managers and employees from every department.

With the new strategy in place, my team and I began working simultaneously with management, the sales force, lead flow, and with the engineering and service departments. While conducting training for each of the appropriate peer groups, we also went to work cleaning up the company's open disputes (the result of substandard product installations and poor service) and initiating the process of collecting $100,000's worth of receivables in efforts to generate cash flow and make the company profitable again.

By the time my team and I were finished, this company was already showing signs of an organization driven with newfound purpose. And that was just the beginning...

In the end, the company experienced 30% growth in sales over the first 12 months for total sales of $11.3 million. Second-year sales jumped 23% to just over $14 million. Our client generated $5.5 million in sales over 24 months, and that doesn't account for the vast improvement in operating income which came from applying strict cost control measures across operations, all for the initial investment of $92,000. Needless to say, my firm's 100% money-back guarantee was not necessary.

That's the power of smart strategy!

*"The best defense is a good offense."*
-Jack Dempsey

**So, what is "strategy?"** *Strategy* can best be defined as the mobilization of power and resources toward the realization of a specific goal or desired result. Strategy is what made Alexander, "great." Strategy is the prism through which businesses can be transformed from the brink of bankruptcy to the height of profitability, often overnight. And it was NFL coach Vince Lombardi's pre-season "training strategies" that turned the Green Bay Packers into a pennant-winning dynasty during the 1960s...

The Green Bay Packers were on an unprecedented losing streak before Vince Lombardi was hired as head coach in 1961.

Lombardi's chief goal was universally understood—to create championship contenders out of a team that had lost all ambition to win. What many people do not know, however, is what strategy Lombardi used to realize his objective.

Lombardi's strategy? "Psychological warfare."

Lombardi set the stage for the Packers' turnaround by targeting a small group of "team stars." Using every resource at his disposal, the crafty coach wielded contract stipulations, threats of trades, warnings of career-ending disgrace, and tough personal challenges to awaken the egos of top players.

Once Green Bay's stars were practicing at maximum intensity, Lombardi openly humiliated any player who failed to produce equal results. Positions were switched to teach players an appreciation for their *own* jobs. Water breaks were used as much as a method of reward as a means of hydration. And grueling penalties were handed down to anyone foolish enough to be the slowest or clumsiest of the bunch.

Before long, the Packers' practices became a predictable display of one player trying to outdo the next. Lombardi's strategy of *psychological warfare* directed at Green Bay's best players enabled the wily coach to create an entire team of NFL stars!

Just one season after Lombardi signed on as head coach, the Green Bay Packers began their decade-long domination of the NFL—forging Vince Lombardi's destiny as one of football's most celebrated coaches.

Smart strategy produces legendary results.

*"Good planning helps make elusive dreams come true."*
-Lester R. Little

Okay, now you know what *strategy* is and how it works.

Although *you* may not be looking to conquer an empire, to turn a company around or to lead a sports team to a national championship, taking a strategic approach to your life and career should be as important to you as it was to the strategists in this chapter.

You see, nothing enables you to reach your goals more directly (or live your life more effectively) than taking a *strategic approach* to living…

# 30

# Life Strategy

*Using What You've Got, to Get What You Want*

*"Have a general strategic plan...about who you are, and about what you aspire to become in the world."*
-Super-CEO Herb Kelleher

Whereas strategy is about mobilizing our powers and resources toward the accomplishment of a specific objective, "Life Strategy" relates to the mindsets and skillsets we use—often over and again—to surmount life's challenges, to deal with (or even influence) other people, and to maneuver skillfully through the best and worst of days, toward the fulfillment of our near and distant goals.

Simply put, *living strategically* is about using what you've got to get what you want, on a regular basis.

For master animator, Walt Disney, the Life Strategy he relied on most was *proactive imagination.*

Born in 1901, Walt Disney grew up on a farm in Kansas City with his parents, brother, and sister. Paid little attention to by his busy parents, Walt took to entertaining himself by retreating to the family's barn with sketchpad and pencil in hand. It was there, drawing cartoons all by his lonesome that young Walt discovered within himself the power to escape to a better reality through the portal of imagination.

Throughout grade school, Disney continued using his primary Life Strategy of escape to his advantage. Graduating from sketching to theater, Walt accepted roles in a series of school plays. The theater gave Walt someplace to go besides home, and someone to be other than an isolated farm boy. Besides that, Walt was quite a good actor. Once, after landing a major role as his hero, Charlie Chaplin, Walt received a standing ovation from the entire school auditorium.

Walt thrived on the applause and attention. The stage provided him with the feeling of importance that he wasn't getting at home.

For the time being, Walt Disney was a star.

*"On the occasion of every incident that befalls you, inquire what power you have for turning it to good use."*
-Epictetus

Things changed for Disney by the time he entered high school at age 15. The starring roles ceased and the applause was silenced. Walt found that he didn't fit in with either the bookworms or the jocks. And being the strange, artsy kid among brutal cliques of teenagers brought ridicule and seclusion. What didn't change for Walt, however, was his Life Strategy of proactive imagination.

Using his potent mind and drawing skills to make the best of another bad situation, Disney landed a job as a cartoonist for the school newspaper and found that he wanted to sketch cartoons full-time. When Walt was 17, he made the life-altering decision to quit school to pursue his dream of running his own animation studio. Following a short stint as an ambulance driver for the Red Cross and a job as a cartoon illustrator on someone else's payroll, Walt opened up shop as the owner of "Laugh-O-Gram."

It was in 1923 that Disney, 22, boarded a train to Hollywood where he launched Disney Studios. Over the next four decades, Walt would use his trusted Life Strategy to build his little studio into a billion dollar empire of movies, theme parks, and merchandise. Throughout his extraordinary life, he never abandoned his childlike imagination.

In 1961, Walt, 60, made headlines by pretending his business ventures were a matter of national security. After deciding to build a second theme park in Florida, Disney orchestrated the purchase of 27,000 acres of swampland under a thick veil of secrecy. Playing the role of secret agent, Walt code-named the purchase "Project X" and created multiple layers of go-betweens to disguise his involvement in the deal.

Why become "secret agent Disney?"

Walt foresaw that the price of the land which he desired would skyrocket if officials learned that the rich and famous, Walt Disney, was the prospective buyer. Only once the deal was sealed, for a steal at $5 million, did Walt reveal his involvement.

Strategic living is highly-effective living!

*"Things alter for the worse,*
*spontaneously,*
*if they are not altered for the better."*
-Francis Bacon

The Life Strategist possesses a keen awareness of his or her *personal powers* and *external resources*, and makes the best use of those powers and resources to get what he or she is after in life and business.

Novelist Agatha Christie, for instance, never attended school. An ambitious young lady, Christie managed to land a job as a nurse during WWII. Trusting her instincts and keeping her eye open to potential, future opportunities, Christie took it upon herself to study the effects of various poisons on the human body. Years later, after making a brazen career leap to mystery writing, Christie called upon her self-taught expertise in toxicology to help stage the plots of her legendary novels—many of which Christie wrote while soaking in a bathtub and eating apples.

That, my friend, is *strategic living!*

## Life Strategy in the Professional World

*How to Position Yourself for Advancement*

A Life Strategist is a master of "self-positioning," that priceless talent for acquiring specific knowledge, producing lucrative ideas, developing necessary skills, finding loopholes, befriending key players, and infiltrating the closed circles that lead to the career roles and salary ranges one has in mind.

For instance, I have personally used the Life Strategy of *self-education* throughout my career in order to compensate for my lack of formal education. By studying up on my fields of choice, I found myself managing multiple multimillion dollar construction projects by age 28, turning around my first company by age 30, being promoted to a national management position less than two years later, and running my own management consultancy (and penning my first book) a few years after that.

While others hope for raises and promotions, the Life Strategist foresees his goal, maps out his next move, and possesses the mental acuity to adjust his approach as necessary along the path to his chosen destinations. And, as a result, this person never fails to remain one step, or even *several* steps, ahead of his peers.

Actress Marilyn Monroe was one such master of self-positioning…

*"Life is a game played between the ears."*
-Michael LeBoeuf, PhD

Born in Los Angeles in 1926, Norma Jean Baker was dumped into the child services system by a mother who refused to take care of her. It was while growing up in foster care and watching movies to pass the time that Norman Jean dared to dream of becoming an on-screen actress.

In 1949, driven by a vision of Hollywood stardom, Norma Jean, 23, posed for a provocative photo shoot in the hopes of earning a quick paycheck and making connections in the entertainment industry. The shoot initially did little for Baker's career and temporarily pigeon-holed her as just another "low-rent," nude model.

Baker didn't let the setback faze her.

As is often the case with resilient and resourceful Life Strategists in pursuit of a specific, energizing career goal, Norma Jean managed to bounce back from her modeling debacle by recalibrating her mental horizons and switching up her strategy. Determined not to let anything or anyone stop her from becoming an actress, Baker changed her name to Marilyn Monroe, and then packed her bags for Hollywood.

While auditioning for movies in 1950, Monroe discovered two, disheartening obstacles to her goals:

- Hollywood was largely controlled by male executives.
- Marilyn lacked the acting skills necessary to stand apart from *other* aspiring actresses.

Determined to land a part, Marilyn compensated for her on-stage inadequacies by batting her eyebrows, flirting with audition managers, and showing male directors just a little more skin than her competition. And guess what—it worked.

In spite of her poor deliveries, difficulty in memorizing lines, constant tardiness, and heated arguments with directors, Marilyn managed to land roles in one Hollywood film after another, even playing "leading lady" to such movie legends as Clark Gable and Sir Lawrence Oliver. Then, in 1955, Monroe's Hollywood dreams came to a defining climax when the world came to know her as the blonde bombshell holding down her air-blown dress in the movie, *"Seven Year Itch."* In little more than one year, Norma Jean Baker repositioned herself from nude model to famous, Hollywood actress. "I want to be the best there is," revealed Marilyn during an interview in 1950. "My daily routine, in matters great and small, is devoted to a larger goal—total self-fulfillment."

Although ridiculed as an egomaniac, it was Monroe's haughty opinion of herself, her insistence on being treated like a star, and her ability to outthink her competition that enabled the actress to make a dramatic transition from foster care to the red carpet.

*"It's common sense to take a method and try it. If it fails, admit it squarely and try another. But, above all—try something!"*
-Franklin Delano Roosevelt

Are you considering reinventing yourself in the workplace? Would you like to position yourself for advancement, in spite of such deficiencies as a lack of formal education or experience?

Marilyn Monroe's self-willed transformation from orphan to movie star shows us that this is entirely possible for the person who knows what he or she wants, and is willing to take a strategic approach to career advancement.

## Life Strategy, "Old Blue Eyes" Style…

Frank Sinatra's disarming smile and hypnotic charm were every bit as instrumental in attracting his cult-like fan base as was the sound of his voice. Sinatra understood the impact of his personal magnetism on others and used his powers wisely.

Just how effective *was* Frank at wielding his advantages in looks and personality?

I was told a story in which an aging Sinatra once invited a young associate to dinner. Knowing that his mother was a huge Sinatra fan, the associate chose to take his mom along. One condition was attached to the outing—don't *bother* Frank.

During dinner, Sinatra noticed the mother star-gazing from across the table and in his big-city vernacular asked, "What's eating you, baby?"

"Mr. Sinatra, I have to ask…"

"Mom, don't do it," nudged the son. But she *had* to.

The mother went on to explain that years ago she'd attended one of Sinatra's shows. She elaborated about the venue and date, and about her certainty that tonight's famous dinner host had noticed her in the audience. Their eyes had met. She'd been bragging to her friends about the encounter for years. And this was her chance to confirm it.

"So, my question is," pressed the woman, "*did* you notice me, Mr. Sinatra?" As the woman's son shrunk in embarrassment, a thoughtful Sinatra pretended to recall the incident.

"Of course, I remember you, baby doll," confirmed a wily Sinatra. Then, employing the same hypnotic charm by which he had amassed an army of loyal fans, Frank added, "And let me tell you, you look even more spectacular tonight than you did the night our eyes first met."

The woman nearly faintly.

That's *Life Strategy,* Sinatra style.

*"I did it my way."*
-Frank Sinatra

Becoming a *Life Strategist* requires the habit of using what you've got, to get what you want.

Living strategically is about understanding your strengths and powers, seizing opportunities, exploiting your unique advantages, and mobilizing your resources in just the right way, at just the right time, to make amazing things happen. It means managing the resources of time, energy, and money wisely. And it requires knowing what tactics to use to outsmart your competition and what approaches to use to win others over.

Strategic living is as much about controlling your mind, exercising your body, and nourishing your soul as it is about educating yourself according to your goals, knowing how to sidestep obstacles, and turning setbacks into new beginnings along the way to your chosen destinations.

Life Strategy is more than a way to meet your important objectives; it's a way of life.

*"Strategy, without tactics,*
*is the slowest route to victory."*
-Sun Tzu

If you're ready to begin approaching life with the legendary effectiveness of the Disneys, Monroes, and Sinatras of this world, it's time to move on to our final lesson in mastering the art of strategic living…

# 31

# The SOAR Mindset

*How to Leverage Your Strengths, Opportunities, Advantages, and Resources*

*"I try to learn from the past, but I plan for the future by focusing exclusively on the present."*
-Donald Trump

What does it take to master the art of strategic living? To become a *Life Strategist* of legendary proportions?

(1) Always know *exactly* what you're after.

(2) Identify your "SOAR" factors—or your strengths (and powers,) opportunities, advantages, and resources.

(3) Develop the ability to exploit your strengths (and powers,) seize golden opportunities, capitalize on your advantages, and mobilize the full range of your resources on a daily basis.

This chapter is designed around the above factors.

Before you're finished reading the next few pages, you will find yourself in a privileged position to begin making full use of a broad spectrum of personal powers and external resources you never even knew you possessed.

## The "SOAR Mindset" in Action

As Demonstrated by Carthaginian General, Hannibal

What's a "SOAR Mindset?" It is a mindset geared toward exploiting one's strengths (and powers,) seizing one's opportunities, capitalizing on one's advantages, and mobilizing the whole of one's resources.

Legendary Carthaginian General Hannibal was the owner of one of history's most calculating *SOAR Mindsets…*

In 218 BC, the Roman Empire began expanding on a collision course with nearby Carthage City. Anticipating an eventual invasion by the Roman army, General Hannibal launched a preemptive seven month long offensive over the Alps, into Italy. Hannibal and his army surprised the Romans and secured an unlikely victory which shook the foundations of the fearsome, Roman Empire.

Hannibal's initial victory, however, was only the beginning of the story.

The Carthaginian army's unlikely win came at a high cost. Less than 50% of its soldiers survived. The remaining soldiers were beaten, hungry, and in no shape to fight again. This was indeed a problem since Roman reinforcements were on their way with forces which outnumbered Hannibal's men by 100's to 1!

That's when Hannibal's methodical mind went to work. Carefully assessing his SOAR factors (or his strengths, opportunities, advantages, and resources,) the general realized that he had one, critical *opportunity* to motivate his troops before the rest of the Roman army arrived. Hannibal seized that opportunity by using a pair of captured Roman prisoners to stage an "exhibition battle" for his weary troops. Hannibal selected two fearsome Roman soldiers and placed them at the head of the Carthaginian army's makeshift camp. After promising freedom to the prisoner who emerged victoriously, a bloody battle ensued. General Hannibal paced among his troops as they watched the two desperate brawlers fight each other with the intensity of 1,000 common soldiers…until a single victor remained.

Following an hours-long exhibition of mortal combat, Hannibal summoned his persuasive leadership abilities (his *strength*) to incite his troops (his *resource.*) "The Romans will be here by morning, and you will be greatly outnumbered," Hannibal shouted to his troops. "And like the warriors who have entertained us tonight, you will be fighting while tired, hungry, and in some cases, wounded."

One can imagine Hannibal pacing among his troops in his crude, body armor and heavy gruff when he pointed to the single prisoner left standing and said, "But if you fight with the intensity with which this warrior has fought before us tonight, you will know victory against a thousand Roman armies!"

Hannibal's troops no doubt exploded into cheers of enthusiasm.

*"Where there is no path, we will make one."*
-General Hannibal

Did Hannibal's strategy facilitate the military *advantage* he was after? The tattered Carthaginian soldiers went on to seize not just the next battle, but a series of unlikely victories against the gigantic, Roman Empire. Want to achieve a series of "unlikely victories" in your life, career, relationships, and finances? Develop a SOAR Mindset!

## Developing a SOAR Mindset

*Your Initiation into the Elite Club of Legendary Life Strategists*

The SOAR Mindset is a force multiplier in the game of peak performance.

The purpose of developing a SOAR Mindset is simple: to make the best use of your strengths (and powers,) opportunities, advantages, and resources in your quest to achieve goals, large and small.

Approaching your personal agenda through this structured, mental prism does two important things. First, it diverts your focus away from perceived weaknesses, missed opportunities, seeming disadvantages, and conditions of lack. And, second, it opens the door to a whole host of new competencies with which to move any goal from mind to matter, more effectively.

In other words, a SOAR Mindset gives birth to a *SOAR Skillset.*

Identifying your distinctive SOAR factors—or your strengths (and powers,) opportunities, advantages, and resources—is the first step to developing a methodical and highly effective SOAR Mindset.

Below, are four guide-lists designed to help you pinpoint the critical SOAR factors that are exclusive to *you.*

## #1) Exploiting Your Strengths (and Powers)

To identify your unique strengths (and powers,) answer the following:

- What great *qualities* do you possess? Are you focused? Well-informed? Bright? Personable? Resourceful? Motivated? Trustworthy? Caring? Persuasive? Resilient? Funny? Hard-working?
- What are your "core competencies?" That is, what do you do exceptionally well? Are you an expert communicator or problem-solver? Are you mechanically inclined? A great parent or effective multi-tasker? An excellent judge of character? What sets you apart from the crowd?
- What odd knowledge, special skills or unusual experience do you have at your disposal? Does your knowledge of the past rival that of seasoned historians? Do you possess organizational skills? Are you bilingual? Tech or social media savvy? Do you have a gift for managing people, children, finances, animals, events or complex business operations?

**Now ask yourself**: Am I putting my strengths (and powers) to work for me in the workplace or marketplace?

If not, brainstorm a few strategies by which to begin exploiting your unique strengths (and powers) more effectively as early as tomorrow.

## #2) Seizing Your Golden Opportunities

To begin seizing the golden opportunities around you, answer the following:

- Have you neglected to seize golden opportunities in the past? What was the *source* of your inaction? Hesitation? Indecision? Fear? Outright laziness?
- What has failing to seize opportunities in the past cost you in terms of money lost, time wasted, progress thwarted, regret created or sleep missed?
- Opportunities respond to big thinking and preparation. What can you learn, ask for, study, practice or pursue in order to become better equipped to seize the very next opportunity Life sends your way?

*"To improve the golden moment of opportunity,*
*and catch the good that is within our reach,*
*is the great art of life."*
-Dr. Samuel Johnson

Is there some wonderful opportunity you can seize *right now* in either your personal, professional or financial affairs? If not, keep searching. Life is generous. There will be plenty more golden opportunities in the days, weeks, and months ahead.

## #3) Capitalizing on Your Unique Advantages

Too many folks fail to leverage their advantages in the name of modesty. Truth is, we all possess advantages of one kind or another over those around us. This is what makes us…us. These unique advantages are designed to be exploited. And we don't have to be patronizing or arrogant in the process.

Of course, to begin capitalizing on your unique advantages, you've got to *identify* them.

- What clear *edge* do you have over most other people? Are you educated? Good-looking? "Connected?" Physically fit? Are you a *likable* person? Do you possess swagger—the ability to light up a room, win people over, and achieve anything you set your mind to?
- What are your special areas of knowledge and expertise? Do you know things or possess skills that an employer or customer base would pay dearly for?
- In what ways are you greatly blessed? Are you in excellent health? Good spirits? Do you have wonderful people in your corner?
- What do you have (perhaps great measure) that other people tend to envy you for?
- What do other people often come to you for? Advice? Ideas? Approval? Solutions? Encouragement? Money? Knowing what others look to you for is a terrific way of discovering your unique advantages.

Make a mental or written list of your exclusive advantages. Then devise a list of matching strategies by which to capitalize on these factors at every chance you get.

## #4) Mobilizing Your Resources

A "resource" may be defined as any person, place or thing that helps you achieve a specific goal or desired result.

Your current, untapped resources may include any the following:

### The 4 Major Resource Categories

**People Resources:** These include your family, friends, neighbors, boss, coworkers, customers, networking associates, advisors, mentors, industry experts, or even a rich uncle.

"People resources" include any relationship that adds value to your life. Who are *your* people resources, and how could you begin making better use of them?

**Places Resources:** These include the local bookstores and libraries where you acquire knowledge. The gym where you condition your body. The church from which you draw spiritual strength. The groups where you meet like-professionals. The institution where you do your banking. And the grocery store where you buy healthy foods.

"Places resources" are all around you. Could some adjustment to your current use of places resources better help you achieve a goal, save time or save money?

**Financial Resources:** These include any assets which carry a monetary value; such as, your property, job, bank accounts, IRA, stocks, bonds, and other investments. Your *liquid assets* include cash, possessions, or any asset that can be quickly converted into cash.

Liquidating (or selling-off) an asset is particularly useful in generating short-term cash to pursue a golden, investment opportunity.

Your financial resources also extend to your credit rating, your bank or credit union, organizations such as the Small Business Administration, the generous people you may have in your corner, and the money you've got in your pocket.

In what ways can you increase the rate of return on *your* financial assets?

**Technological Resources:** Tech resources include the internet which enables you to stay connected, your PC, the laptop that allows you to get work done on the fly, your smartphone, and the GPS that increases your efficiency while on the road.

Tech resources extend to goodies such as: software programs, gadgets, apps, PowerPoint, YouTube, and any internet-based service or network which enables you to do business, or live life, more effectively.

If you've completed the preceding exercises, you are now in a terrific position to begin exploiting your strengths (and powers,) seizing opportunities, capitalizing on your advantages, and mobilizing the whole of your resources on a daily basis.

In order to maximize the effectiveness of the *Goal Realization System (GRS)* from the previous section, simply apply your SOAR Mindset to the goals you have for your life, career, relationships, and finances.

In doing so, you will exponentially improve your ability to move goals from mind to matter, and you will begin operating at a level of life-effectiveness that rivals that of legends past and present.

And this, after all, is what it means to be a master strategist.

*"There must be a translation from strategic thought to strategic action."*
-Dr. Fred R. David

## Mastering the Art of Strategic Living

*A Quick Review*

.

Okay, you now know what strategy is, and you understand how to use *Life Strategy* to dramatically increase your level of life-effectiveness. You've identified the SOAR factors that are critical to your success, and you know how to leverage your strengths (and powers,) opportunities, advantages, and resources to accelerate the goal actualization process.

You're now prepared to begin operating at a level of performance in life and business equal to that of a *dozen* ordinary people.

In your quest to transform your wildest dreams into your waking reality, there's only one thing left for you to do.

*Take action unto excellence...*

# Take Action unto Excellence!

*The Final Element of the Dream Acquisition Formula (DAF)*

John Echols

# 32

# Action!

*Dream Acquisition Formula Activator*

*"Whatever you can do, or dream you can do, begin it. Boldness has genius, power, and magic within it."*
-Johann von Goethe

"Master Your Mind" is the *precursor* to the Dream Acquisition Formula found exclusively in *Mind Contrology* ®. By combining what you've learned about mind control with an active application of the first six elements of the DAF, you can easily attract into your life such fortuities as: helpful people, favorable events, open doors, guiding signs, and more. However, unless you *interact* with your helpers, *seize* the moment when the timing is right, *walk through* the doors that are opened for you, and *follow* the signs that lead to your chosen destinations, your boldness in daring to dream and any preparation you may have made will have served no real purpose of good.

Without a concerted effort in the direction of your dreams and goals, the Mind/Reality Relationship cannot work its magic and the process of moving your objectives from mind to matter cannot occur. In other words, *action* is the activating ingredient of the formula for transforming dreams into reality.

Sometimes, even the smallest efforts can trigger a response from the Universe which is so precise to the designs of our dreams and goals that it boggles the mind.

For instance, some time ago, I decided I wanted to buy a horse. At the time, I had no idea what would be involved in terms of up-front costs, stabling, vet bills, feed, and so on. However, shortly after putting this goal to paper (a very small action step,) I *just happened* to cross paths with an interesting fellow with an upbeat attitude. While making small talk, I asked, "What do you do for a living?"

As if he should've been gift-wrapped and tied with a bow, my living, breathing representative of the Mind/Reality Relationship answered back, "I 'break' thoroughbreds for upscale clients."

"You're kidding me," I said.

After picking my new friend's brain, I was fully informed, newly enthused, and thoroughly prepared to take the next step in making my equestrian goal real.

*Action* represents the critical juncture in the dream acquisition process at which your plans begin to take on unmistakable, physical characteristics and irreversible, forward motion. The Universe eagerly rewards the man or woman who exercises faith by stepping out confidently in the direction of his or her dreams and goals.

One of my favorite examples of a human being mastering the relationship between mind and matter, transforming fiction into fact as a result of a few small, strategic efforts in the direction of a monumental objective, took place more than two centuries ago in Rhode Island…

*"Genius is the fruit of labor and thought."*
-Alexander Hamilton

## Nathanael Greene

*The Handicapped Mill Worker Who Changed History*

In 1774, a 32 year-old, crippled tradesman was preparing to realize an impossible dream, a dream that, once fulfilled, would enable him to alter the course of history.

Nathanael Greene was born in Kent County, Rhode Island, in 1742. While working in his family's foundry as a young boy, Nate suffered a horrible accident which left him with a mauled leg and a painful, permanent limp. Greene was also illiterate. However, Nate, a chubby Quaker who did not ascribe to the concept of self-pity, outright refused to allow his disadvantages to define him.

During his 20's, Greene decided that he wanted to learn how to read. So, after a long day's work at the mill—and in spite of asthma attacks which often drove him to his knees—Nate began trekking 40-plus miles (each way) to a bartering post in Boston, where he bought books and began the painstaking process of educating himself to read. First, Nate read pages. Then books. Then *piles* of books.

*"Do what you can,*
*with what you have, where you are."*
-Theodore Roosevelt

Following his father's passing in 1770, Greene, 28, took over the family business. Nate, however, disliked the extensive manual labor that his role required, and he wanted out. So, while continuing to uphold his obligations at the mill over the next four years, Nate immersed himself in the study of politics and law with his eye on a career in which he could use more of his mind and less of his damaged body.

Greene received his wish in 1774, when his hometown of Coventry took its place among the growing number of American colonies edging toward a full-scale revolt against Great Britain. It was then that Nate began entertaining the possibility of a command post on the battlefield. More specifically, he saw himself becoming a *general*—and he wasted no time taking swift, strategic action.

Laying the foundation for military command, Greene's trips to Boston became entirely devoted to purchasing rare and expensive books based on battle strategy. Along his journeys, Nate overheard enchanting stories about George Washington, the Virginian governor who'd taken charge of the newly forming Continental Army.

The more Greene heard about Washington's heroism and growing popularity, the more spellbound he became. Each night, after managing the mill, Nate would sit on the rocking chair in his small, private library, pouring over battle plans by candlelight, and dreaming about his glorious future in the rebel Rhode Island militia. The harder Greene studied and the longer he rocked, the more his knowledge of war planning grew and the higher he raised the bar on his goals. Before long, Nate not only desired a role in the revolution, he craved a top position by Washington's side.

At last, under the spell of Mental Identity, and self-educated according to his master plan of homeland patriotism, Nate abandoned the family mill, bought a musket, and enlisted in the Rhode Island militia as a lowly private.

Greene's courageous efforts would be rewarded both quickly and handsomely...

*"It's amazing how the thoughts we plant in our minds can eventually materialize into actions."*
-Chuck Norris

On May 8, 1775, after spending just *six months* running drills and preparing for battle among the local militia's rank and file, the Mind/Reality Relationship, working in cooperation with Nate's vision of military command, delivered him with the very miracle he'd been working toward.

While conducting a regional inspection of the Rhode Island regiments, Continental Congressman Samuel Ward stumbled across a particularly enthusiastic and visibly disabled soldier who was sporting a homemade uniform and brandishing a store-bought rifle.

"Tell me your name, private," said Ward.

The soldier responded, "Nathanael Greene, Sir."

Following their meeting, Ward, for reasons unknown, placed Greene in charge of the 2,500-soldier Rhode Island regiments. At 33 years of age, Nate was suddenly the youngest brigadier general in the new, American military!

Does the fact that Greene, a crippled tradesman with severe health problems and zero battle experience, managed to get himself promoted to general within six months of joining the Rhode Island militia convince you that small, concerted efforts in the direction of one's dreams can make miracles happen? If not, maybe the following facts will.

Within six *weeks* of his promotion, George Washington swept through Greene's field of command on horseback. Greene instantly fell into Washington's good graces.

Throughout the eight, ensuing years of the Revolutionary War, General Nathanael Greene consistently translated his self-taught expertise in military strategy into a genius command of the Southern Campaign. After becoming one of Washington's favorite generals and closest friends, Greene was appointed to Washington's coveted War Cabinet and promoted to major general—making Greene the highest-ranking general next to Washington himself. Through his triumphs in more than a dozen major battles, Greene repeatedly proved himself indispensable both to George Washington, as well as to the cause of American Independence.

Interestingly enough, it was Greene's battlefield victory that cleared a path for Washington's historic, icy crossing of the Delaware River!

*"If one advances confidently in the directions of his dreams,*
*and endeavors to live the life which he has imagined,*
*he will meet with unexpected success in common hours."*
-Henry David Thoreau

A compelling dream articulated into a personal agenda of specific goals is often all the motivation we need to take those important initial steps which set the unstoppable forces of the Mind/Reality Relationship into motion on our behalf.

Other times, the best method for initiating decisive action is to consider what we'll *lose* by failing to act…

## Our Client's $3.5 Million Dollar Incentive

Recently, my firm was hired by the president of a 40 year-old, seven-unit chain of sandwich shops in New Jersey. The chain's 65 year-old founder requested our *Strategic Masterplan* service, a service that includes a full day of training for ownership, as well as the development of a 36-month strategic plan specifically designed for the client's business.

After spending the morning with the president and his top people, the consultant who administered the service recommended the following:

- Relocating one marginal unit situated in a deteriorating area
- Launching a new, targeted M&A campaign
- Opening two additional shops over the next five years, roughly 32 months apart
- Removing 10 of the least purchased menu items
- Committing to product development by doubling his menu selection over the next 12 months
- Offering catering services to supplement off-peak hours of operation

After unveiling this strategy to the client, our consultant called me from the client's main facility to inform me that there was a problem. The client didn't agree with the recommendations being set forth and wanted to speak to me directly. After initiating a video conference, I listened to the president tell me all the reasons why he wanted to stay the course. "I built this company from nothing to more than $5 million using my current market approach," this client protested. "Why should I change directions now?"

The president went on to tell me that he didn't want to expand into new markets, didn't want to risk a large investment, and didn't want to add any new items to his menu. Convincing this client to capitalize on a combination of his company's local brand power and evolving consumer trends was largely a matter of explaining what he would be missing out on by not pursuing an aggressive growth strategy.

I spent some time explaining the proven effectiveness of the "best practices" currently being exploited by the top brands in his industry. I also explained the evolution of several new consumer trends which necessitated the introduction of an expanded menu. I then provided multiple case studies demonstrating the likely results of pursuing the recommendations being set forth.

Finally, to conclude my presentation, I wrote a number on a napkin and held it up to the camera so that the president could see it. The number was $3,500,000.

"This is the minimum of what you stand to *lose* over the next three years by sitting on your hands and doing nothing," I assured the president. I watched the president's eyes burst open in illumination. At last, the executive was primed to take action.

*"If a man would move the world,*
*he must first move himself."*
-Socrates

As you begin the process of transforming your dreams into reality, take the time to consider not only what you will gain by *taking action*, but what you may lose by *failing to act.* Once you've got the incentive to move forward with your plans and you begin taking steps in the direction of your dreams and goals, you will have activated the transmutation process by which these dreams and goals are made real.

Although there may be times when it seems that your efforts are not producing results, you can rest assured that the *Law of Suspended Returns* is at work and on your side. Galatians 6:9 instructs us, "Let us not lose heart in doing good, for in due time we will reap if we do not grow weary." Remember, every effort you make represents a "cash payment" on the total cost of that which you desire to do, have, and become.

Moreover, while even small efforts toward our objectives can lead to great results in our life, career, relationships, and finances, large and daring actions often lead us to results that come to prove legendary…

# Abraham Lincoln

*Man of Revolutionary Action*

Abraham Lincoln wasn't only a man who, at times, possessed a degree of mental clarity bordering clairvoyance; he was also a man of *revolutionary action.* And Lincoln's daring efforts during the Civil War would bring about historic consequences.

On March 4, 1861, following a series of career leaps he foresaw in great detail and predicted out loud, newly elected President Lincoln assumed command of a United States violently divided over the issue of slavery. While abolitionists on one side of the issue hurled rocks at the Executive Mansion in an attempt to get Lincoln to end human indenture, slavery supporting thugs on the other side of the issue threatened to assassinate Lincoln if he dared try to abolish the age-old trade.

Whichever way he turned, Lincoln found his life under daily threat. And that was just the beginning of Lincoln's troubles.

Refusing to forfeit the right to own slaves, 13 of America's southern states began to secede from the Union one by one. Self-appointed Confederate President, Jefferson Davis, took center stage as Lincoln's arch nemesis. Then, under the orders of opposing presidents, northern and southern generals faced off in what would become a series of the bloodiest battles ever fought on U.S. soil.

Opening battles proved Davis' southern forces superior to Lincoln's north. Northern forces came under heavy fire, costing the Union both soldiers and ground, as Confederate troops advanced toward the nation's capital in their attempt to seize control of Lincoln's Executive Mansion. By the winter of 1862, Abe's forces were sheared by 13,000, and Union losses continued to mount.

Lincoln was pacing the floors of his office, surrounded by advisors and aides, when someone called out, "Why does this north continue to falter?"

Lincoln postured by a window, returning, "The fact is that the people haven't yet made up their minds that we are at war with the south. The people haven't yet made up their minds, I tell you!"

Lincoln, on the other hand, understood that the fate of the country was at stake. He became entirely convinced that democracy and slavery could not peacefully coexist, and he realized that the time for *decisive action* had arrived…

*"Act—and God will act, too."*
-Joan of Arc

On January 1, 1863, President Lincoln walked to his desk, sat down, and grasped a pen. Sprawled out before him was a large document representing even larger ramifications—the Emancipation Proclamation.

"My mind is made up," announced Abe to the closest members of his cabinet. "It must be done. I am driven to do it." Against fierce opposition and under the threat of assassination, Lincoln courageously swept his signature across the document which would outlaw slavery across America.

Following that incident, something very *strange* began to happen…

As if hinged upon Abe's very signature, a Union military campaign spearheaded by General Ulysses S. Grant shifted the balance of power on the battlefield from southern forces to Lincoln's army. By the spring of 1865, following a series of pivotal Union victories, Lincoln's generals were able to secure the unconditional surrender of the Confederacy. At last, the Civil War, along with all of its 620,000 casualties, was no more. In Lincoln's mind and heart, however, another battle was taking place.

Although the Civil War was over, the staggering number of casualties had taken an enormous toll on the president's well-being. Consumed by the heartache of so many lives lost, Lincoln's mind soon became burdened by visions of his *own*, untimely demise.

"I am sure that I will meet with some tragic end," Lincoln assured his grief-stricken wife, Mary. "Assassination is always possible, and will come if they are determined upon it."

During his final weeks, becoming increasingly comfortable with the prospect of martyrdom, Abe's lifelong resolution to succeed increasingly gave way to the willful surrender of his very existence. Just hours before his fateful trip to the theater, a somber Lincoln prophesied to his distraught wife and chief of security that his "life's work" was nearing its end.

On the evening of April 14, 1865, Abe's morbid premonition was realized in an echo of gunfire. At 7:22 am the next morning, Lincoln passed into the pages of history—and an American legend was born.

*"Honor and rewards fall to those who show good qualities in action."*
-Aristotle

## How to Activate the Dream Acquisition Formula

*Just Add Action!*

*Action* is an absolute prerequisite to the end result of transforming dreams into reality. In fact, the realization of all that you now seek is largely hinged upon the *very next step* you take in the direction of your vision for your future. Consider Nathanael Greene, my firm's hesitant client, and Abraham Lincoln...

Nathanael Greene *began* transforming his impossible dream of military command from mind to matter during the very first step of his journey to Boston, where he bought a book based on the art of war. Greene's enlistment in the Rhode Island militia, his six-month promotion to brigadier general, his 6-week promotion to major general, his promotion to Washington's War Cabinet, and his legacy in history were all hinged upon the very first steps Greene took in the direction of his "unachievable" objectives.

Remember the hesitant president from the previous story? His fortune in converting his seven-shop chain to a nine-shop chain, the additional revenues he generated, the talented GMs he managed to recruit, and the new customers who would come to enjoy his food were all contingent upon his very first call to my firm.

Finally, let's turn to Abe Lincoln. It was only after Lincoln committed his signature to the Emancipation Proclamation that the cruel winds of battle shifted in his favor. Could the two have been related? Could Abe's signature have been the activating ingredient in the formula for the North's ensuing victories?

Furthermore, is it possible that Lincoln's powerful mind, after becoming consumed with thoughts of assassination and martyrdom, served to facilitate the events surrounding his untimely demise, just as his thoughts had once been the source of his self-willed evolution from illiterate farm boy to president of the United States? Although careful study of Lincoln's final months raises some interesting questions about the extent of the president's role in his own untimely passing, the issue must remain one of speculation.

What is *not* speculation, however, is that concerted efforts in pursuit of your dreams and goals can create a ripple effect of favorable results which begin connecting you to your chosen destination in life and business, almost overnight.

*"Oh, Lord, thou give us everything at the cost of effort."*
-Leonardo da Vinci

## Tomorrow Never Comes

*The Time to Act Is* Now!

The ideal time to begin chiseling the undefined stone of your destiny into the kind of masterpiece you've got in mind is *now*.

Every day, millions of people all over the world *hope* for bigger bank accounts, *pray* they'll overcome some lifelong struggle, and *wish* for any number of vague results which never materialize. Why do these folks remain broke, defeated, and confounded, in spite of their good intentions? Because success, in any form, does not answer to hopes, to wishes, or to the prayers of those who ask God to grant them a miracle that they are fully equipped to perform for themselves. Success responds to the *Mind Contrologist* who dares to dream, infuses it with imagination, fuels it with passion, backs it by belief, fashions it into specific goals, matches those objectives to smart strategies, and then pursues his or her vision for the future with *decisive action!*

It all comes down to this: If you want to pilot an aircraft, drive to the nearest training center, take a course, and earn a license. Dream of becoming a famous musician? Buy an instrument, create a song, and then book a recording studio. And if it's vast wealth you seek, commit to a specific amount and deadline, come up with a plan that supports this figure, and then *implement* your strategy with the help of your boss, employees, agent, supplier, publisher, partner, advisor, lender or money manager. But, above all, do something to make what you want to happen, happen.

*"All of our dreams can come true,*
*if we will have the courage to pursue them."*
-Walt Disney

Decide right now what calls you can make, meetings you can schedule, image you can perfect, plans you can draw up, websites you can visit (or build,) books you can buy, classes you can take, brains you can pick, avenues you can pursue, places you can go, changes you can make, alliances you can forge, experts you can model, or resources you can mobilize to begin realizing your potential, fulfilling your dreams, improving the lives of your loved ones, and changing the world for the better.

Then give your intentions wheels, and set them in motion!

**GURU'S TIP:** Action is the activating ingredient in the formula for transforming your dreams into reality.

Bold efforts let your Creator know that you're committed to your plans. And, in response, the Heavens above will commit to them, too. The stars will eagerly align for you once you take the first steps of your journey in faith.

Well, what are you waiting for? Tomorrow never comes; it will always remain *tomorrow.* You have only this day to undertake the process of revolutionizing your life.

"Cognition is incomplete until discharged into action," wrote the great Dr. William James. Whatever your dreams may be, *immediate action* is required.

And, if at first you don't succeed, try, try again…

# 33

# Relentless Execution

*Cracking the Code of Your Dreams*

*"Perseverance is a great element of success."*
-Henry William Wadsworth

Great dreams and important goals are not typically fulfilled by average measures or overnight undertakings.

For instance, it may take weeks to win over your boss in your pursuit of the promotion you desire. Sculpting your ideal physique may require months of exercise and smart eating habits. A five-year commitment may be necessary to generate your first million—or next $10 million—in income or revenues. And it can take the better part of a *lifetime* (including multiple setbacks, numerous failed attempts, countless revised approaches, and a seemingly endless series of realized short-term goals) to "crack the code" of your chosen Ultimate Identities in life and business.

Simply put, the spectacular results we seek often require persistence.

In this chapter, you will find out what it means to crack the code of peak performance by reviewing the case studies of four *Mind Contrologists* who struggled long and hard before, at last, fulfilling their dreams.

## Charles Dickens

*Literary Fame Against All Odds*

Charles Dickens was born in the slums of Port Sea, England in 1812. When Charles was 12, his father was carted away to a debtor's prison after accumulating piles of unpaid debt. Prematurely thrust into a role as the family's chief provider, Charles, the eldest of seven Dickens children, quit school and took on 12-hour shifts at a local shoe factory. Just like that, Charles went from sitting in a classroom to waving to his former classmates as he walked by the schoolhouse on his way to work.

The children in the window, however, had no idea of the horrors to which young Dickens was being exposed.

At the factory where he worked, Charles slaved from morning until night beside a smelting furnace, where he earned just pennies a day for his service. The factory was brutally hot, and reeked of greasy machinery, toxic chemicals, and human suffering. In fact, many of the boys and girls who worked alongside Dickens had been reduced over many months and years to nothing more than skin and bones.

At some point during his exposure to the horrors of child labor, Dickens developed a palpable distaste for manual labor. And it was while manning his work station alongside the town's poor, with their underutilized brains and malnourished bodies, that young Charles Dickens vowed that he would one day ascend from the hellish pits of his living nightmare to the height of respectability.

Charles dreamed of becoming a *distinguished* Englishman.

*"Some minds seem almost to create themselves, springing up from every disadvantage, and working their solitary but irresistible ways through 1,000 different obstacles."*
-Washington Irving

Out of dedication to his family, Dickens managed to continue working at the factory for three, grueling years. Then, when Dickens was 15, his father returned home from prison. And that's when Charles made his move.

Yearning to find a place among the learned, Dickens quit his job, contacted the Law Offices of Ellis & Blackmore, and begged for a job. Hired as a clerk, Charles was responsible for taking notes and running errands. Although he viewed his "office job" as an exciting step in the direction of his dreams, Charles made it known that he intended to remain a clerk only until an opportunity to move up presented itself. Playing his part in expediting that opportunity, Charles persuaded his boss's secretary to teach him the ins-and-outs of administrative work.

Within 18 months of starting his new job, Charles was ready to move on to bigger and better things.

After tailoring some snazzier duds to wear, Dickens convinced his boss to provide a character reference which enabled him to land a job as a copyboy for a regional newspaper. At his new job, Dickens served as assistant to a group of seasoned reporters. Wasting no time in climbing the corporate ladder, Dickens learned everything he could about researching, writing, and reporting. Charles also became a master at imitating the distinguished journalists for which he worked.

It was after deciding that journalism was the best way to reach the next rung of the workplace ladder that Dickens marched into the editor's office and requested his own writing assignments. After more than five years since he'd vowed to acquire a distinguished position in the world, Dickens was, at last, promoted to "journalist" and given a substantial raise. Charles soon gained local celebrity through a series of widely-read articles.

Just 20 years old, Dickens was already more successful than 90% of his peers. Of course, Charles had only scratched the surface of the wealth and fame he would soon come to know…

*"Continuous effort—not strength or intelligence—*
*is the key to unlocking our potential."*
-Winston Churchill

In 1832, Dickens made a decision to shift his focus and energies to the craft of story writing.

While working by day as an editor, Charles began spending his nights writing colorful stories. Sitting at a desk by the window of his suburban home and gazing out over the slums from which he had risen, Dickens found the inspiration to churn out three books which included "Oliver Twist"—a tale loosely based on Dickens' own struggles with, and triumph over, poverty. Oliver Twist was an instant hit. Publishing advances, book sales, and stage translations earned Dickens enough coin to assume a full-time role as a writer.

Finally, after nearly a decade spent paying such dues as the humiliation of a father in prison, the sadness of having to quit school and abandon his friends, the strife of child labor, and the methodical planning and waiting involved in climbing the workplace ladder from law office errand boy to best-selling story writer, Dickens had *cracked the code* of success as he chose to define it.

After publishing his masterwork "A Christmas Carol" in 1843, Charles Dickens would exhaust the next 27 years traveling between England and America, penning 15 would-be classics, directing hit plays, fathering a family of ten, and assuming his destiny as one of the world's most distinguished authors!

Regardless of your starting point, there is no station in life or financial status you cannot attain through the process of relentless execution.

*"Austere perseverance, harsh and continuous,*
*may be employed by the least of us*
*and rarely fails its purpose, for its silent power*
*grows irresistibly greater with time."*
-Johann von Goethe

## Charles Lindbergh

*Persistence in the Open Skies*

Charles Lindbergh was just 25 years old when he imagined flying a single engine aircraft from New York to Paris, a feat that had never before been accomplished.

Experienced pilots assured Lindbergh that crossing the Atlantic alone was suicide. Staying awake and alert at the controls for more than one full day was, in the estimation of many, physically impossible. But Lindbergh could not be talked out of it. The young aviator was convinced that he possessed the mental conditioning, physical stamina, and piloting skills necessary to pull off a transatlantic flight.

What's more, Lindbergh decided on doing it alone.

On May 20, 1927, Lindbergh packed a lunch of sandwiches and water, jumped into a single engine aircraft named "Spirit of St. Louis," and then took off from New York's Roosevelt Field on course to Paris…

*"To be thrown upon one's resources*
*is to be cast into the very lap of fortune,*
*for our faculties undergo a development and display an energy of which they were previously unsusceptible."*
-Benjamin Franklin

Lindbergh's flight would prove every bit as mentally and physically demanding as others had warned.

Along the 3,610 mile trip, Charles became so consumed with anxiety that he couldn't eat, so lonely that he began talking to himself to break the silence, and so exhausted that he allowed his plane to lose altitude and nearly crashed into the ocean. Just seconds before plummeting to a watery grave, Lindbergh yanked back on the controls and wrestled the aircraft back to a safe altitude.

After more than 30 punishing hours in flight, Lindbergh trembled in weakness and fought against heavy eyelids. In a last-ditch effort to stay awake, the pilot scarfed down a sandwich, and then opened a window to force air into his lungs. Nothing Charles did helped for long and he wondered if he would ever see land again.

With each passing moment, the prospect of failing—of dying—grew frighteningly more certain. Dangling from a fraying thread of consciousness, Lindbergh resorted to slapping himself in the face, and was just about to surrender his will and his mission, when he spotted a flock of birds in the distance, evidence that land was not far off. A short time later, after 33 hours and 29 minutes in flight, the ecstatic aviator found himself circling the Eiffel Tower. Back in the States, Charles Lindbergh would become a national hero.

Unceasing determination in the face of difficult circumstances is the factor that most often determines whether or not we reach our chosen destinations.

*"However high the price of courage and self-determination, the rewards are ultimately much greater."*
-J. Paul Getty

## Harry Truman

*Relentless Execution over the Course of Four, Long Decades*

Born in 1884, Harry S. Truman grew up on a 160-acre farm in Missouri. The four agonizing years Truman spent in high school created within him an aversion to formal education. What he did enjoy, however, was studying the lives of legendary figures of the past. Through his personal studies of history, Truman sensed his own spirit of greatness stirring within him, and, before long, he began to dream about doing something remarkable with his own life.

The question was...what? Truman would spend the next 40 years in search of the answer.

After graduating high school in 1901, Truman considered going to West Point, but poor eyesight prevented him from applying. He later enrolled in a local business school, but dropped out after only one semester. Over the next decade, Truman would hold such positions as a farm hand, railroad worker, mail clerk, and bank teller. He also served as a soldier in the Army National Guard, a position Truman reportedly finagled by memorizing the eye chart which he otherwise had no chance of deciphering. None of these roles, however, sparked Truman's enthusiasm. *Maybe I'd make a good family man,* thought Harry, but the woman he proposed to said no.

Not much was working out the way Harry Truman had hoped.

Entertaining the prospect of a career in the military, Truman—likely resorting to his old eye chart memorization trick—enlisted in the Army at age 33. At the end of his tour, however, Captain Truman chose *not* to reenlist. Trying his hand at business instead, Harry opened a men's clothing store in Missouri, but the recession of 1921 eventually drove the business into bankruptcy. Down, but not out, Harry pressed on.

Truman seemed to have finally found his calling in 1922, when, by some merciful act from Above, he got himself elected as a judge in Jackson County. Harry was enjoying his career in politics, until his failure to get reelected in 1934 threw another wrench into his ideas about his future. The loss hit Truman hard. At age 50, Truman again found himself in search of a career. Contemplating a future as an attorney, he enrolled in night classes at Kansas City Law School. Before long, however, Harry's childhood distaste for classrooms resurfaced. Enduring yet another failure, he dropped out of school before earning his degree.

At this point, many men might've thrown in the towel and given up on life. However, Harry Truman, a short and balding, 50 year-old, college dropout whose lifelong job-hopping, numerous failures, and high school education encapsulated everything that is "ordinary" in a man, had no intentions on relinquishing his bold aspirations of finding his special place in the world.

Instead of giving up, Harry did something *extraordinary.* He kept searching…

*"I do not think there is any quality so essential to success of any kind as the quality of perseverance. It overcomes almost everything, even Nature."*
-J. D. Rockefeller

In 1935, Truman decided to shoot for the stars by organizing a run for the Missouri State Senate. He won. At last, the tides of fortune seemed to be shifting in Truman's favor. Between 1935 and 1945, Truman would serve on the Missouri State Senate before being offered the position of vice president under Franklin Roosevelt.

Then, on April 12, 1945—after just 82 days in office as the vice president—Harry was sworn in as the 33rd president of the United States, following President Roosevelt's untimely passing.

In the end, Harry Truman's long and arduous quest for greatness led him to the White House, where, at age 61, the college dropout and failed businessman found himself in charge of the CIA, FBI, and the world's mightiest military. Whenever he was alone in the Oval Office, Truman found himself gazing up at the portraits of famous presidents past, many of whom had inspired Harry's hard-won and unlikely ascension to president of the United States.

If only those portraits could speak, they'd say, "Nothing justifies the dreamer like relentless execution."

The triumphs won by Dickens, Lindbergh, and Truman teach us that there is no level of achievement that cannot be bought at the affordable cost of perseverance.

Next, we'll learn how the habit of *relentless execution* can help you position yourself up the workplace ladder in the face of such obstacles as an uncooperative boss, insufficient experience, industry prejudices, and more.

## Unrelenting Spirit, Inc.

*How to Use Persistence to Land Your Dream Job*

I once had an employee who would *not* take "no" for an answer.

Epiphany was an office manager who'd become enamored with the prospect of joining our Client Acquisitions Division, a division traditionally dominated by men. For weeks, Piff had been telling me all the reasons why she was the right person for the job. However, because this particular division catered primarily to mature, male business owners, I feared that our prospects would be leery of signing large contracts that were being pitched by a young, sales...*woman.*

After denying her request several times, I thought the issue was over. However, Piff was *not* one who easily gave up. It was just days after her last attempt to win me over that Epiphany caught me in my office in Philadelphia. Suddenly, she was at it again.

"John, I want you to reconsider my transfer," Piff barged into my office to announce. She sat down and then threw a resume on my desk, as if we were conducting a scheduled, formal interview.

"Piff, leads cost money. First-round closes are critical. And you have zero experience selling," I explained. "So, again, no."

"I want this position!" she demanded.

"I admire your enthusiasm, but it ain't happening. You're an office manager. We need you inside."

Piff stormed out. For the life of me, I could not understand this girl's insistence on ditching her secure, administrative position to go contract-hunting on commission, with a bunch of cigar-smoking salesmen who were typically twice her age.

I hoped she would soon come to her senses. Epiphany had other plans…

*"Perseverance and spirit have done wonders throughout the ages."*
-George Washington

A week later, I was halfway across the country visiting the president of a distant branch when I received a call from my secretary in Philadelphia. Epiphany was quitting. At Piff's request, I set up a videoconference through Skype. As Epiphany and I were being connected, I expected a rant. Instead, I received a *sales presentation.*

Treating me as a prospective client, Piff "sold me" on the company and explained the firm's complex service portfolio like a true pro. She explained the benefits of each service and supplied information about the results I could expect to receive by becoming a client. She even offered me a video commercial of our team in action, a clever selling strategy which we weren't currently employing.

"Piff, I'm impressed," I conceded. "But I thought you were quitting."

"I had to do *something* to get your attention," she said.

"Well, you got it. You also got the job. We'll work out the details when I get back."

**GURU'S TIP**: Reluctant bosses, lack of experience, industry prejudices, and other similar obstacles are far less responsible for one's inability to advance in the workplace than is a lack of persistence. The "yes" or positive outcome you seek is often hidden behind your very next effort. If at first you don't succeed, ask another question, try a new approach, or tap a different resource.

Execute *relentlessly* until you get what you're after!

*"The secret of success is constancy of purpose."*
-Benjamin Disraeli

## "Cracking the Code" of Your Dreams

The grand prizes you seek from Life are typically long-range results which take time to fully transition from mind to matter. These results may be viewed as Life's guarded treasures. "Cracking the code" to these realities requires a specific *combination* of smart personal efforts and favorable external events. The most certain method for discovering this magic combination of efforts and events, and for winning Life's favor in the process, is relentless execution.

Below is a guide for using persistence to *crack the code* of your dreams for your life, career, relationships, and finances.

Tip #1) **Take Action**: The quality of persistence is, in its purest sense, an ongoing commitment to taking action.

Giving your dreams and goals 100% effort on a daily basis is the best guarantee for success over the long-run.

Tip #2) **Discover the *Magic Combination* of Personal Efforts and External Events**: Every outcome you seek is guarded by some magic combination of smart personal efforts and favorable external events. It's your job to discover the *precise combination* of efforts and events that unlocks the door to your dreams and goals.

Tip #3) **Never Give Up!** Thomas Edison was one of the greatest Mind Contrologists of the 20th century. Edison once said, "Many of life's failures are men who did not know how close they were to success when they threw in the towel."

Do *you* have the habit of giving up the instant pressure begins to mount? Big mistake. Resistance represents a splinter in the wall of the dam of progress. You will often trigger a deluge of desirable results and long-awaited rewards by pushing *just beyond* your supposed "breaking points." Never give up!

*"I know the price of success: dedication, hard work, and an unceasing devotion to the things you want to see happen."*
-Frank Lloyd Wright

## A Biblical Promise to the Persistent

Man's ability to crack the code of success, and win Life's favor in the process, is no new revelation. A promise related to the rewards of persistence has existed in the pages of scripture for thousands of years.

Luke 11: 5-9 reads, "And the Master said to them, 'Which of you shall have a friend and go to his home at midnight and say to him: Friend, lend me three loaves of bread, for another friend of mine has come to me on his journey, and I have nothing to feed him.

"And he will answer from his window and say: Do not trouble me, *the door is locked now*, and my children are sleeping. I cannot rise and give you what you ask.

"I say to you that if you *continue to knock*, although he will not rise to give you what you need because you are his friend, *because of your persistence*, he will rise and give you as much as you want.

"So, I say to you, ask and you shall receive; seek, and you shall find; *knock*, and the *door will be opened unto you*'."

No matter which doors in life you seek to enter, *persistence* is your key!

*"To him that overcometh*
*will I give of the Tree of Life to eat."*
-Revelations 2:7

**GURU'S TIP:** Once you have discovered the magic combination of smart personal efforts and favorable external events that unlocks the door to your chosen outcomes, you will have cracked the code of success.

Then, having deciphered the code of your ideal realities, you will arise one morning to the magnificent realization that you are standing on the threshold of a society of elite *Mind Contrologists* who represent less than 1% of the world's population.

You will be standing upon the threshold of the *"Realm of Excellence"—the place where dreams and reality merge...*

# 34

# Entering the Realm of Excellence

*The Place Where Dreams and Reality Merge*

*"To few comes the gift of excellence."*
-Theognis

The *Realm of Excellence* is the place where dreams and reality merge. To achieve excellence in your life, career, relationships, and finances is to begin operating at a level of peak performance that very few individuals on this planet will ever come to enjoy. It is also the natural consequence of regularly practicing in its entirety the Dream Acquisition Formula (DAF) found exclusively in *Mind Contrology*®.

So, what does "excellence" look like in the real world? How can you vastly increase your chances of attaining it? And what life-altering rewards can you expect to receive when you do?

The next two chapters aim to answer these questions and more.

Let's begin by reviewing a case study on excellence as demonstrated by famous Harvard psychologist, Dr. William James.

## The Art of Excellence

*As Demonstrated by Legendary Psychologist William James*

The odds were against William James from the beginning. In 1842, James was born in a hotel room in New York to dysfunctional parents who, at times, didn't seem to care whether he lived or died.

When William was just a boy, his father, an eccentric and gypsy-like salesman, began moving the family from one shabby home to the next. By the time he was 15, William and his siblings had resided at 20 different addresses—including a dozen, month-long hotel stays—throughout Boston, Rhode Island, and beyond. William's father also held paranoid beliefs about the American education system and the "self-righteous intellectuals" who ran it; thus he placed little value on schooling his children. As a result, William and his siblings were ritualistically enrolled and then withdrawn from a series of grade schools, and then high schools.

Never quite sure what his address would be next month or what classroom he'd be walking into next week, William James, a quiet boy with an appetite for knowledge, turned to reading both to escape from the mayhem of having no place to call home and to acquire the education he was largely deprived of by his caregivers.

James certainly could've used his misfortunes or the constant, physical illnesses he experienced as a result of them, as an excuse to drink alcohol, smoke cigarettes or ditch school, as troubled teenagers often do. Yet, he didn't. Instead, James took the tough breaks he continued to receive throughout high school, applied to them high personal standards, and then redirected them into his education.

After graduating from high school with honors, James then shot for the stars and attempted to enroll at Harvard.

*"Hold yourself to a higher standard than anyone else expects of you."*
-Henry Ward Beecher

In 1861, after convincing the college dean that he was Cambridge material and borrowing tuition money from his father, James, 19, earned himself a seat in the Lawrence Scientific School at Harvard University. The thrill of entering an academy as prestigious as Harvard did wonders for James' confidence and outlook on life. And after parting ways with his father, William's health improved dramatically.

After studying hard and contemplating his future over the next two years, William informed his sister that he was entertaining three, distinct career possibilities: history, the arts or medicine. Swayed by the value he placed on financial security and on making a difference in the lives of others, James chose medicine. He enrolled in medical school in 1864, and received his degree in 1869 after a total of eight, tough years of schooling.

At age 27, William James, the kid from nowhere in particular, was now Dr. William James of Harvard University.

James barely had time to enjoy his victory when Minnie, James' girlfriend of two years, fell suddenly ill and passed. Minnie's death devastated William. The fact that he—a licensed doctor—could do nothing to save his sweetheart destroyed William, and the host of infirmities that had haunted him as a child returned in full force.

Over the next two years, James would suffer recurring episodes of dark depression, self-loathing, and a series of illnesses which included migraine headaches, blurred vision, flu, insomnia, and angina.

It was a fateful night in 1871, while locked in his bedroom in the grips of a bout of psychogenic anguish which pushed him to the brink of taking his own life, that James, 29, had an epiphany. The recurring bouts of madness and illness he'd been experiencing over the past two years could be attributed to only one true source—his own *mind.* James suddenly realized that he'd let negative thoughts get the best of him and he was paying the price. Furthermore, theorized James, if an *absence* of "mind control" had altered his circumstances for the worst, a *mastery* of the mind's powers was most assuredly the key to returning to sanity, to regaining his health, and to setting the life he'd let spin out of control back on track again.

In his own words, James suddenly realized that "reality is congenial to the powers you possess." Simply put, Dr. William James had awakened to the existence of the Mind/Reality Relationship.

*"With regard to excellence, it is not enough to know; we must try to have it and use it."*
-Aristotle

In 1872, on a quest to unlock the mysteries of mentality, James, 30, familiarized himself with the research that was being conducted in Europe in the highly-unchartered field of "psychology." After channeling this research through the complex prism of his own, vast intellect, the doctor foresaw the potential implications of legitimizing the field on American soil, and began discussing the idea with his colleagues in the States.

Fascinated with how the mind works and with the extent to which one's thoughts govern one's world, James ditched his medical career and devoted himself to studying the human psyche full-time.

In 1873, James began pushing the administration at Harvard to commit a portion of its financial resources to developing a psychology curriculum, and then began teaching his colleagues about the mind and healing patients of their psychogenic infirmities, as if born to be a psychologist. Then, through an ongoing stroke of genius between the years of 1873 and 1875, James penned the series of revolutionary theories of psychology that branded him as an unparalleled expertise in the field.

At the age of 34, Dr. William James was a certified, Harvard celebrity.

In 1876, James was appointed professor of psychology, a field James had almost single-handedly imported to America and developed into a working science. And James was just getting started. Over the next two decades, James' pioneering work in the field of psychology would usher the issue of the human mind's untapped powers to the forefront of the American consciousness. And while some minds tarnish with age, James' brilliance seemed only to grow sharper with time.

By 1897, William James, 55, was just beginning to operate at the top of his game. While juggling teaching commitments at Harvard, Stanford, and Yale, James found the time to author his first ground-breaking book and had a dozen more on the way. Far from his days as a young med school student, James was considered a national authority on matters of the human psyche.

By the turn of the 20th century, Dr. William James' legacy as the "father of American psychology" was being permanently etched upon the scrolls of history.

*"Living and working at our best makes a difference not only to ourselves, but also to the world around us—the company, the community, the family."*
-Dr. Charles Garfield

## The Anatomy of Excellence

"Excellence" is a relatively straightforward concept. As is reflected in the simple diagram below, excellence may be defined as the combination of high standards, superiority in *doing,* and superiority in *being*. Put another way, excellence is the result of operating at the highest levels of performance in life and business.

**The Anatomy of Excellence**

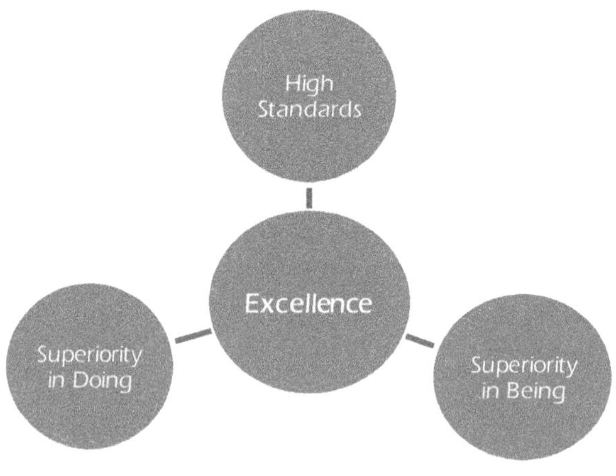

Excellence can be earned by filling a dream or realizing a goal which creates a positive impact in one's life, in the lives of others, or in one's world. Excellence can also be achieved on a primarily moral level as is accomplished by, say, delivering groceries to an elderly neighbor who lives on a fixed income, and expecting nothing in return.

In your quest to attain excellence in your own life, it may help to ask yourself the following simple question each morning: Do I practice the habit of infusing the *highest possible standards* into all that I *do*, and all that I *am?*

If you're not happy with your answer, make the necessary adjustments one day at a time. However, if your answers consistently turn up as yeses, you are undoubtedly on the road to an honorable legacy in life and business.

*"Aim at sincerity in every word and action,*
*the most amiable excellence in a rational human being."*
-Ben Franklin

Entering the Realm of Excellence typically doesn't happen overnight. Reaching the highest plateaus of performance in your life, career, relationships, and finances requires an extraordinary commitment to going above and beyond the norm, and to constantly holding yourself to a standard superior to that being exercised by virtually everyone else around you.

## Your Road to Excellence Begins Here and Now...

You are no different than Dr. William James in that you were born with all of the mental, physical, and spiritual resources you need to achieve everything you want out of life and to gain access to the coveted Realm of Excellence.

All that is required is a daily commitment to superiority in doing and being.

So, perhaps you're psyched about the prospect of assuming your Ultimate Identities in life and business and about operating at the highest levels of performance morning, noon, and night. You're geared up about becoming a world-class spouse, parent, or friend. And you're thrilled about the prospect of banking your first—or next—million and giving back to others in your own special ways. You're also determined that you've got what it takes to make it happen.

But, you're human, and like the rest of us, you're looking for some incentive to marshal the mental, physical, and moral resources necessary to transcend mediocrity and achieve excellence over the months and years ahead.

Fair enough. Allow me to unveil your motivation.

I call it the *"7 Rewards of Excellence"*...

# 35

# The 7 Rewards of Excellence

*A Guide for Earning the Payoff of a Lifetime*

*"Every good and perfect gift is from Above, and comes down from your Father of Lights."*
-James 2:17

Excellence comes to those who know what it takes to be the best, and are willing to pay the price. Is the "Realm of Excellence" worth the price of admission? You be the judge.

Following, are seven ultimate rewards you can expect to receive by applying the highest standards to your quest to lead your field or become a millionaire (or billionaire,) to become the "world's best" mom or dad or perform some "impossible" physical feat, to become an indispensable friend or change the world, or whatever your dream may be.

## The 7 Rewards of Excellence

### The 1st Reward of Excellence
**UNLIMITED POWER!**

Milton Hershey was born in 1857 and grew up in Lancaster, Pennsylvania.

When Milton was 12, he quit school. Two years later, he began an apprenticeship with a local caramel maker called, "Mr. Joe." Fascinated with the process of making candy, Milton eagerly absorbed Mr. Joe's trade secrets. Over the next four years, Milton worked hard and saved every penny he earned. Then, upon expiration of his apprenticeship with Mr. Joe, Milton, 19, opened a caramel shop of his own in 1876.

Over the next seven years, Hershey would operate three failed businesses in five different cities before finally getting it right. It was after moving back to Lancaster in 1883 that Hershey opened the Lancaster Caramel Shop. Between 1883 and 1890, Hershey's company grew to employ 1,500 across two factories. While attending a manufacturer's expo in Chicago in 1890, Hershey discovered the latest, high-tech, chocolate making equipment which was being sold out of Germany.

Envisioning a future in chocolate, Milton sold his company, reinvested all of his cash in expensive chocolate making machinery, and then relocated to Derry Church, Pennsylvania, where he opened Hershey Chocolate Company. Hershey spent the next ten years perfecting his Hershey Bar, inventing Kisses, and developing regional distribution channels across the country. Hershey's company grew so large, so quickly, that before long the factory had attracted an entire infrastructure of homes, businesses, schools, and churches. By age 43, Milton Hershey was an experienced CEO who envisioned building an *empire* made of chocolate. Guided by the dream of becoming the world's largest chocolate manufacturer, Milton purchased some additional land, built a massive plant, and pioneered a process for mass-producing his chocolate bars.

By 1909, the "Hershey Bar" alone was hauling in over $5 million per year, and Hershey's operation could no longer support the market's demand for product. Hershey again expanded his plant in Derry Church. The entrancing scent of processed chocolate permeated the area, and the town fell so deeply in love with Milton's delicious product that Derry Church was renamed "Hershey, Pennsylvania."

At last, after years of manufacturing the world's highest-quality confectionaries, Milton Hershey's dream of running a chocolate empire had become an edible reality!

*"Power is a form of wages received as a result of long and arduous labor."*
-James Allen

In 1907, Hershey opened an amusement park with the goal of giving back to the local community which had supported his dream. Then, in 1918, Hershey began searching for more noble ways to invest his wealth and launched the Hershey School for Orphans. The school was founded to provide less fortunate boys and girls with the education Hershey himself had not received. The Hershey School would go on to provide educations for thousands of orphaned boys and girls each year.

In 1976, in a poetic twist of fate, William Dearden, a Hershey executive who had grown up in Hershey's orphanage, took over as CEO of the company.

Milton Hershey achieved excellence by dreaming big, by insisting on producing only the highest-grade products, and by regularly sharing with his family, friends, coworkers, and fellows the riches he worked so hard to generate.

That, my friend, is what I call *power.*

**GURU'S TIP:** Power in its most functional form is the ability to live fully and give in extraordinary ways. Want unlimited power to live and give? Strive for excellence in all that you do, and all that you are. Power is a byproduct of a quest for high achievement!

## The 2nd Reward of Excellence
## ETERNAL DEMAND

After graduating from college in 1986, Katherine Brosnahan landed her dream job at "Mademoiselle Magazine." By 1991, Kate's superior work ethic and gift for fashion had elevated her to a position as senior fashion editor. Unable to turn a blind eye to newly developing opportunities in her field, Kate recognized an untapped segment in the market for women's handbags, the segment for sophisticated, well-crafted bags at an *affordable* price. Next came Kate's genius idea: "Why not fill this niche…myself?"

Venturing into entrepreneurship with the help of her boyfriend, Andy Spade, Kate began designing her idea of the quintessential woman's handbag. While Kate focused on a product line and start-up issues, Andy put his marketing background to work. Then, in 1993, Kate's bright idea became Kate Spade Handbags.

Obsessed with quality, Kate and Andy spent the next few years staffing the company with high-level executives who could help grow the firm without diluting quality. In 1996, Kate Spade opened its first upscale boutique in SOHO. Retail operations quickly exploded into Boston, Georgetown, Chicago, and Los Angeles. By 1999, increasing demand for Kate's premium handbags fueled growth into a global market, including shops in Tokyo, Australia, Ireland, and the Bahamas. The world, it seemed, couldn't get enough of what Kate Spade was selling.

In recent years, Kate Spade has blossomed from the mental seedling of one woman's imagination into a multimillion, global harvest of highly sought-after products.

As of 2015, more than 170 Kate Spade boutiques existed worldwide.

*"Your best security on the world*
*is your own ability to make a contribution.*
*And if you're really good, people will want you."*
-Super CEO Al Dunlap

**GURU'S TIP:** Nothing entitles you to "eternal demand" like becoming the *best* there is at what you do!

## The 3rd Reward of Excellence
## THE NOTORIETY FACTOR

In 1908, Napoleon Hill, a 25 year-old newspaper reporter with a reputation for professionalism was granted an interview by famous industrialist, Andrew Carnegie. Upon arrival at Carnegie's estate, Hill was escorted to the steel baron's private library where Carnegie lit a cigar and then began to reveal to Hill his vision for introducing to the masses the world's first, comprehensive "motivational manual."

Of course, Carnegie, CEO of the largest steel company in the country, had neither the time nor writing experience by which to realize such a lofty, literary goal. And that's where Hill came in.

One can imagine Hill's awe as he sat in Carnegie's library, surrounded by pricey books, rare paintings, and the scent of money mingling with cigar smoke, when suddenly the steel magnate popped the question. "Son, would you be willing to travel the world, for as long as it takes, to interview my rich and famous friends, and produce the motivational book I long to see materialized?"

Hill, surely taken aback by the prospect of picking the brains of the rainmakers of his day, took just seconds to reply, "Yes, I'll do it."

It was at this very moment that Carnegie reportedly produced the golden timepiece he'd been using to time Hill's answer. Carnegie went on to explain that his dealings with many men over the years had taught him that those who were slow to commit themselves to an endeavor were usually quick to abandon it. Hill, however, had passed the test.

*"That aim in life is highest which requires the highest and finest discipline."*
-Henry David Thoreau

Hill would prove a master at both rendering swift decisions and at carrying out a monumental undertaking. Determined not to quit until his manuscript was completed to the best of his abilities, Hill would exhaust the next 20 years scouring the nation on a quest to interview such legends-in-the-making as Henry Ford, Thomas Edison, and J.D.

Rockefeller before, at last, publishing his would-be classic, the *"Law of Success,"* in 1928.

Transcending his former, limited role as an unknown reporter, Hill's pioneering literary masterpiece would earn him fame as an author and success coach, allow him to forge friendships with the world's most enduring figures, and enable him to command the national spotlight as an advisor to presidents Wilson and Roosevelt.

**GURU'S TIP**: Want notoriety, perhaps even national or international fame? Apply rigorous standards to your relentless pursuit of success as you choose to define it.

In the words of Andrew Carnegie, "Aim for the highest!"

## The 4th Reward of Excellence
## **THE GENIUS LABEL**

Extraordinary success in one area of life tends to translate to superior performance in other areas of life. Edgar Allan Poe was the exception to this rule…

Born in Baltimore in 1809, Edgar Poe was still an infant when his father abandoned him and his mother. A short time later, Edgar's mother died of pneumonia, and Edgar landed in an orphanage.

Fortunately for Edgar, he was soon adopted by a wealthy do-gooder named John Allan. Treating the boy as his own son, Allan gave Poe love and gifts, and enrolled him in the finest schools where he acquired a palate for poetry. Writing poetry, Edgar found, was like a spiritual elixir which quelled the demons of angst and self-pity that had taken up residence in his soul as a result of his inability to process the events that had led to his adoption.

Wanting only the best for his son, Allan paid Edgar's tuition at the University of Virginia, but the return of Poe's demons cut the young poet's education short. Edgar's drinking and gambling problems forced the teen out of college and became the tinder for explosive arguments between the boy and his surrogate father. By the time he was 18, Poe left home and ventured out on his own.

While bouncing around Baltimore over the next few months, Poe drank, worked, and wrote in manic intervals. Searching for his place in the world, Edgar joined the army in 1827 with a five-year commitment, but quit after two years in order to attend West Point. In a final attempt to reconcile with his son, Allan financed Poe's entrance into West Point. However, in 1831, Poe was brought up on charges of gross insubordination and was kicked out of the military academy. Just 22 years old, Poe was out on the street again. This time, Allan wanted nothing to do with him.

Back in Baltimore in 1833, Poe, 24, entered a poetry contest to try to win some extra cash. To his surprise, he won $50 and was offered a job at a local magazine. Over the next three years, Poe would sharpen his writing skills first as proofreader, then editor, and by 1836 Edgar was earning a handsome $800 a year. Poe showed clear potential for a rewarding career in journalism; however, Poe's hot temper in the workplace and romance with liquor ended up getting him fired from nearly every job he ever held.

At age 27, Poe added fuel to his fiery trials when he married his 13 year-old cousin, Virginia. It was while living with Virginia's mother (his aunt) over the next several years that the would-be poet quietly penned the collection of stories and poems that would earn him a legacy as one of the greatest literary geniuses of all time. After Virginia's sudden passing in 1847, Poe became a loyal customer of the local taverns where he attempted to drink away the sorrows of his self-generated misfortunes.

Sadly, Poe's decision to drink would prove fatal...

*"Mental excellence is a splendid and lasting possession."*
-Sallust

In 1849, Poe went on a drunken bender which lasted for days. Desperate for cash, Poe reportedly got involved in a voting scam at an election hall in Baltimore. The escapade ended with the poet beaten and hospitalized. He died four days later, never to enjoy the "genius label" and worldwide acclaim his wizardry of words would earn him.

Poe was just 40 years old.

### The Moral to Edgar Allan Poe's Story

The lesson to Poe's story is this: Edgar wasted the large majority of his life making poor decisions and chasing quick fixes.

In fact, Poe applied *exceptional standards* to only one relentless pursuit during his 40 years on Earth—writing. However, that singular pursuit of excellence was all that was required to earn Edgar a legacy as one of the most beloved literary geniuses of all time.

Is there *one* particular field or endeavor into which you are willing to exhaust the innermost parts of yourself?

If so, you, too, may be entitled to the *Genius Label!*

## The 5th Reward of Excellence
## PRICELESS SATISFACTION

History is brimming with inspiring examples of those who've attained euphoric victories after struggling long and hard in their quest to fulfill their dreams and goals. In fact, these incidents of *priceless satisfaction* are often so perfectly timed for the recipient, so spectacular in nature, that they appear to be staged by the Heavens above.

For instance, Walt Disney quit school at age 17 to pursue his dream of running his own animation studio. It was a decision that Disney often regretted. It would be nice, thought Walt, to have experienced the joy of graduating high school, of attending his prom, and of having a diploma to hang on the wall at his studio in Hollywood.

Disney, however, never let his regret sour him. Along his journey to greatness, Walt paid his workers above average wages, launched the careers of countless artists, and used his movies to bring joy to the hearts of millions of children. Still, the fact that he'd dropped out of school remained a regret which gnawed at Disney's soul much of his life. Apparently, the God of the Universe was aware of Walt's grief. So, in 1939, Disney was granted his own, personal miracle.

As a direct result of his quest for excellence in film-making, Walt was presented with honorary degrees from Harvard and Yale

Universities. Then, further redeeming the high school dropout, Walt was appointed the head of the National Committee for Education by President Eisenhower during the 1950s!

> *"The price of victory is high, but so are the rewards."*
> -Paul Bryant

Chuck Norris also has experienced the *5th Reward of Excellence.*

It was while serving in the U.S. Air Force between the ages of 18 and 22 that Carlos "Chuck" Norris discovered his calling—martial arts. During his tour in Korea, Norris served as a military policeman, and attended an off-site martial arts school where he earned a black belt in Tae Kwon Do.

After returning home in 1963, Norris entered the professional martial arts circuit—and utterly dominated it. Over the next seven years, Norris would win an astonishing 12 World Champion victories and become *Black Belt* magazine's "Fighter of the Year" before retiring undefeated in 1970.

Not one to let potential go to waste, Norris exhausted the 70's and 80's by launching 32 martial arts schools across the west coast, and writing, producing, and starring in, more than a dozen martial arts films. Then during the 90's, Norris took on the role of a crime-fighting cop in the hit television series, "Walker, Texas Ranger," which has since become the longest-running show in the history of television.

Norris' fascinating career is eclipsed only by his personal commitment to charity. In addition to launching such programs as "Kick Start" and "Kick Drugs out of America," Norris' contributions to humanity include acting as a spokesperson for disabled vets, making celebrity appearances on behalf of "Make-A-Wish," as well as mentoring troubled children around his hometown of Rolling Hills, California. And after many years of selfless service, Norris, at last, received the *priceless satisfaction* of an award he truly deserved.

In 1997, old-school badass Chuck Norris became the first man in the western hemisphere to receive the coveted "8th Degree Black Belt Grand Master" title in Tae Kwon Do!

*"Happiness is the full use of your powers along lines of excellence."*
-John F. Kennedy

**GURU'S TIP:** The road to excellence is paved with special surprises your Creator has in store especially for you. You may claim your reward by continuing to do your best in life and business until such time as your effort and good deeds are remunerated.

## The 6th Reward of Excellence
## THE ABUNDANT LIFE

If you could have one extravagant, material wish granted within the next 24 hours, what would it be? A brand new Maserati in your driveway? A pre-paid Ivy League college education for your kids? Your own helicopter?

Whatever your wish may be, there's probably only one thing standing between you and your heart's desire: *money.*

Of course, you are not alone. Consider this…

The average American family income for 2016 was just over $50,000. Each adult in this family carries about $12,000 in personal debt (excluding mortgages,) has no retirement investments in place, and spends half the waking day chained to the cubicle at a job that offers little chance for near-term advancement. This is not living; it's bondage. Truly living requires an ability to call your own shots (at least to a degree you perceive as acceptable,) a level of financial resources necessary to enjoy the best life has to offer, and the option to work long hours because you love what you do, not because your boss or unpaid bills demand it.

Nothing improves one's ability to live fully like substantial, financial wealth.

*"It is a wretched taste to be satisfied with mediocrity when the excellent lies bountifully before us."*
-Isaac D'Israeli

Money isn't everything. Family, friends, health, and happiness are all essential to living a truly rich lifestyle. However, it's nearly impossible to live life to the fullest and take care of your family when you're constantly, financially strapped. As someone who's been "broke," who's been caught up in the 9-to-5 grind, and who's felt the pain of not being able to provide my family with the wonderful gifts they deserved, I can assure you that abundance is infinitely better than lack.

So the question is: How do you make the transition from your current, financial position to a position in which you are free to experience life in full measure and are able to provide your loved ones with all that they deserve? Generally speaking, you must strive for excellence in who you are and what you do. My experiences with numerous CEOs, doctors, and self-made millionaires have taught me that a quest to "best the best"—at who you are as a person and how you earn your living—is the surest guarantee for generating power, creating demand, gaining notoriety, winning satisfaction, and *acquiring wealth*, all of which enable you to live your life as it was meant to be lived…abundantly!

## The 7th Reward of Excellence
## **A LEGENDARY LEGACY**

The obstacles surmounted by George Washington after assuming command of his ragtag Continental Army in 1775 would come to represent one of the most inspiring stories of triumph over circumstance in recent centuries.

When the 400-ship British armada sailed into the port of New York, ready for battle at the start of the Revolutionary War, Washington's "troops" (many of whom were nothing more than old drunks or inexperienced teens) began deserting in droves.

During one British offensive, Washington's rebels reportedly ran off into the woods without firing a single shot. Washington, outraged to the point of self-sacrifice, charged the enemy alone on horseback. It took two of Washington's aides to chase the general down, pry away the reigns, and force him to safety.

Plagued by disloyal soldiers, extreme temperatures, scarce food supplies, depleted ammunitions, and rampant disease, Washington's army suffered numerous battle losses and more than 4,400 casualties. Once, following the capture of 2,800 of his soldiers, Washington was seen weeping uncontrollably. Then, as if the commander's plate wasn't full enough, Benedict Arnold, one of Washington's generals, became enraged after being passed over for a promotion. In retaliation, Arnold defected to the British, and then organized a series of bloody battles against his former, American compadres.

Washington wasn't even safe around his own men. During one of multiple coups, a group of power-hungry foot soldiers tried to overtake Washington and seize control...by killing him. Washington's survival was secured only by a heroic rescue staged by his loyal underling, General Nathanael Greene. Finally, in 1783—eight agonizing years after swearing allegiance to the cause of American independence—Washington managed to engineer the final battle strategy that broke the spirits of the occupier, and won America its freedom.

Washington's reward? As a result of his unwavering commitment to the United States and his diligence in effecting its liberation, Washington was elected as America's first president, an 8-year post for which he *refused* to be compensated!

*"The quality of a person's life will be in direct proportion to their commitment to excellence, regardless of the chosen field or endeavor."*
-Vince Lombardi

**GURU'S TIP:** Ask yourself: *How do I want to be remembered? What legacy will I leave behind in life and business?* Remember, you have no Ultimate Identity except that which you engineer for yourself, either by default or design.

The content and quality of the objectives you pursue today will become the legacy you leave behind tomorrow. Exercise your spirit of greatness, the spirit by which George Washington earned a lasting legacy as America's first, and greatest, president.

Take action unto excellence!

## Taking Action unto Excellence

*Lessons to Take With You*

*The Final Element* of the Dream Acquisition Formula (DAF)—"Take Action unto Excellence"—has taught us three important things:

(1) Desired results, one and all, require *action!*

(2) *Relentless execution* forms the basis for a 100% success rate.

(3) By consistently infusing *impeccable standards* into what you do and who you are, you are sure to find yourself, one glorious day, among those elite members of the coveted *Realm of Excellence.*

*"The idea is to prove at every foot of the way*
*that you are one of the anointed ones who has the right stuff*
*and can move higher and higher—and ultimately, one day—*
*that you might be able to join the few at the very top."*
-Thomas Wolfe

Over the past three chapters, you've discovered the Final Element of the Dream Acquisition Formula (DAF) found exclusively in *Mind Contrology ®.*

In the next chapter, we'll review this formula in its entirety and I'll extend a special invitation to *you*, the reader…

# Epilogue

# The Dream Acquisition Formula (DAF)

*And a Special Invitation to You, the Reader*

*"Somehow, I can't believe that there are any heights that can't be scaled by a man who knows the secret of making dreams come true."*
-Walt Disney

The fulfillment of your dreams begins in your mind. Mastering your thinking sets the stage for a successful application of the Dream Acquisition Formula (DAF) found exclusively in *Mind Contrology*®.

The inspiring case studies of the 500 fascinating figures presented throughout the *Mind Contrology*® series provide irrefutable evidence that an active application of the DAF is the most effective method for transforming your dreams for your life, career, relationships, and finances into reality—with *scientific* precision.

Let's restate the formula one more time in its entirety, shall we?

## The Dream Acquisition Formula

Dream Formula Precursor: **Master Your Mind**

The 1st Element: **Awaken Your Imagination**

The 2nd Element: **Become a Visionary**

The 3rd Element: **Ignite Your Passions!**

The 4th Element: **Harness the Force of Belief**

The 5th Element: **Become a Goal Scientist**

The 6th Element: **Master the Art of Strategic Living**

The 7th Element: **Take Action unto Excellence!**

## Your Invitation to the Life of Your Dreams

It is my sincere hope that your experiential journey through the pages of *Mind Contrology* ® has been one that sets the stage for ground-breaking transformation in your life, career, relationships, and finances.

The time has come to entrust you with the greatest secret of the ages, a secret once known only by the wisest, richest, most powerful figures on Earth. That secret is this: *Within you right now exists unlimited power to master your mind and to transform your wildest dreams into your waking reality.* And there is no more effective method for awakening and summoning forth this God-given power than an active application of the Dream Acquisition Formula (DAF) found exclusively in *Mind Contrology* ®.

Perhaps you sense that you've been changed for the better during our time together. Maybe you sense the potent forces of goodness and greatness stirring within you, waiting to be unleashed. And perhaps you can't wait to close this book and take revolutionary action unto excellence.

If this is the case, then I suppose I've accomplished my purpose.

I consider it an honor to have served you. I'd wish you luck, but "luck" is irrelevant to someone like you, a 21st century *Mind Contrologist* who possesses the ability to achieve anything and everything you set your mind to. You are now tasked with scripting the living details of the greatest success story ever told—your own.

Go now, my friend, your destiny as you choose to define it awaits...

Wishing you success in all that you set your mind to!

John Echols

# About John Echols

## *John Echols is Among the Nation's Leading Authorities in Matters of Mind and Business*

---

For 15 years, John has been helping companies and their CEOs achieve peak performance.

An accomplished CEO coach and management consultant, John has been sought-after by such global and national powerhouses as: ***Exxon/Mobil, New York Life, telecom giant WPCS, U.S. Facilities & Maintenance, Marshall's & T.J. Maxx, Five Below, Roto-Rooter*** and more.

CEO of Mindbiz Coaching & Consulting, Inc., John has become the go-to coach and consultant of clients ranging from top-flight CEOs and business college board members to board certified surgeons and numerous small business owners.

A highly sought-after mind guru, business expert, author, and speaker, John's mission is one of helping people across the globe master their minds and fulfill their dreams.

"***Mind Contrology***"® is now available in 53 countries.

**In 2017, John Echols continues to set the standard for all things mind and business in the 21st century.**

*To Learn more about John Echols, visit...*

***JohnEchols.Online***

**The Mind Guru's**
# "Make Me Famous Sweepstakes!"

## Want to become famous?
Here's your chance...

The ***Mind Guru's "Make Me Famous" Sweepstakes*** is your chance to become an overnight celebrity by becoming a featured story in John Echols' next book!

- *Do you have an incredible story of personal triumph?*
- *Have you overcome a life-threatening illness or personal barrier?*
- *Do you wish to nominate someone you know to become a featured story in John Echols' next book?*

Send your story to...

**MakeMeFamous@JohnEchols.Online**

Entries will be reviewed and owners of stories selected for publication will be contacted by email and/or telephone in order to schedule a formal interview regarding submission and to obtain permission to print submission.

**If selected, you could become a featured story in John Echols' next book!**

***IMPORTANT!*** Please provide contact information (name, phone number and email) where you can be reached should your entry be selected for publication.

# Author's Acknowledgements

The *Mind Contrology*® series (installments II and III scheduled for future release) has been a monumental undertaking that has required nearly 10 years and more than 15,000 hours to complete. No task of this magnitude takes place without the help of a large team of amazing individuals.
The list of wonderful people who helped make *Mind Contrology*® possible includes…

My Creator; the God of the Universe, of Life, of Love, and of Success. Thank you for my family and friends, for health and wellness, and for the bountiful blessings bestowed upon me from above. Thank you for the amazing people you place into my life on a daily basis, and for guiding me to the fulfillment of my dreams and goals.

My parents, John and Monica, who believed in me and made great sacrifices for many years so that I might have every opportunity to become as successful in life and business as I chose to become. This book is as much yours as it is mine.

My wife and love of life, Denise; our children Haley and Tyler; and our Rottweiler, Odie. You are the Beacons of Light who have seen me through my darkest days. You are what make life worth living to me. You are my highest purpose and greatest source of happiness. You are my heart and soul—God's greatest gift. Without you, I am nothing more than an empty shell. All my love, always.

My brother, Mike. My best friend, coach, and a living example of class and magnanimity. Words cannot express what you mean to me. Your unwavering friendship and selflessness throughout the years is a testament to your impeccable character. Many of my greatest my memories are those with you by my side. My hope is that we will share countless more of those moments for years to come. And my prayer is that I may be to you in the years to come the friend that you have been to me in years passed.

My sister, Danielle. In appreciation of your hard work, professionalism, encouragement, and support. Thank you for your extraordinary insights in putting the final touches on this project. Your role in bringing *Mind Contrology®* to life has been indispensable.

My favorite Aunt Cindy. Always the optimist. Always on my side. Always the first to lend a hand. Always my favorite.

My grandparents, George and Barbara. My loudest and greatest fans. Thank you for your unwavering support and encouragement throughout the years.

Uncle Blaise, for instilling in me the work ethic that got the ball rolling. That work-ethic is integrated into every page of *Mind Contrology* ® and is the foundation of everything I do at Mindbiz Coaching & Consulting, Inc.

Tony Campisi, president of Campisi Construction. The boss who taught me how to be a boss. I owe my entrance into the business world to what you saw in me when I was a younger, more foolish version of myself.

Frank Recchio, CEO, American Home Owner's Association. My first mentor in the business world and the man who entrusted me with the challenge of my first turnaround experience.

Al Dunlap. The ultimate turnaround expert and a mentor who inspired me to reach for the stars. Your business expertise is unparalleled.

Anthony Robbins. The master of mind and behavioral science whose work in the latter 20th century has paved the path for others like me.

Napoleon Hill. The Father of Mind Science. A man whose work in the field of positive psychology has touched the lives of millions of people in a profound way. You are a true example of a tree that bears good fruit.

Dr. Fred R. David, my intellectual hero and author of the most important business books of all time, "*Strategic Management*." Thank you so much for your wisdom and inspiration over the years, for your important role in my career development, and for your personal support in bringing this project to fruition.

Dr. Dennis Kimbro, one of my greatest motivators. For your insights and encouragement in completing this project.

Dr. Karyl McBride, PhD, renowned psychologist and author. For your interest in my work, encouragement, and assistance in bringing this project to fruition. You are amazing. I will remain forever grateful.

Danny Creed, best-selling author of *"A Life Best Lived"* and CEO of FocalPoint Business Coaching of Arizona. I must offer special thanks to you, my friend, for your guidance and support in bringing this project to light. As a best-selling author, a 6-time winner of the Brian Tracy Award of Excellence, and a Master Business Coach, you have touched the lives of countless business owners, executives, and readers in a positive way. I count myself among this list. Thank you for your friendship and support.

Dr. Travis Bradberry; Lac D. Su, Psychologist, Director, TalentSmart, Inc.; Dr. Christopher McGrath, Professor of the College of Business at Strayer University; and Dr. Katherine Sherif, Professor and Vice Chair, Academic Affairs, Department of Medicine Director, Thomas Jefferson University, for your interest in my work and inspiration to press forward.

Andy Hildalgo, CEO, WPCS. For your early interest in what I had to offer to you and your company. Your encouragement and involvement in my professional development remains one of the highlights of my career.

Our team of talented Area Relationship Managers at Mindbiz Coaching & Consulting, Inc. Thank you for your hard work in educating clients, in forging relationships, and in driving customer satisfaction.

Our team of top-flight consultants at Mindbiz Coaching & Consulting, Inc. Every day, you help to enlighten and empower our clients and propel these important individuals beyond the next level of performance. The gravity of your role at the company and within the business community cannot be overstated.

Kristin Swarcheck, nationally recognized leadership expert. Thank you for your class, support, assistance, and professionalism. You are truly a world-class individual.

Victoria Ipri, nationally recognized social media expert. In appreciation of your amazing attitude, support, insights, and inspiration.

Michael Grover, President, G-6 Turnaround Consulting and Six Sigma Black Belt operations expert. Your kind critique and insights related to Jack Welch and GE were welcome additions to this project. Thank you for your support, professionalism, and assistance.

Bob Senske, Jr., RSM, Bayard Printing Group. Bob, thank you for your brilliant and selfless assistance in developing the client acquisitions system at Mindbiz, Inc. and for the friendship we have developed along the way. You are a rare gem among a stretch of common stones. I count myself fortunate to have met you.

Chris Zenack, tech wiz and graphics designer extraordinaire.

Kate at A Dying Art, Ltd. Your design capabilities are extraordinary. Your customer relations skills are exceptional. And your professionalism is unparalleled. Thank you for your role in bringing this project together.

Rick Potts, graphic artist and tech expert. Thank you for your ability to see into my mind and produce the images and graphics that make Mindbiz Coaching & Consulting, Inc. recognized across the business universe.

The team at 1and1. You're the best.

# Index

www.ingramcontent.com/pod-product-compliance
Lightning Source LLC
Chambersburg PA
CBHW021037090426
42738CB00006B/130

* 9 7 8 0 6 9 2 8 1 0 1 5 6 *